TEPS in
TEPS

650독해

박기혁

서울대학교 졸
(현) 메가스터디 어학센터 TEPS 강사
(현) SLA 학원 TEPS 대표 강사
(현) 중앙일보 영자 신문 중앙 데일리 교육 분야 객원 논설위원
(현) 한국 생산성 본부 영어 전임 강사
(현) PTT(Park's TEPS Teacher's Group) 대표 강사
-TEPS의 최고를 지향하는 강사들의 모임

TEPS in TEPS 650 독해 2nd Edition

저자 | 박기혁
초판 1쇄 발행 | 2009년 5월 25일
개정 6쇄 발행 | 2016년 7월 11일

발행인 | 박효상
총괄이사 | 이종선
편집장 | 김현
기획 · 편집 | 박혜민
디자인 | 손정수
마케팅 | 이태호, 이전희
디지털콘텐츠 | 이지호
관리 | 김태옥

Special Staff

표지 | 장선숙
내지 | 홍수미
편집 | 조혜정
조판 | 김선자

출판등록 | 제10-1835호
발행처 | 사람in
주소 | 121-839 서울시 마포구 서교동 378-16번지 4F
전화 | 02) 338-3555(代)   팩스 | 02) 338-3545
e-mail | saramin@netsgo.com
Homepage | www.saramin.com

:: 책값은 뒤표지에 있습니다.
:: 파본은 바꾸어 드립니다.

ⓒ박기혁 2009

ISBN 978-89-6049-190-8 13740
      978-89-6049-175-5 (세트)

사람이 중심이 되는 세상, 세상과 소통하는 책 **사람in**

TEPS in
TEPS

650 독해

박기혁

사람in
saram in.com

Preface

영어 시험을 둘러싼 여러 가지 환경 변화에 의해서 TEPS의 중요성은 나날이 강조되고 있고 그 특징 또한 뚜렷이 변화를 겪고 있다.

첫째, 갈수록 문제가 다양화되고 있고 더욱더 세련되어지고 있다.
둘째, 시험을 치르는 대상 연령층이 자꾸 낮아지고 있다.
셋째, 특목고나 외고, 로스쿨이나 의학전문대학원 진학 등 그 쓰임새가 더욱 광범위해졌다.

이러한 세 가지 변화에 발맞추어, TEPS 교재도 다양화되고 진화되어야 하는데, 현재의 교재 시장은 그러한 가시적인 변화에 능동적으로 대처하지 못하는 것이 사실이다. 이에, 이번 TEPS in TEPS 시리즈를 통해서 진화하는 TEPS에 가장 적합한 패러다임을 제시하고자 한다.

TEPS는 참으로 복잡하고 미묘한 시험이다. TOEFL처럼 학문적인 점에 초점을 맞추는 것도 아니고, TOEIC처럼 실용 언어적인 측면만을 강조하는 시험도 아니다. 어쩌면 이 둘의 장점만을 모아 놓은 시험이라 할 수 있겠다.

학문적인 내용들을 풀어가되 좀 더 현실성을 부여하여 실용적으로 쓰이는 영어들을 묻는 것이다. TEPS가 최근 시험 시장에 지각 변동을 일으키고 있는 이유는 이런 장점이 토대가 되었다고 볼 수 있다.

TEPS는 실제로 회화를 하다가 혹은 네이티브가 보는 외국 신문 등을 읽다가 느끼는 애로사항을 잘 해결해 줄 수 있는 시험이다. 어휘력의 측면에서 보아도 실생활에서 우리는 이런 어려움을 겪는다. '단어 하나하나의 해석은 되는데 왜 전체적으로는 독해가 안 되고 해석이 안 될까?', '이 상황에서 저 말은 대체 무슨 뜻으로 쓰이는 걸까?'

그것은 바로 간단한 단어라도 초보적으로 배웠던 사전적 지식 외에 실생활에서는 다양한 뜻으로 활용되기 때문이다.

이처럼 네이티브와의 가장 적절한 의사소통에 초점을 둔 TEPS는 지극히 영어수험과 영어실용의 접목이라는 공인영어시험의 목적에 가장 합당한 인증시험이라 하겠다.

TOEIC이 점수 인플레로 상위권 수험생의 변별력을 상실했다는 비판이 많다. TEPS는 TOEIC과 같은 패턴의 지속적인 반복만으로는 해결할 수 없는 시험이다. 이에 학습자들도 이런 TEPS에 대한 관심과 욕구가 더욱 늘어나고 있는 현실이다.

필자는 좀 더 실용적이고 영어 실력 향상에 도움이 되는 TEPS에 대한 관심이 높아지고 있는 것은 고무적인 일이라 생각한다. 그리고 그런 TEPS를 연구하고 학습하는데, 이 'TEPS in TEPS 시리즈' 가 선구자적인 역할을 하길 진심으로 바라는 마음으로 문제 하나 설명 하나에 세심한 신경을 쓰면서 작업에 임하였다.

혼자서는 할 수 없었던 작업에 언제나 도움이 되었던 분들께 감사의 마음을 전할까 한다. 늘 미안한 마음이 드는 가족들과, 사람in 출판사의 박효상 사장님, 김상호 팀장님, 조승주 대리님 그리고 이 책의 출간에 물심양면으로 도움을 주신 류건 선생님, 신일섭 조교, 윤이랑 조교에게도 아울러 감사의 뜻을 표하고 싶다.

PPT(Park's TEPS Teacher's Group) 대표 강사

박 기 혁

학생들의 자습서와 학원 교재의 성격을 둘 다 가질 수 있게 만들었다. 그래서 학원에서의 강의는 물론 독학용으로 사용하도록 준비했다.

1. 상세한 해설을 통해 정답을 공략하는 법과 함께 오답을 피할 수 있는 Skill들을 제시하여 좀 더 높은 점수로의 도약이 가능하게 하였다.

2. TEPS의 4대 영역(독해, 어휘, 청해, 문법)과 기준 점수대별로 학습 목표와 가장 효율적인 방법들을 제시하여 좀 더 전문적이고 체계적인 학습자 맞춤형 학습이 가능하도록 하였다.

3. 애매모호한 이론이나 군더더기 설명을 최대한 배제하여 학습 시간 대비 효율성을 극대화하도록 구성하였다.

TEPS in TEPS

1. TEPS 독해 유형을 완전하게 익힐 수 있는   Type A

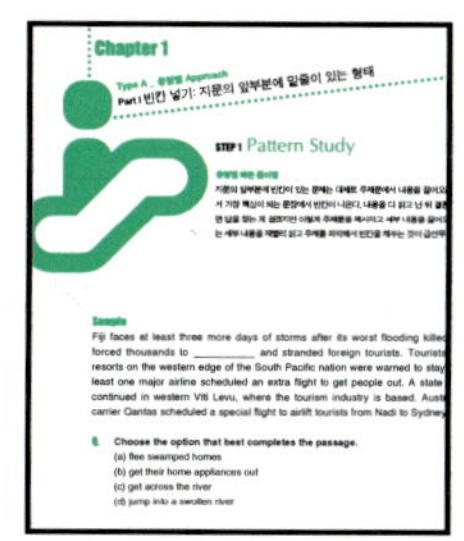

TEPS 독해 유형 9가지를 집중적으로 분석하고 이에 따른 빠르고도 정확한 해결법을 제시하였다. 출제 패턴을 철저히 분석하고 Clinic을 통해 올바른 풀이법은 물론 오답에 빠지지 않는 요령까지 섭렵할 수 있도록 하였다.

2. TEPS 테마의 완벽한 분석과 해결법을 제시한   Type B

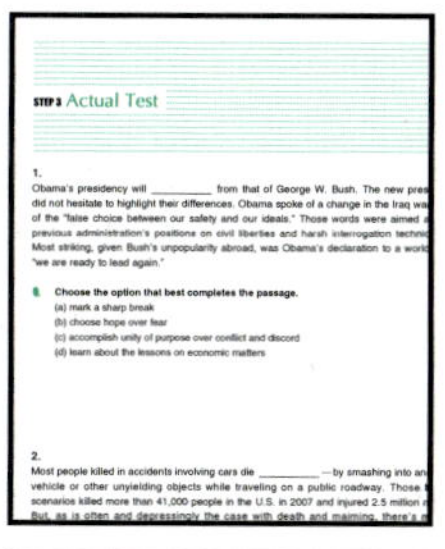

TEPS 독해에 잘 나오는 소재들을 테마별로 나누어서 분석하고 해결법을 제시하였다. 각 테마별로 독해에 적용할 수 있는 필수 어휘들을 챙겨 익히도록 하여 TEPS에 가장 적절한 독해법을 완성하였다.

3. 자신만의 해결 노하우를 만들어가는   Actual Test

Type A와 Type B를 통해 TEPS 전문가의 독해법을 익히고 이를 실전문제에 적용하여 자신만의 문제 해결 노하우를 만들 수 있도록 하였다.

4. 실전보다 더 실전 같은   Final Test

TEPS와 가장 가까운 문제들만 엄선하여 학습자로 하여금 실전 감각을 최고조에 이를 수 있도록 하였다. 기존의 TEPS 문제들을 철저하게 분석함은 물론 앞으로 출제가 예상되는 부분까지 반영하여 언제 시험을 보더라도 자신감 넘치게 대처할 수 있도록 하였다.

Contents

Chapter 1

Chapter 2

Chapter 3

Chapter 4

Chapter 5

Chapter 1

Type A

Part I 빈칸 넣기: 지문의 앞부분에 밑줄이 있는 형태

Type B

Whale 고래

Chapter 1

STEP 1 Pattern Study

유형별 빠른 풀이법

지문의 앞부분에 빈칸이 있는 문제는 대체로 주제문에서 내용을 끌어오는 경우가 많다. 따라서 가장 핵심이 되는 문장에서 빈칸이 나온다. 내용을 다 읽고 난 뒤 결론을 정리하는 문제라면 답을 찾는 게 쉽겠지만 이렇게 주제문을 제시하고 세부 내용을 끌어오는 유형의 문제에서는 세부 내용을 재빨리 읽고 주제를 파악해서 빈칸을 채우는 것이 급선무이다.

Sample

Fiji faces at least three more days of storms after its worst flooding killed nine people, forced thousands to ___________ and stranded foreign tourists. Tourists in dozens of resorts on the western edge of the South Pacific nation were warned to stay inside, and at least one major airline scheduled an extra flight to get people out. A state of emergency continued in western Viti Levu, where the tourism industry is based. Australia's national carrier Qantas scheduled a special flight to airlift tourists from Nadi to Sydney.

Q. **Choose the option that best completes the passage.**

(a) flee swamped homes
(b) get their home appliances out
(c) get across the river
(d) jump into a swollen river

 **풀이 적용**

이 글에서는 빈칸 뒤의 stranded foreign tourists가 큰 힌트가 되고 있다. 맨 앞에 보면 폭풍우로 인해 현재 비극적인 상황이 펼쳐지고 있다는 것을 짐작할 수 있으며 뒤에 나오는 지문 역시 비슷한 내용이다. 따라서 stranded foreign tourists와 병렬적으로 놓일 수 있는, 폭풍우에 의한 비극적 상황을 묘사한 내용을 찾는다면 정답이 (a)임을 쉽게 알 수 있다.

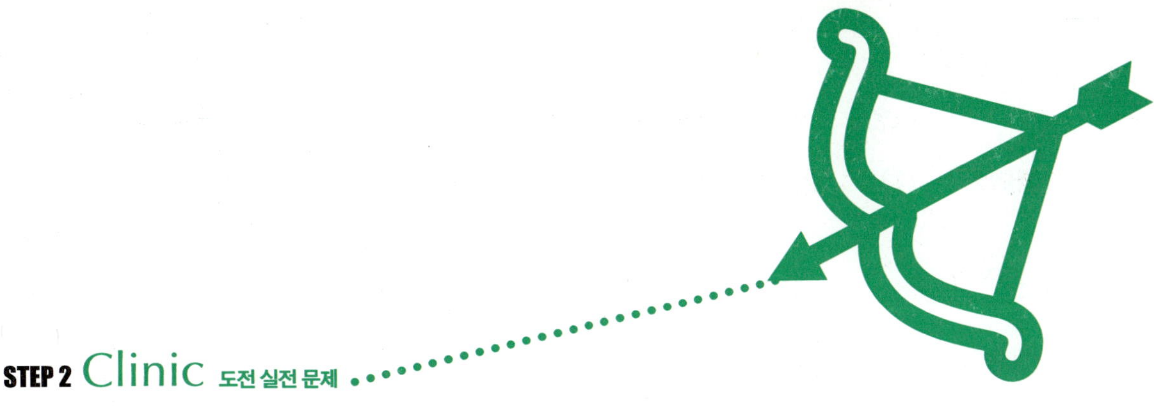

1.

Apple's dynamic CEO Steve Jobs said he would ___________ , a decision viewed by investors as a potential blow to the company's visionary thinking while also raising questions about succession planning. Apple's stock tumbled 7 percent in after-hours trading, amid predictions from analysts that shares would suffer in the short term, much as it has every time there have been reports of Jobs having health problems. He had a bout of pancreatic cancer in 2004 and more recently announced he had a hormone imbalance that led to weight loss.

Q. Choose the option that best completes the passage.
    (a) make every single decision at Apple
    (b) grow market share for key products
    (c) remain at work
    (d) take medical leave

2.

Metallica will reach its 28th anniversary later this year as a band that has transcended its heavy metal origins and ___________ full of controversies, tragedies and near breakups. Through the '80s, Metallica's brutal, brazen brand of speed metal blasted through the underground and turned them into mainstream stars. In the '90s, they started experimenting with different styles of less frenzied music and momentarily lost their mojo. But the band recovered with the *Death Magnetic* album which has the spirit of their hard-and-fast '80s music. Though not quite matching those standards, the quartet is playing as ferociously as ever.

Q. Choose the option that best completes the passage.
    (a) endured a roller-coaster ride
    (b) criticized their behaviors
    (c) defended their choices
    (d) playing music

1.

Apple's dynamic CEO Steve Jobs said he would ___________, a decision viewed by investors as a potential blow to the company's visionary thinking while also raising questions about succession planning. Apple's stock tumbled 7 percent in after-hours trading, amid predictions from analysts that shares would suffer in the short term, much as it has every time there have been reports of Jobs having health problems. He had a bout of pancreatic cancer in 2004 and more recently announced he had a hormone imbalance that led to weight loss.

Q. **Choose the option that best completes the passage.**
  (a) make every single decision at Apple
  (b) grow market share for key products
  (c) remain at work
  (d) take medical leave

오답과 정답 분석

정답 분석
뒤에 나오는 호르몬 불균형(hormone imbalance) 등을 보면 분명히 건강에 이상이 생긴 것이고, 이에 수반해서 생긴 문제들에 대한 내용이기에 leave, 즉 '휴가' 그것도 '건강상의 휴가' 인 medical leave를 받아야 마땅하다. 그래서 답은 (d)이다.

오답 분석
일단 바로 뒤에서 potential blow라는 표현을 썼다는 것은 부정적인 평가를 내려야 할 사실이다. 따라서 (b)나 (c) 는 해당 사항이 없다. 혼자서 독단적으로 경영 결정을 내리겠다는 (a)도 부정적인 여지는 있지만 뒤에서 잡스 개인 의 건강에 대한 우려의 문제로 귀결되기에 (d)가 답이 된다.

2.

Metallica will reach its 28th anniversary later this year as a band that has transcended its heavy metal origins and ___________ full of controversies, tragedies and near breakups. Through the '80s, Metallica's brutal, brazen brand of speed metal blasted through the underground and turned them into mainstream stars. In the '90s, they started experimenting with different styles of less frenzied music and momentarily lost their mojo. But the band recovered with the *Death Magnetic* album which has the spirit of their hard-and-fast '80s music. Though not quite matching those standards, the quartet is playing as ferociously as ever.

Q. **Choose the option that best completes the passage.**
   (a) endured a roller-coaster ride
   (b) criticized their behaviors
   (c) defended their choices
   (d) playing music

오답과 정답 분석

정답 분석

역시 주제문의 판단에서 중요한 것은 긍정적이냐 부정적이냐에 대한 판단이다. 따라서 바로 뒤의 full of 이하에 나오는 사항들이 controversies와 같은 부정적인 이야기들로 가득 찼다는 내용이기에 '심한 굴곡을 겪었다' 는 (a)가 정답이다.

오답 분석

문장 전체를 채우는 것이 아닌 이러한 부분적인 채우기는 답을 찾기가 다소 수월하다. 이럴 때는 긍정적이냐 부정적이냐의 다소 이분법적 논리로 답을 단순하게 찾아가는 것이 효과적이다. (b)를 제외한 나머지 (c), (d)는 다분히 긍정적인 서술이고 이는 뒤에 나오는 내용들과는 어울리지 않는다. 특히 밴드가 겪었던 여러 가지 우여곡절 등의 뒤에 나오는 사항으로 볼 때 이는 roller-coaster라는 표현과 다분히 맞아떨어진다.

1.

Obama's presidency will ___________ from that of George W. Bush. The new president did not hesitate to highlight their differences. Obama spoke of a change in the Iraq war and of the "false choice between our safety and our ideals." Those words were aimed at the previous administration's positions on civil liberties and harsh interrogation techniques. Most striking, given Bush's unpopularity abroad, was Obama's declaration to a world that "we are ready to lead again."

Q. Choose the option that best completes the passage.
(a) mark a sharp break
(b) choose hope over fear
(c) accomplish unity of purpose over conflict and discord
(d) learn about the lessons on economic matters

2.

Most people killed in accidents involving cars die ___________ —by smashing into another vehicle or other unyielding objects while traveling on a public roadway. Those basic scenarios killed more than 41,000 people in the U.S. in 2007 and injured 2.5 million more. But, as is often and depressingly the case with death and maiming, there's more. According to a new study, mishaps that involved cars but aren't classified as traffic accidents on public roads claimed the lives of more than 1,700 Americans in 2007 and injured an additional 841,000.

Q. Choose the option that best completes the passage.
(a) at the other situation
(b) the way you would expect
(c) in non-crash incidents
(d) by overheated radiators

3.

Splashtopia is the newest, ____________ of any resort in the desert, encompassing almost two acres of aquatic fun and thrills. Drift away in the 425-foot lazy river; go sliding down one of the two 100-foot long water slides, build a castle and play on our expansive sandy beach before taking the zero entry right into the river! Splashtopia also features unique water-play zones with fountains and sprinklers, a raging waterfall off our very own mountains, plus a mountainside Jacuzzi and a huge swimming pool!

Q. **Choose the option that best completes the passage.**

(a) most incredible water feature
(b) most safe place to enjoy
(c) most unique sandy beach
(d) most clean fountains

4.

Another three members of ____________ in Texas have been indicted. The case sprang from an April raid of the group's compound near El Dorado. A Schleicher County grand jury indicted two people on bigamy charges and a third on charges of conducting an unlawful marriage ceremony with a minor. The names of the new defendants have not yet been released. The grand jury has also issued an additional charge of aggravated sexual assault against Jeffs. He's already been charged in Texas with bigamy and aggravated sexual assault of a child.

Q. **Choose the option that best completes the passage.**

(a) a criminal organization
(b) a polygamist group
(c) a murderer group
(d) a teenager group

Whale 고래

출제 경향 파악

고래의 기본적인 특징은 외관상으로는 어류처럼 보이지만 실제로는 포유류(mammal)라는 점에 있다. 고래는 그와 같은 특성, 즉 어류처럼 생겼지만 계통적으로는 포유류라는 점 때문에 TEPS에서 예컨대, 다른 동물들과의 상대적인 비교 등을 묻는 문제로 자주 출제된다. 특히 고래가 먹이인 오징어(squid)를 잡는 습성이라든지 어류 이상의 뛰어난 지능을 가진 점이 나오기도 하고, 환경과 관련해서는 고래잡이(whaling)의 남획 및 그에 따른 종의 보호에 관한 문제도 자주 나온다.

STEP 1 Theme Research

Fill in the blanks with suitable words.

1.

Flamingos and whales have something in common: both are sus___nsion fe___ers. They obtain food by taking in large quantities of water and ejecting it through a fil___ring system, thus extracting prey or plants that are too small to be hunted individually.

2.

Communication through in___asound is not limited to giraffes. Over the last few decades, biologists have found that whales, elephants, and some other animals also use this extremely low-pitched sound to communicate. This infrasound, as a means of communication, has special merit: It can travel a greater distance than higher-p___tched noise. Such long-distance communication is a must for animals such as giraffes or elephants that roam over wide areas.

Translation

1. 홍학과 고래는 공통점이 있는데 바로 둘 다 물에 뜬 부유물을 먹고 산다는 점이다. 그들은 많은 양의 물을 마신 뒤 여과 장치를 통해 이를 다시 내뿜어서 개별적으로 사냥하기에는 너무 작은 먹이나 식물을 추출해냄으로써 먹이를 얻는다.

2. 초저주파음을 통한 의사소통은 기린에게만 해당되는 것은 아니다. 지난 수십 년에 걸쳐 생물학자들은 고래와 코끼리 그리고 몇몇 다른 동물들도 의사소통을 하기 위해 초저음을 사용한다는 것을 알게 되었다. 의사소통의 수단으로서의 이 초저주파음은 특별한 장점을 갖고 있는데 그 소리는 고음보다 훨씬 더 먼 거리를 갈 수 있다는 점이다. 그와 같은 원거리 의사소통은 넓은 지역을 돌아다니는 기린이나 코끼리 같은 동물들에게는 필수적이다.

STEP 2 Words and Expressions

어구 해설

flamingo 홍학
suspension 부유(浮遊)
extract 뽑아내다, 추출하다
prey 먹이
infrasound 초저주파 불가청음
roam (정처 없이) 돌아다니다

POP Quiz

다음 어휘나 어구의 뜻을 빈칸에 써 넣으시오.

1. sperm whale ___________________
2. squid ___________________
3. suspension feeder ___________________
4. harpoon ___________________

ANSWERS

STEP 1 1. suspension feeders / filtering system
2. Communication through infrasound / higher-pitched noise

STEP 2 1. 향유고래 2. 오징어 3. 부유물을 먹는 동물 4. 작살

1.

The sperm whale feeds almost entirely on squid. To catch these swift creatures, the whale dives deep and stays down for long periods of time—a unique trait of the species. The sperm whale's hunting strategy relies less on active pursuit than on silent hovering followed by a quick pounce into a passing shoal of squid. Little or no daylight penetrates the hunting depths, but most of the squids on which the whale preys are luminescent. In its effort to catch the swift invertebrates, a still, silent whale may well have the advantage over a swimming one.

Q. Where does the sperm whale usually catch squid?

(a) wherever it finds them
(b) near the surface
(c) deep in the ocean
(d) in areas where daylight penetrates

오답과 정답 분석

정답 분석

지문에서 핵심은 향유고래가 적극적으로 먹이를 찾아 나서기보다는 잠복해 있다가 먹이를 습격한다는 부분이다. 이 특징에 따라서 고래는 빛이 거의 스며들지 않거나 아예 빛이 없을 정도의 깊은 바다에서 사냥을 한다. 즉 답은 (c)가 된다.

오답 분석

향유고래의 사냥 습성에 따르면 (a)와 같이 발견할 때마다 사냥을 한다는 것은 부적절하다. 깊은 곳에서 은둔하는 존재라는 전체적인 습성을 파악했다면 쉽게 가려낼 수 있는 오답이다. 마찬가지로 (b), (d)도 그러한 사냥 습성을 이해한다면 오답 파악이 용이하다. 특히 (d)처럼 빛이 잘 들어오는 곳이라면 은둔하고 있다가 사냥감을 습격한다는 것은 불가능할 것이다.

2.

The evidence for the connection includes the fact that the narwhale's tusk bears a striking resemblance to the unicorn's mythical horn and ____________ the fact that northern European fishermen sold narwhale tusks reputed to have magical properties to apothecaries in the fifteenth century.

Q. Choose the option that best completes the passage.
  (a) in view of
  (b) in terms of
  (c) thus
  (d) because

오답과 정답 분석

정답 분석

unicorn이 등장하는 등 전반적으로 신화적인 분위기가 유지되고 있다. 앞에서는 unicorn과 narwhale의 연관성을 이야기하면서 뒤에서는 선원들이 미술적 효능이 있다고 소개되는 것을 팔았다는 내용이기에 서로 간에 순접적 연결 관계가 이루어지고 있다. 연결사 문제의 핵심은 앞뒤의 내용이 순접인지 역접인지 빨리 파악하는 것인데 여기서는 순접의 연결사 thus가 적합하다.

오답 분석

(d)는 순접이기는 해도 앞뒤 내용이 인과적으로 연결되어야 하는데, 뒤의 내용이 앞 내용의 원인이 되지 못하기에 부적합하다. 또한 '~의 관점에서' 라는 뜻을 가진 (a)와 (b)도 문맥에 어울리지 않는다. 특히 and를 중심으로 두 개의 the fact가 서로 병치되는 이 문장의 구조에도 안 맞는다.

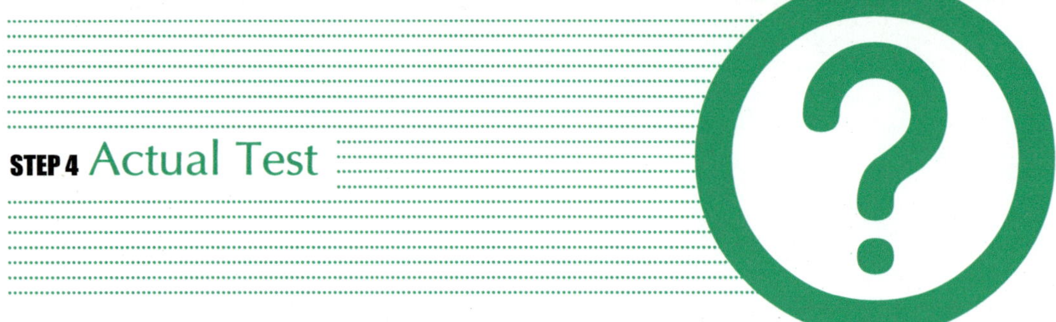

1.

One of the most unusual musical albums was made by a whale. (1) This album contains songs sung under the sea by a talented fifty-five-ton whale. (2) According to those who have heard them, the songs are both beautiful and sad. (3) The number of whales has rapidly declined over the past ten years and we need to take action to protect them. (4) The recordings were made underwater off the coast of Bermuda.

Q. **Identify the option that does NOT belong.**

    (a) (1)

    (b) (2)

    (c) (3)

    (d) (4)

2.

Looming like a submarine, a young blue whale off the coast of Sri Lanka measures about 45 feet long. With maximum lengths of nearly 100 feet, blue whales easily outstrip dinosaurs as the largest animals ever to live on earth. The whale's size and speed discouraged harvesting until steam-powered ships and guns that fired explosive-tipped harpoons were introduced in the late 1800s. Subsequent slaughter reached a peak in 1931, when 30,000 were killed.

Q. **Which of the following is correct according to the passage?**

    (a) Blue whales are often larger than dinosaurs.

    (b) Dinosaurs are the largest animals ever to live on earth.

    (c) Blue whales swim faster than dinosaurs because they are larger.

    (d) Blue whales weigh about 200 pounds at birth.

Section Switch

Chapter 1에 나와 있는 TEPS 필수 어휘입니다.

- ☐ **after-hours trading** 시간 외 거래 (폐장 이후의 거래)
- ☐ **aggravated sexual assault** 가중 성폭행
- ☐ **airlift** 항공기로 대피시키다
- ☐ **apothecary** 약제사
- ☐ **bigamy** 중혼(죄), 이중 결혼
- ☐ **blow** 타격
- ☐ **blue whale** 흰긴수염고래
- ☐ **bout** 발병, 발작
- ☐ **brazen** 시끄러운
- ☐ **brutal** 난폭한, 사나운
- ☐ **claim a life** 목숨을 빼앗다
- ☐ **compound** 구내, 주택군
- ☐ **defendant** 피고
- ☐ **encompassing** 아우르는
- ☐ **ferociously** 사납게, 맹렬하게
- ☐ **frenzied** 열광적인, 광포한
- ☐ **grand jury** 대배심
- ☐ **hard-and-fast** (규칙 등이) 엄격한
- ☐ **harpoon** 작살
- ☐ **harsh** 가혹한
- ☐ **hover** 맴돌다, 어슬렁거리다
- ☐ **indict** 기소하다, 고발하다
- ☐ **interrogation** 심문
- ☐ **invertebrate** 무척추동물
- ☐ **lazy** (유속이) 느린
- ☐ **loom** 어렴풋이 나타나다
- ☐ **luminescent** 발광성의
- ☐ **maim** 불구로 만들다
- ☐ **mishap** 사고, 재난
- ☐ **mojo** 마력, 힘
- ☐ **mountainside** 산기슭
- ☐ **much as** ~와 같은 정도로
- ☐ **narwhale** 일각돌고래
- ☐ **outstrip** 능가하다

- ☐ **pancreatic cancer** 췌장암
- ☐ **pounce** 갑자기 달려들기, 급습
- ☐ **presidency** 대통령의 지위[임기]
- ☐ **property** 특성, 속성
- ☐ **quartet** 4인조
- ☐ **raging** 맹렬한, 거센
- ☐ **raid** 급습, 불시 단속
- ☐ **shoal** 떼, 무리
- ☐ **slaughter** 도살, 학살
- ☐ **sperm whale** 향유고래
- ☐ **squid** 오징어
- ☐ **steam-powered ship** 증기선
- ☐ **strand** 오도 가도 못하게 하다
- ☐ **subsequent** 그후의
- ☐ **suffer** 손해를 입다, 나빠지다
- ☐ **swamp** 침수되다, 물에 잠기게 하다
- ☐ **swift** 재빠른, 신속한
- ☐ **swollen** 물이 불어난
- ☐ **trait** 특징
- ☐ **transcend** 초월하다, 능가하다
- ☐ **tumble** (가격이) 폭락하다
- ☐ **tusk** 입 밖으로 튀어나온 길고 뾰족한 이
- ☐ **unyielding** 단단한, 견고한

Chapter 2

Chapter 2

STEP 1 Pattern Study

유형별 빠른 풀이법

빈칸이 지문의 중간이나 끝에 있다는 것은 주제문에서 약간 벗어난 내용이라는 것을 의미한다. 여기서 벗어났다는 말은 주제문을 세부적으로 서술해서 표현했다는 뜻이다. 이때는 앞부분에서 빨리 주제문을 파악해서 대강의 내용과 전체 취지를 파악한 뒤 그에 따른 세부적인 내용을 선택해야 한다.

Sample

Tibetan monks have disrupted a tour of Lhasa by foreign journalists. The journalists were the first to be allowed back to Tibet since protests erupted two weeks ago. About 30 monks shouted pro-Tibetan slogans and defended the Dalai Lama as journalists toured the Jokhang Temple. China has accused the Dalai Lama of masterminding the protests, but the US has urged Beijing to ___________. Foreign journalists were expelled from Tibet at the height of the unrest, but China allowed a group of about two dozen reporters into Lhasa for a three-day escorted visit.

Q. **Choose the option that best completes the passage.**
(a) dialogue with Tibet's exiled spiritual leader
(b) bring down the rebellion of Tibetan monks
(c) let the press write their article
(d) allow more journalists to Tibet to cover the protests

풀이 적용

'티베트 승려들이 외국 언론인들의 라사 방문 중 돌발 시위를 벌였다' 는 첫 문장에 나타난 주제를 바탕으로 빠르게 내용을 읽어 나간다. 그 결과 중국과 미국의 반응이 상반되게 나오게 된다는 점을 파악한다면 (a)가 답이 된다는 것을 쉽게 알 수 있다.

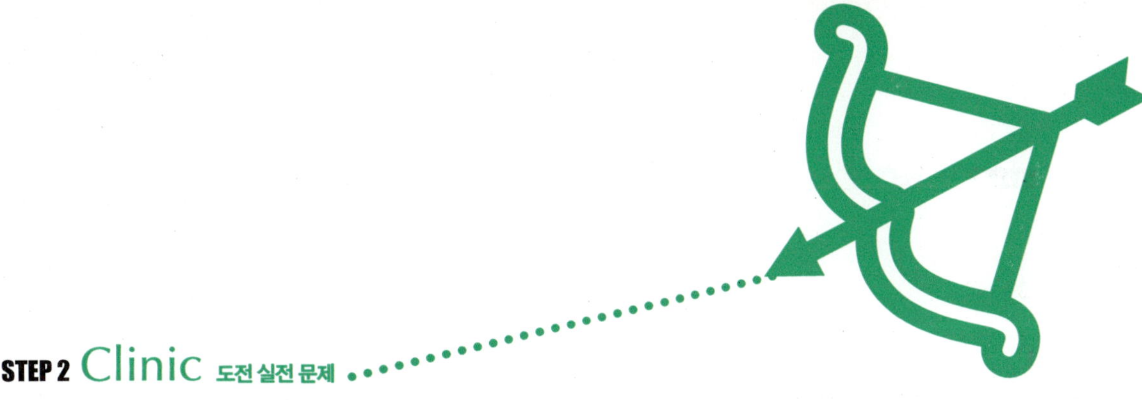

1.

Lots of products promise to restore thinning or disappearing hair. One intriguing option is the HairMax LaserComb, a laser device that supposedly revives hair follicles. Hailed on TV news programs as a "cure for baldness," the device received FDA clearance in 2007. Unlike drugs, most medical devices can be approved ___________. A company must merely persuade the FDA that the new device is "substantially equivalent" to other products already on the market.

Q. **Choose the option that best completes the passage.**
(a) through rigid investigation
(b) without complex processes
(c) without rigorous testing
(d) in a relatively short period

2.

Hillary Clinton said that she intends to revitalize the mission of diplomacy in American foreign policy, calling for a "smart power" strategy in the Middle East. At a confirmation hearing, President-elect Barack Obama's choice for secretary of state sailed smoothly through an array of non-contentious questions. She encountered no challenges to her basic vision for foreign policy. Clinton, who will ___________ in the Senate when confirmed, spoke confidently of Obama's intentions to renew American leadership in the world and to strengthen U.S. diplomacy.

Q. **Choose the option that best completes the passage.**
(a) become a vice president
(b) relinquish her seat
(c) become a secretary of state
(d) be reelected as senator

1.

Lots of products promise to restore thinning or disappearing hair. One intriguing option is the HairMax LaserComb, a laser device that supposedly revives hair follicles. Hailed on TV news programs as a "cure for baldness," the device received FDA clearance in 2007. Unlike drugs, most medical devices can be approved ___________. A company must merely persuade the FDA that the new device is "substantially equivalent" to other products already on the market.

Q. **Choose the option that best completes the passage.**
   (a) through rigid investigation
   (b) without complex processes
   (c) without rigorous testing
   (d) in a relatively short period

오답과 정답 분석

정답 분석

빈칸 뒤의 문장에서 FDA에게 그 새로운 기구가 이미 시장에 출시된 다른 상품과 비슷하다는 것만 설득하면 된다고 했으므로 (c) 엄격한 테스트를 거치지 않는다는 내용이 적합하다. 지문 중간에 빈칸이 있는 문제는 주로 다음에 나오는 문장을 통해서 빈칸에 들어갈 내용을 찾을 수 있으며, 설혹 중간에 연결사가 없어도 해석을 통해서 확인이 가능하다.

오답 분석

빈칸 뒤에 어떤 것이 (b) '복잡한 과정' 인지 모호하다. 특히 다음 문장의 부사 merely가 복잡하다는 말과는 정면으로 배치되는 결정적 힌트가 되고 있다. 새로운 기구가 다른 제품만큼 안전하고 효과적이라는 것만 FDA에게 설득하면 된다고 한 것이 (d) 짧은 기간 내에 허가를 득한다는 이야기는 아니다.

2.

Hillary Clinton said that she intends to revitalize the mission of diplomacy in American foreign policy, calling for a "smart power" strategy in the Middle East. At a confirmation hearing, President-elect Barack Obama's choice for secretary of state sailed smoothly through an array of non-contentious questions. She encountered no challenges to her basic vision for foreign policy. Clinton, who will ___________ in the Senate when confirmed, spoke confidently of Obama's intentions to renew American leadership in the world and to strengthen U.S. diplomacy.

Q. Choose the option that best completes the passage.
(a) become a vice president
(b) relinquish her seat
(c) become secretary of state
(d) be reelected as senator

오답과 정답 분석

정답 분석

국무부 장관과 상원의원을 겸직할 수 없으므로 인준이 확정되면 현재의 연방 상원의원직을 사퇴해야 할 것이다. 전체적인 문맥 파악 외에 기본적인 논리성과 배경 지식으로 풀 수 있는 문제이다. 더불어 다소 난이도가 있는 단어인 relinquish의 의미도 같이 묻고 있다.

오답 분석

(a), (d) 부통령, 상원의원과 국무부 장관의 겸임은 불가능하다. (c) 국무부 장관이 되면 국무부 장관직을 사퇴한다는 것은 논리적으로 말이 안 된다. 전체적인 논지를 파악하지 못해도 기본적인 상식과 문장을 섬세하게 읽어 나가는 힘이 있다면 지문 중간에 빈칸이 있는 문제는 풀어낼 수 있는 여지도 많다. 

1.

Specialty retailer Cost Plus Inc. said that it was closing 26 stores and exiting eight media markets in response to the challenging retail environment. The company would also implement other _____________ like laying off some employees. Cost Plus did not specify which locations would be closing. The company currently operates 296 stores in 33 states now. The chain sells mainly home decor such as furniture, bedding and candles.

Q. **Choose the option that best completes the passage.**
(a) new marketing strategies
(b) cost-cutting measures
(c) promotional approaches
(d) boosting measures

2.

The six-party talks, in which North Korea committed to end its nuclear program in return for aid and diplomatic benefits, are stalled over Pyongyang's failure to accept a verification plan for the nuclear declaration it made last June. North Korea said it would _____________ its small arsenal of nuclear weapons until the United States normalized relations with it and drops what was termed a "hostile" policy toward the communist state.

Q. **Choose the option that best completes the passage.**
(a) hold on to
(b) take away with
(c) do away with
(d) open to the world

3.

Insurance can be bought through insurance or travel agents and tour operators. The Internet has made it easy to research and purchase insurance. Sites such as Insuremytrip.com, Squaremouth.com and Totaltravelinsurance.com offer side-by-side comparisons, including prices. Before embarking on an overseas vacation, travelers should check their medical policy to _______________. American healthcare providers may not cover costs out of the country. Medicare generally does not provide coverage unless a supplement is purchased.

Q. Choose the option that best completes the passage.
(a) know how much the premium is
(b) ask when you should purchase the insurance
(c) see what is covered
(d) see how you buy travel insurance

4.

The UN special envoy to Burma, Ibrahim Gambari, has ended his latest visit to the country without meeting military leader Than Shwe. He did meet detained opposition leader Aung San Suu Kyi, but requests for talks with top generals were denied. Gambari has been pressing Burma's authorities for political reforms, ___________. Burma has rejected his call for independent observers to monitor a referendum on the new constitution. It also refused to consider changing the constitution to allow Aung San Suu Kyi to take part in proposed elections.

Q. Choose the option that best completes the passage.
(a) but with little apparent progress
(b) and accomplished their objectives
(c) and Burma has changed little by little so far
(d) but Burma proposed an alternative solution

출제 경향 파악

담배를 피우는 게 건강에 좋지 않다는 것을 모르는 사람은 아무도 없다. 그래서 금연과 관련해서 TEPS에서는 단순히 건강에 좋지 않다는 측면보다는 특히 어떤 점이 건강에 좋지 않은지에 대한 부분이 많이 출제된다. 그러나 담배는 기호 식품이므로 지나치게 금연을 강요하면 정신 건강에 좋지 않다는 일부 반론적인 주제도 시험에 출제된다. 최근에는 금연의 사회적 분위기와 맞물려 금연을 하지 않으면 생길 취업상의 불이익에 대한 것까지 출제된다.

STEP 1 Theme Research

Fill in the blanks with suitable words.

1.

Smoking damages include almost all aspects of se___al, rep___ductive and child health, a hard-hitting report by the British Medical Association said on Wednesday. The report estimated around 120,000 men aged 30-50 were im___tent because of smoking. "The sheer scale of damage that smoking causes to reproductive and child health is shocking," said Dr. Vivienne Nathanson, the BMA's Head of Science and Ethics.

2.

The BMA called on the government to ramp up its anti-smoking drive and introduce legislation to make enclosed public places smoke-free. Women who smoke are twice as likely to be inf___tile as non-smokers, the report said. Furthermore, smoking is linked to up to 5,000 mis___rriages a year and around 1,200 cases of malignant cer___cal cancer. "Women are generally aware that they should not smoke while pregnant, but the message needs to be far stronger," Nathanson told reporters. "Men and women who think they might one day want children should stop smoking."

Translation

1. 영국 의학 협회는 흡연이 성적 건강과 생식 능력, 어린이의 건강을 포함한 거의 모든 면에 피해를 준다는 충격적인 보고서를 수요일에 발표했다. 이 보고서는 30-50세 연령의 약 12만 명의 남성들이 흡연 때문에 성 불능이라고 추정했다. "흡연이 생식 능력과 어린이 건강에 끼치는 피해의 순수한 규모는 충격적이다"라고 BMA의 과학 윤리 과장 비비엔 나단손 박사는 말했다.

2. BMA는 정부에게 금연 운동을 강화하고 폐쇄된 공공 공간을 금연 구역으로 만드는 법을 도입할 것을 촉구했다. 보고서는 담배를 피우는 여성들이 담배를 피우지 않는 여성들보다 불임이 될 가능성이 2배 더 높다고 말했다. 게다가 흡연은 연간 5,000건에 이르는 유산과 약 1,200건의 악성 자궁 경부암과 관련이 있다. "여성들은 대개 그들이 임신 중일 때 담배를 피우지 말아야 한다는 것을 알고 있지만 그 메시지는 더 강력해야 한다"고 나단손 박사는 기자들에게 말했다. "언젠가 아이를 원할지도 모른다고 생각하는 남성이나 여성들은 담배를 끊어야 한다."

STEP 2 Words and Expressions

어구 해설

hard-hitting 충격적인, 효과적인
association 협회
sheer 순수한, 순전한
reproductive 생식의
ramp up 강화하다, 늘리다
legislation 입법, 법률 제정
malignant 악성의

POP Quiz

다음 어휘나 어구의 뜻을 빈칸에 써 넣으시오.

1. stop smoking _______________
2. reproductive _______________
3. pregnant _______________
4. kick the habit _______________
5. secondhand smoke _______________

ANSWERS

STEP 1   1. sexual, reproductive and child health / impotent
2. infertile / miscarriages / cervical cancer

STEP 2   1. 담배를 끊다 2. 생식(력)의 3. 임신 중의 4. 습관을 버리다 5. 간접흡연

1.

Job seekers are discovering that smoking can endanger their careers. Newspaper classified advertisements frequently specify that employers are looking for nonsmokers only. One of the first questions asked of job applicants at Vanguard Electronic Tool in Redmond, Washington, is "Do you smoke?" If the answer is Yes, the interview is over. That is perfectly legal.

Q. **What can be inferred from the passage?**

(a) You don't have to kick the habit of smoking until it endangers your career.

(b) It is getting very difficult for employers to hire nonsmokers.

(c) Many newspapers advertise only for the employers looking for nonsmokers.

(d) If you smoke, you'd better not apply for a job at Vanguard Electronic Tool.

오답과 정답 분석

정답 분석

윗글에서 흡연이 구직자들의 경력에 해를 입힐 수 있다는 내용과 뱅가드 일렉트로닉 툴이 흡연자를 좋아하지 않는다는 내용으로 보아 흡연자라면 뱅가드 일렉트로닉 툴에 지원할 필요가 없다는 것을 추론할 수 있다. 그래서 had better not(~하지 않는 것이 좋겠다)의 내용이 지문 후반부에서 추론이 된다.

오답 분석

(a) 경력에 해가 되기 전에 나쁜 버릇을 고쳐야 하는 것은 당연하다. (b) 비흡연자를 고용하는 어려움에 관한 내용은 지문에 없다. (c) 신문사 입장에서 담배를 피우지 않는 사람을 찾는 고용주만을 위해서 광고를 한다는 것은 이 글에서 추론될 수 있는 사항, 즉 금연을 하는 사람이 취업에 유리하다는 점을 훨씬 더 넘어서는 사항이다.

2.

Unfortunately not everyone has her willpower. Some may want to quit for the sake of their loved ones or for their own well-being, but the power of nicotine addiction is too great. Others claim to enjoy their cigarettes and have no desire to give them up. If you can't or won't quit, there is still a great deal you can do to safeguard those around you. Never allow anyone to smoke in your home or car, even when there are no children present. Explain to people that they must respect your right not to smoke involuntarily. Toxins linger in the air, even though you may not be able to see or smell them. If you are a smoker, take it outside or smoke in an area where the ventilation system is separate from that of your home.

Q. **What is the main idea of the passage?**
(a) How to stop smoking
(b) The method to prevent indirect smoking
(c) The toxicity of smoking
(d) How we can enhance our health

오답과 정답 분석

정답 분석

마지막 문장의 take it outside ~ separate from ~ 에서 흡연자와 거리를 두라고 하는 취지의 글임을 알 수 있다. 주지하는 대로 최근에 더욱 더 부각되는 것은 간접흡연이다. 이 글은 전체적으로 직접적인 흡연보다는 간접흡연의 위험성에 대해서 주로 언급하고 있다.

오답 분석

사람들에게 비자발적으로 흡연하지 않을 당신의 권리를 존중해달라고 말하라는 내용과 담배의 독성이 공기에 오래 머문다는 내용으로 보아 위 지문은 간접흡연에 관한 내용임을 알 수 있다. 따라서 (a) 금연하는 방법, (c) 담배의 유해성, (d) 건강 증진은 지문과는 관계가 없다. 특히 담배의 유해성은 direct smoking, 즉 '직접 흡연' 이 주제일 때 전형적으로 나올 것이다.

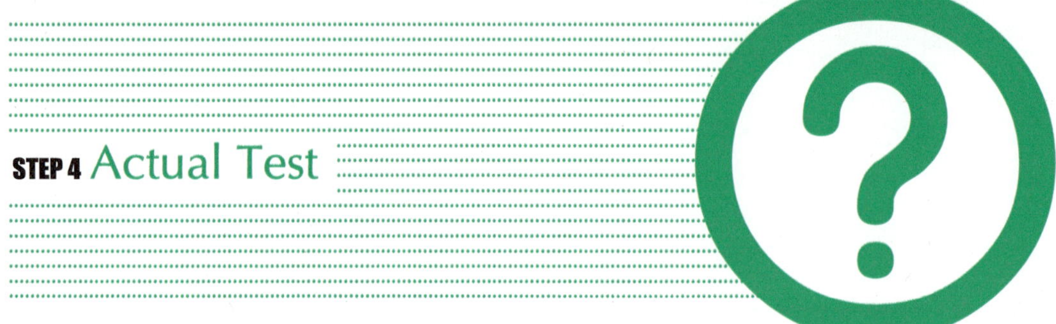

1.

Asia has long been the home of inveterate smokers. To millions of them, cigarettes are the stuff of daily social intercourse. Nothing is done without them—no task unrewarded, no meal concluded. Everybody knows that Asia is supposed to be the last great frontier of the tobacco industry, a place where vast numbers continue to expose themselves to the risks of lung cancer, cardiovascular disease, emphysema and other smoking-related illnesses. And yet, across the region, an Asian antismoking movement is quietly but inexorably gathering strength. It isn't large yet, but it is starting to have a dramatic impact from fresh legal wins in unlikely quarters to tough bans on smoking in public places. The Framework Convention on Tobacco Control (FCTC), a treaty sponsored by the World Health Organization (WHO) became binding law on Feb. 27 in the first 40 countries to ratify it. A third of these countries are in Asia, and more Asian nations are expected to adopt the treaty's tough antismoking provisions over the coming months.

Q.   Which can be inferred from the passage?
   (a) Smoking brings Asian nations to an economic crisis.
   (b) Smoking-related illnesses were eradicated in Asia.
   (c) Antismoking movements cost Asian nations lots of money.
   (d) Asian nations are beginning to recognize that the situation must be addressed.

2.

It has long been understood that cigarette smoking is a health hazard to the smoker. However, recent tests have made it clear that secondary smoking is dangerous to nonsmokers. Secondary smoking is particularly disgusting in a room, such as in restaurant. There, innocent people are forced to eat their meals enveloped in the harmful nicotine fog that inconsiderate smokers send their way. Many people want new laws to be introduced to create non-smoking areas. What's taking the lawmakers so long?

Q.   What is the purpose of the article?
   (a) To praise
   (b) To apologize
   (c) To confess
   (d) To demand

- [ ] **an array of** 일련의, 연이은
- [ ] **arsenal** 무기고
- [ ] **binding** 구속력 있는
- [ ] **cardiovascular** 심장 혈관의
- [ ] **classified advertisement** 구인 광고, 3행 광고
- [ ] **clearance** 인가, 허가
- [ ] **confirmation hearing** 인사청문회
- [ ] **coverage** 보상
- [ ] **disgusting** 메스꺼운
- [ ] **disrupt** (일시적으로) 혼란시키다
- [ ] **embark on** ~에 나서다, 착수하다
- [ ] **emphysema** 폐기종
- [ ] **encounter** 마주치다, (위험 · 곤란 등에) 부닥치다
- [ ] **envelop in** ~으로 싸다
- [ ] **envoy** (외교) 사절, 특사(特使)
- [ ] **equivalent** 동등한
- [ ] **erupt** (폭동 등이) 발발하다
- [ ] **expel** 내쫓다, 추방하다
- [ ] **hail** 환호하여 맞이하다
- [ ] **hair follicle** 모낭(毛囊)
- [ ] **hazard** 위험
- [ ] **hostile** 적대적인
- [ ] **implement** 실행[실시]하다
- [ ] **in response to** ~에 대응하여
- [ ] **in return for** ~에 대한 보답으로
- [ ] **inconsiderate** 남을 배려할 줄 모르는, 무관심한
- [ ] **inexorably** 움직일 수 없이, 엄연히
- [ ] **intercourse** 교제, 왕래
- [ ] **intriguing** 흥미를 자아내는
- [ ] **inveterate** 뿌리 깊은, 만성적인
- [ ] **lay off** 해고하다
- [ ] **linger** 남아 있다, 좀처럼 사라지지 않다
- [ ] **mastermind** 주모자로서 지휘하다
- [ ] **media market** 중개 시장

- [ ] **noncontentious** 논쟁[논의]의 여지가 없는
- [ ] **president-elect** (취임 전의) 대통령 당선자
- [ ] **quarter** 지역
- [ ] **ratify** 비준하다
- [ ] **referendum** 국민 투표
- [ ] **retailer** 유통업체, 소매점
- [ ] **revitalize** 부활시키다
- [ ] **safeguard** 보호하다
- [ ] **sail through** 무사히 치르다, 통과하다
- [ ] **secondary smoking** 간접흡연
- [ ] **Senate** 상원
- [ ] **six-party talks** 6자 회담
- [ ] **stall** 오도가도 못하게 하다
- [ ] **supplement** 추가, 보충
- [ ] **toxin** 독성, 독소
- [ ] **unrest** 불안
- [ ] **ventilation** 통풍, 환기
- [ ] **willpower** 의지력, 정신력

Type A

Part I 빈칸 넣기: 연결사 찾기

Type B

Darwin 다윈과 진화론 vs. 창조론

Chapter 3

STEP 1 Pattern Study

유형별 빠른 풀이법

연결사란 문장과 문장을 이어주는 매개체가 되는 것이다. 따라서 문장의 흐름이 이어지다가 역접이나 예시, 비유 등 내용이 전환될 만한 여지가 있는 곳에 연결사가 들어가게 된다. 특히 '그러나' 라는 식으로 이전 내용의 흐름에서 완전히 전환을 꾀하는 경우가 많기 때문에 연결 접속사 중에서도 주로 역접의 접속사가 TEPS에서는 출제 비중이 높은 편이다.

Sample

Patients with Parkinson's disease who received deep brain stimulation showed greater improvement in movement and quality of life after six months than those treated with medication, a new study shows. The deep brain stimulation patients, ___________, had an almost four times greater risk of serious side effects such as depression, infections, falls or heart problems. Although most side effects could be treated, one patient suffered a brain hemorrhage and died.

Q. **Choose the option that best completes the passage.**

(a) for instance
(b) however
(c) in fact
(d) moreover

 **풀이 적용**

TEPS에서는 주로 역접의 접속사가 많이 출제된다는 전제 하에서 글을 읽어 나가야 한다. 윗글에서도 앞 부분은 greater improvement라는 매우 긍정적인 분위기에서 시작하다가 이후 almost four times greater risk라는 부정적인 분위기로 바뀐 만큼 역접의 접속사를 사용한 (b)가 정답이다.

1.

Nine Americans and one Russian will share Thanksgiving aboard the International Space Station tomorrow. The food may be irradiated, freeze-dried and vacuum-packed, ___________ Endeavour astronaut Steve Bowen says the menu is down-to-earth. NASA sent along only enough Thanksgiving food for the shuttle crew, but the astronauts have raided the space station's pantry to come up with enough traditional items for their ISS friends.

Q. Choose the option that best completes the passage.

(a) and
(b) then
(c) but
(d) so

2.

For some, it's not the holiday decorations at the mall that say Christmas is coming, but something else that's red and green. Cups have returned to Starbucks, marking the unofficial start of the holiday season for millions of coffee drinkers. The Seattle-based coffee chain began offering their holiday-theme drinks, like the Gingersnap Latte and Peppermint Mocha Twist yesterday. Starbucks says the holiday shopping season is their busiest time of the year. Unlike yesterday's freebies, ___________, you do have to pay for the fancy Christmas drinks.

Q. Choose the option that best completes the passage.

(a) moreover
(b) in the end
(c) for somehow
(d) however

1.

Nine Americans and one Russian will share Thanksgiving aboard the International Space Station tomorrow. The food may be irradiated, freeze-dried and vacuum-packed, ___________ Endeavour astronaut Steve Bowen says the menu is down-to-earth. NASA sent along only enough Thanksgiving food for the shuttle crew, but the astronauts have raided the space station's pantry to come up with enough traditional items for their ISS friends.

Q. **Choose the option that best completes the passage.**
   (a) and
   (b) then
   (c) but
   (d) so

오답과 정답 분석

정답 분석

추수감사절이 가져다주는 풍성한 음식의 이미지와 냉동 건조된 진공 포장은 어딘지 모르게 어울리지 않는 측면이 있다. 그러나 우주비행사의 말을 빌어서 down-to-earth, 즉 현실적이거나 아니면 중의적으로 earth(지구)에서 먹는 것과 같다는 식의 표현을 한 것이라면 빈칸 앞뒤의 내용이 상반되기에 역접의 접속사가 와야 한다.

오답 분석

(a)는 대등, (b)는 전환, (d) 역시 전환의 접속사로서 해당 지문에서는 답이 될 수 없다. 앞에서 말한 대로, 특히 여기에서는 down-to-earth가 나타내는 의미가 크다. 앞과 달리 현실적이라는 내용을 담아야 하기에 역접의 접속사가 아닌 것들은 오답으로 처리해야 한다. 

2.

For some, it's not the holiday decorations at the mall that say Christmas is coming, but something else that's red and green. Cups have returned to Starbucks, marking the unofficial start of the holiday season for millions of coffee drinkers. The Seattle-based coffee chain began offering their holiday-theme drinks, like the Gingersnap Latte and Peppermint Mocha Twist yesterday. Starbucks says the holiday shopping season is their busiest time of the year. Unlike yesterday's freebies, ______________, you do have to pay for the fancy Christmas drinks.

Q. Choose the option that best completes the passage.
   (a) moreover
   (b) in the end
   (c) for somehow
   (d) however

오답과 정답 분석

정답 분석

연결사 문제는 다른 문제들보다는 수험자의 부담이 없기에 가끔은 결정적인 단어 또는 난이도 있는 단어를 연결사의 앞뒤에 두고는 한다. 본 문제에서는 freebie가 free(공짜)에서 유래한 단어라는 것을 파악하는 것이 주요 포인트이다. 빈칸의 앞뒤 내용이 상반된 내용이기에 빈칸에는 역접의 접속사가 와야 한다.

오답 분석

freebie(공짜)가 have to pay(비용을 지불해야 한다)로 연결되기에 역접의 의미가 필요하고 나머지 접속사는 (a) 심화, (b) 결론 제시, (c) 전환의 의미로서 해당 사항이 없는 오답이다.

1.

Afghan officials have accused the Taliban of a massacre. The government reports that 31 out of 50 civilians who were on the bus that was stopped by the militant group were killed. The Taliban claim that they killed 27 Afghan soldiers traveling through the country's south. The Afghan Ministry of Defense, ____________, said that there were no soldiers on board, and that everyone killed had been a civilian.

Q. **Choose the option that best completes the passage.**
(a) however
(b) in the end
(c) as well
(d) instead

2.

Fixing a pipe leak isn't difficult if you're home when the pipe bursts and have solder, flux and a propane torch in the toolbox. That's for copper pipe. It's even easier with plastic. But things can turn ugly at 3 a.m. when you stumble down the basement stairs searching for that gushing sound and step into ankle-deep water. ____________ it will probably be a cold night when an air leak near a pipe turns standing water into solid ice.

Q. **Choose the option that best completes the passage.**
(a) But
(b) Indeed
(c) Instead
(d) As a result

3.

Joseph Pritchard is eight years old and he loves playing soccer very much. He plays soccer with his friends every day. ___________, he is an excellent soccer player. His dream is to become a goalkeeper in the England Premier League. But there is a little problem. So, what's his problem? Joseph was born with only six fingers—three fingers on each hand. But don't worry. He is very healthy, and he has a special talent as a goalkeeper. However, it was hard for him to find goalkeeper gloves that fitted his hands. The gloves kept on coming off. So his father decided to get a special pair of gloves for him.

Q. **Choose the option that best completes the passage.**
(a) In fact
(b) However
(c) By the way
(d) In spite of

4.

I totally understand your problem. I briefly had a full-time job in retail. But you don't realize how important comfortable shoes are ___________ you are standing over eight hours a day in them. In the majority of office jobs it doesn't matter since you are sitting down most of the time. I love Aerosoles. That's where I get most of my shoes. They have all different heel heights, their soles are flexible and have good cushioning and they are very stylish.

Q. **Choose the option that best completes the passage.**
(a) when
(b) until
(c) because
(d) since

출제 경향 파악

다윈의 진화론(the theory of evolution)은 늘 공격을 받고 또 결론이 쉽게 나지 않는 주제인데 그 핵심은 자연 선택(natural selection)이다. 캠브리지 대학 출신인 그의 저서 '종의 기원' (The Origin of Species)에서 처음 제기된 이 이론은 적자생존(survival of the fittest) 이론에 바탕을 두고 있다. 자연 선택 이론에서 말하는 선택은 인간의 뜻대로 이루어지는 의도적이고 인위적인 선택이 아니라 자연 세계에서의 자유로운 선택이라는 의미를 담고 있다.

STEP 1 Theme Research

Fill in the blanks with suitable words.

1.

Charles Darwin, the author of the influential book *The Or___in of Spe___es*, lamented that nobody seemed to understand that na___ral sel___tion is a process without purpose, that is, without a preo___ained ou___ome and without an active selection process as in "man's selection."

2.

I believe that this aspect of Darwin's idea has never become wi___ly und___stood and that instead, history and culture have dictated that evolution, as an active conscious selector and an inevitably pro___essive fo___e, is widely thought to represent natural selection.

1. '종의 기원'이라는 영향력 있는 책의 저자인 찰스 다윈은 자연 선택이 목적이 없는 과정, 즉 운명적으로 예정된 결과나 "인간의 선택"에서와 같은 적극적인 선택 과정이 없는 과정이라는 것을 이해하는 사람이 아무도 없는 것 같다면서 비통해했다.

2. 나는 다윈 사상의 이 같은 측면이 한 번도 널리 이해된 적이 없으며 그 대신 역사와 문화가, 적극적인 의식을 가진 선택자이자 불가피한 진보의 힘으로서 진화가 자연 선택설을 대변하는 것으로 널리 여겨지도록 만들었다고 믿고 있다.

STEP 2 Words and Expressions

어구 해설

lament 통탄하다, 비통해하다
natural selection 자연 선택
preordained 이미 정해져 있는
outcome 결과
dictate 영향을 끼치다
progressive 진보적인

POP Quiz

다음 어휘나 어구의 뜻을 빈칸에 써 넣으시오.

1. Origin of Species   _______________
2. natural selection   _______________
3. differential fertility   _______________
4. creationist   _______________

ANSWERS

STEP 1   1. Origin of Species / natural selection / preordained outcome
               2. widely understood / progressive force

STEP 2   1. 종의 기원 2. 자연 선택 3. 차별적 번식력 4. 창조론자

1.

Since antiquity, philosophers have argued that higher mental abilities—in short, thinking and language—are the great divide separating humans from other species. The lesser creatures, Rene Descartes contended in 1637, are little more than automatons, sleepwalking through life without a mote of self-awareness. The French thinker found it inconceivable that an animal might have the ability to "use words or signs, putting them together as we do." Charles Darwin delivered an unsettling blow to this doctrine a century ago when he asserted that humans were linked by common ancestry to the rest of the animal kingdom.

Q. **What is the best title for the passage?**
(a) The Origin of Language and Thought
(b) Philosophical Trends in France in the 17th Century
(c) Do Animals Have Intelligence?
(d) The Nature of Animal Communication Systems

 오답과 정답 분석

정답 분석

이 글의 주제를 파악하기 위해서는 첫 번째 문장의 mental abilities라는 용어를 주의 깊게 기억해둘 필요가 있다. 그것을 나중에 선택지 (c)의 intelligence와 함께 연결해서 생각하면 정답은 쉽게 도출된다. 이 글은 인간만이 지적인[정신적] 능력을 지니고 있다는 관념에 대한 다윈주의의 도전을 소개하고 있다.

오답 분석

윗글 뒷부분의 내용에 비추어보면 인간만이 지적 능력을 지닌 것이 아니라는 것을 알 수 있고 그 내용이 윗글의 요지가 되므로 (a) 언어와 사상, (b) 17세기 프랑스의 철학 사상 등은 윗글과 관계가 없다는 것을 알 수 있다. 

2.

Darwin's theory of natural selection is based not on the idea of death for the unfit and longevity for the fit, but on the notion of differential fertility. Differential fertility is the claim that the more fit individual in every generation will leave ___________. Darwinism raised a series of tantalizing questions for future generations: If other vertebrates are similar to humans in blood and bone, should they not share other characteristics, including intelligence?

Q. **Choose the option that best completes the passage.**
   (a) more offspring than the survived
   (b) a few more precursor than the dead
   (c) a few more offspring than the unfit
   (d) a few more children than the fit

 오답과 정답 분석

정답 분석

주어인 the more fit individual과 대비되는 것을 빨리 찾는 것이 목표이다. 그 대상은 죽은 자(the dead)나 (이미 주어로 쓰여졌던) 적자(the fit) 자신이 될 수는 없기에 결국에는 부적자(the unfit)에서 찾아야 할 것이다. 그래서 정답은 (c)가 된다.

오답분석

결론적으로 unfit이 fit보다 열등하다. 그 주장의 뒷받침으로 fit이 unfit보다 어떤 점이 우월하고 좋은지에 대한 판단에서 결국에는 fit이 더 많은 후손, 즉 offspring을 번식시킨다는 점이 강조되고 있다. 그래서 이 문제는 precursor(선조)와 offspring(후손)의 관계를 어떻게 잘 처리해서 논리적으로 오답을 골라내는가가 관건이 된다. 따라서 (c)를 제외하고는 전부 오답이다. 

1.

Environment is the factor that ultimately determines which species will survive. Adaptation to environment is the basic requirement of life. The creature that fails in this, __________ it remains true to the ways of its own kind, is bound to perish. But the creature that is in sync with this will flourish and at last make the majority of the certain species.

Q. **Choose the option that best completes the passage.**

(a) though
(b) but
(c) however
(d) in addition

2.

In the public mind, challenges to Darwin's theory of evolution are associated with biblical creationists who periodically remove their children from schoolrooms where they are being taught that __________. What most people do not know is that for much of this century, and especially in recent years, scientists have been fighting among themselves about Darwin and his ideas.

Q. **Choose the option that best completes the passage.**

(a) god created man
(b) creationism surpasses evolution
(c) man evolved from monkeys
(d) Darwin's theory is supported by all scientists

- ☐ **accuse** 비난하다, 고발하다
- ☐ **adaptation** 적응
- ☐ **antiquity** 고대, 태고
- ☐ **assert** 단언하다, 강력히 주장하다
- ☐ **automaton** 자동 장치, 로봇
- ☐ **biblical** 성서의, 성서와 관련된
- ☐ **bound to** 반드시 ~하게 되어 있는
- ☐ **come off** 벗겨지다
- ☐ **come up with** ~을 마련하다
- ☐ **contend** (강력히) 주장하다, 논쟁하다
- ☐ **deliver** (타격 · 공격 등을) 주다, 가하다
- ☐ **depression** 우울증
- ☐ **divide** 분수령, 분계
- ☐ **down-to-earth** 현실적인
- ☐ **fertility** 번식력
- ☐ **flux** 용매제
- ☐ **freebie** 공짜
- ☐ **gushing** 분출하는, 넘쳐흐르는
- ☐ **hemorrhage** 출혈
- ☐ **inconceivable** 상상할 수도 없는
- ☐ **infection** 감염
- ☐ **in sync with** ~와 조회를 이루는
- ☐ **irradiate** 방사선 처리하다
- ☐ **leak** 누출
- ☐ **longevity** 장수
- ☐ **massacre** 대량 학살
- ☐ **medication** 약물 치료
- ☐ **militant group** 무장 단체
- ☐ **mote** 티끌, (한 점의) 먼지
- ☐ **natural selection** 자연 선택
- ☐ **offspring** 자손
- ☐ **pantry** 식료품 저장실
- ☐ **periodically** 주기적으로, 정기적으로
- ☐ **perish** 사멸하다, 사라지다

- ☐ **raid** 급습하다, 쳐들어가다
- ☐ **solder** 땜납
- ☐ **sole** (신발의) 바닥, 밑창
- ☐ **standing** 고여 있는
- ☐ **stimulation** 자극
- ☐ **stumble** 비틀거리며 걷다
- ☐ **tantalizing** 애타게 하는
- ☐ **theory of evolution** 진화론
- ☐ **torch** 발염(發炎) 방사 장치
- ☐ **ultimately** 궁극적으로
- ☐ **unfit** 부적당한
- ☐ **unsettling** 동요시키는
- ☐ **vertebrate** 척추동물

Chapter 4

STEP 1 Pattern Study

유형별 빠른 풀이법

제목이나 대의를 찾으라는 문제는 전체적인 주제에서 한 단계 더 나아가 글의 중심을 이루는 핵심 대의를 한두 마디의 말로 분석하는 것이 중요하다. 따라서 빠른 속도로 주제를 찾아 내용 파악을 하되 그에 맞춰 제목을 짚어내야 하기 때문에 다소 시간이 걸리는 편이다.

Sample

A year-old mystery may be ending. Officials confirmed it was the wreckage of Steve Fossett's plane found in a part of eastern California. Madera County Sheriff John Anderson affirmed the finding; the confirmation coming after a hiker found a pilot's license and other items in the Sierra Nevada. Officials say no human remains have been found. Millionaire adventurer Fossett vanished in a solo flight in a borrowed plane after taking off from Nevada more than a year ago.

Q. **What is the best title for the passage?**
(a) The Pilot's License and Other Items
(b) Plane Parts Found May Be Fossett's
(c) The Wreckage of Steve Fossett's Plane
(d) The Crash in the Sierra Nevada

 **풀이 적용**

전체적으로 지문을 읽으면서 파악한 대의는 '사건 해결 → 의문의 죽음의 해결 → 백만장자의 소지품 발견' 식으로 전개되고 있다. 따라서 그 백만장자가 누구인지 그리고 그의 무엇에 관한 이야기가 제목이 될지를 쉽게 알 수 있다.

1.

Ford unveiled a new transmission that should increase fuel efficiency and performance, while reducing maintenance. Dubbed "PowerShift," the new six-speed automatic transmission would be Ford's first implementation of a dual-clutch or automated-manual gearbox in North America. Ford expects its PowerShift transmission to be 9% more fuel efficient and weigh 30 pounds less than the four-speed automatic transmission. Ford wants to equip the gearbox to a compact car by 2010.

Q. What is the best title for the passage?
(a) How to Equip the Gearbox to a Compact Car
(b) Ford's Gearbox Will Be Requiring No Regular Maintenance
(c) Ford Introduces New Efficient Transmission
(d) How to Increase Fuel Efficiency Using New Transmission

2.

The first flight of an experimental aircraft. Seeing the system you designed enter the fleet. Success stories like these are why Northrop Grumman is a leader in the aerospace, defense, and technology industries. If you're searching for a career where you can be part of a big achievement, take a look at everything we have to offer. For decades, Northrop Grumman Integrated Systems has provided aircraft and systems for government, and guaranteed substantial opportunities for engineers and business operations professionals.

Q. What is the purpose of this passage?
(a) To recruit applicants to the company
(b) To boast the company's achievement
(c) To explain the company to their investors
(d) To demonstrate how the company has developed

1.

Ford unveiled a new transmission that should increase fuel efficiency and performance, while reducing maintenance. Dubbed "PowerShift," the new six-speed automatic transmission would be Ford's first implementation of a dual-clutch or automated-manual gearbox in North America. Ford expects its PowerShift transmission to be 9% more fuel efficient and weigh 30 pounds less than the four-speed automatic transmission. Ford wants to equip the gearbox to a compact car by 2010.

Q. **What is the best title for the passage?**
(a) How to Equip the Gearbox to a Compact Car
(b) Ford's Gearbox Will Be Requiring No Regular Maintenance
(c) Ford Introduces New Efficient Transmission
(d) How to Increase Fuel Efficiency Using New Transmission

오답과 정답 분석

정답 분석

자동차 부품에 조예가 없는 수험자는 다소 당황할 수도 있지만 이 글은 첫 문장부터 transmission, 즉 '변속기' 로 시작해서 끝나는 부분도 gearbox, 즉 '변속기' 에 대한 글로 마무리하고 있다. 따라서 이 글은 일관되게 포드의 새로운 변속기에 대해 소개하는 글이라는 정답을 끌어낼 수 있다.

오답 분석

지문에서는 변속기 장착의 효과 등을 다루고 있지 (a) 어떻게 장착을 시킬 것인가를 다루는 것은 아니다. (b) 기대 효과 중에서 정기적인 유지 보수가 필요 없다는 내용은 없다. (d) 새로운 변속 장치가 연료 효율성을 증가시킨다는 내용이 있긴 하나 그 방법에 대해 언급하지는 않았다. 이러한 제목 찾기 문제에서 출제자는 정답과 유사한 몇 가지 단어를 오답 보기 속에 넣고 수험자가 그것을 고르도록 유도한다.

2.

The first flight of an experimental aircraft. Seeing the system you designed enter the fleet. Success stories like these are why Northrop Grumman is a leader in the aerospace, defense, and technology industries. If you're searching for a career where you can be part of a big achievement, take a look at everything we have to offer. For decades, Northrop Grumman Integrated Systems has provided aircraft and systems for government, and guaranteed substantial opportunities for engineers and business operations professionals.

Q. What is the purpose of this passage?
(a) To recruit applicants to the company
(b) To boast the company's achievement
(c) To explain the company to their investors
(d) To demonstrate how the company has developed

오답과 정답 분석

정답 분석

윗글은 Northrop Grumman에 대한 소개 및 직원 채용을 위한 안내 글이다. 글의 전반적인 대의나 취지는 앞에서 언급되는 경우가 많지만, 이 글의 성격상 (사람을 뽑는다는 면에서) 너무 직접적인 언급보다는 비전 제시 등을 통해서 관심을 고조시키고 할 말은 뒤에서 하는 구조가 자연스럽다.

오답 분석

(d) 회사의 업적에 대해 간략히 이야기는 했지만 글 중간에 '~한 직업을 찾으신다면' 이라는 내용이 있어 답이 될 수 없다. 이러한 유형의 문제에서 출제자가 오답을 만드는 전형적인 방법은 부분적으로는 취지에 합당해도 전체적으로나 궁극적인 취지에는 맞지 않는 선택지를 제시하는 것이다. 회사의 업적 제시도 결국에는 구인을 위한 중간 제시라는 점에서 전형적인 오답이다.

1.

Kidney donors now can stop worrying about the long-term effects such a donation might have on their health and longevity. The long-term study of kidney donors has found that people who give kidneys to others not only have a normal life span, they also have fewer kidney problems than the general population. "We've suspected all along that kidney donation is a safe practice, but there has never been a long-term study with large numbers of patients in the United States," said Dr. Hassan N. Ibrahim of the University of Minnesota Medical School, who led the study.

Q.　**What is the best title for the passage?**
(a) Kidney Donors Have a Normal Life Span
(b) Kidneys Are the Most Commonly Transplanted Organ in the United States
(c) Kidney Ttransplants Grew Increasingly Popular
(d) The Donors Simply Feel Much Better about Themselves

2.

The *Los Angeles Times* is cutting 300 positions and will shrink the number of daily sections to four from five. The paper's publisher Eddy Hartenstein informed staff in a memo. Editor Russ Stanton said in a second memo that the cuts will include a 70-person reduction across the editorial department in the coming weeks. Hartenstein said the move to reduce the number of sections was intended to reap efficiencies in operations, production and distribution. The Times is owned by Chicago-based Tribune Co., which has filed for bankruptcy.

Q.　**What is the best title for the passage?**
(a) The Number of the Employees Fired from the Chicago Tribune
(b) The Los Angeles Times to Cut 300 Jobs
(c) The Effect of the Layoff
(d) The Chicago Tribune Has Filed for Bankruptcy

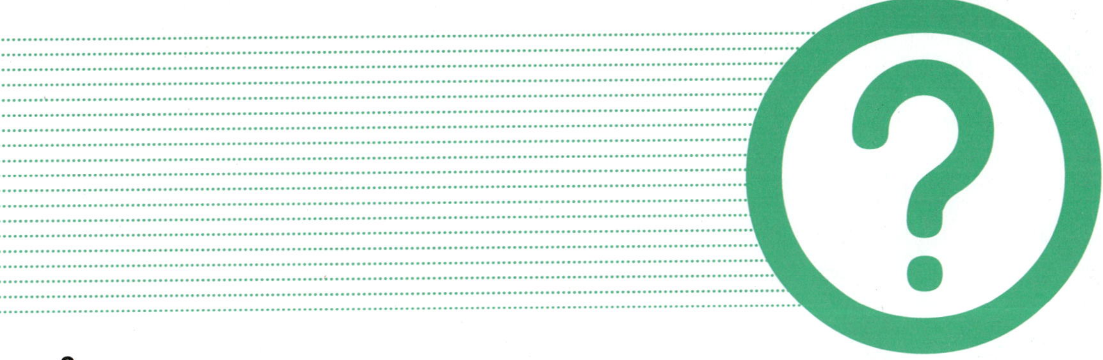

3.

If you are worried about your job or your future, you owe it to yourself to learn as much as you can about non-traditional ways to bring in a rock solid income. Remember, lots of regular people just like you are using the Internet to make money. You don't need any high-tech expertise to use Altavista to generate income. Our kit will show you how easy it can be to use Altavista to make money. Even if your job is secure, wouldn't it be great to have more money to put into savings to help with your retirement or pay off some bills? That's why so many millions of Americans are using work-from-home plans like Altavista to make money.

Q. **What is the purpose of the passage?**
(a) To teach people how to make money on the Internet
(b) To advertise the Altavista kit
(c) To recommend a job at home
(d) How to make savings

4.

More than a thousand eager shoppers flocked today to an airport hangar in Santa Monica with bad mirrors and no dressing rooms in the hopes of snagging some fashion treasure at a huge discount. It was opening day of the twice-yearly Barneys Warehouse Sale, which draws Southern California's fashion cognoscenti to this unlikely place in the hopes of getting expensive, fashion-forward dresses, shoes, men's suits and other sought-after items at bargain basement prices. The items gathered here at the Barker Hangar once adorned the floors of the rarefied retailer, Barneys New York, at its stores across the country. The 12-day sale continues through Feb. 16.

Q. **What is the best title for the passage?**
(a) Shoppers Flock to Barneys Warehouse Sale
(b) Fashion Treasure Decrease at a Bargain
(c) The Effect of National Recession to Fashion
(d) Shoppers Professed to Exercising More Caution, Buying Less

Urbanization 도시화

도시는 영어로 city지만 형용사형으로는 urban을 주로 쓴다. 도시는 나름의 장단점을 갖고 있으며 TEPS에는 주로 그 장단점에 관해 많이 출제된다. 장점으로는 도시화가 됨으로써 인프라가 개선되고 물자가 한 곳에 집결되어 있어 편리한 생활을 할 수 있다는 것이다. 그러나 단점으로는 인구의 도시 집중으로 농촌이 공동화되고, 도시에도 슬럼이나 빈민가 형성, 빈부 격차 심화 등의 문제가 파생된다는 것을 명심해야 한다.

STEP 1 Theme Research

Fill in the blanks with suitable words.

1.

Great cities have been built with no regard for us. The shape and dimensions of the skys___apers depend entirely on the necessity of obtaining maximum income per square foot of ground. This caused the construction of gigantic buildings where too large ma___es of human beings are crowded together.

2.

While they enjoy the comfort and banal luxury of their dwelling, they do not realize that they are deprived of the necessities of life. Obviously, it has not been planned for the good of its inh___itants.

Translation

1. 대도시는 우리를 전혀 고려하지 않은 채 만들어졌다. 고층 건물들의 모양과 크기는 전적으로 1평방피트 단위 면적당 최대한의 수입을 올리기 위한 필요에 따른 것이다. 이런 필요성 때문에 지나치게 많은 사람들로 빽빽하게 들어차 있는 거대한 건물들을 짓게 되었다.

2. 그들은 자신이 살고 있는 집의 안락함과 평범한 화려함을 즐기지만 정작 삶에 있어 필수적인 것들을 빼앗기고 있다는 사실은 깨닫지 못한다. 도시가 거주민들의 편의를 위해 계획되지 않았다는 것은 분명한 사실이다.

STEP 2 Words and Expressions

어구 해설

dimensions 크기, 규모
maximum 최대의
gigantic 거대한
banal 평범한
dwelling 거처, 사는 집
be deprived of ~을 빼앗기다
obviously 명백하게, 분명히

POP Quiz

다음 어휘나 어구의 뜻을 빈칸에 써 넣으시오.

1. urban   ___________________
2. urbanization ___________________
3. necessities of life ___________________
4. dwell   ___________________
5. inhabitant   ___________________
6. rural   ___________________
7. skyscraper   ___________________

ANSWERS

STEP 1 1. skyscrapers / masses of human beings
2. inhabitants

STEP 2 1. 도시의 2. 도시화 3. 생활의 필수 요소 4. 거주하다 5. 거주자 6. 시골의 7. 마천루, 고층 빌딩

1.

City parks were originally created to provide the local populace with a convenient refuge from the crowding and chaos of its surroundings. Until recently, these parks served their purpose admirably. City parks were a tranquil spot in which to unwind from the daily pressures of urban life. They were places where people met their friends for picnics or sporting events, and they were also places to get some sun and fresh air in the midst of an often dark and dreary environment, with its seemingly endless rows of steel, glass, and concrete buildings.

Q. **What is the main topic of the passage?**

(a) Parks were built in order to preserve plant-living cities.

(b) Parks were designed with the needs of city residents in mind.

(c) Parks were supposed to help people make new friends.

(d) Parks were intended to allow natural light to filter into cities.

오답과 정답 분석

정답 분석

도시의 공원은 원래 지역 주민들에게 북적대고 혼란스러운 주위 환경으로부터 편안한 피난처를 제공해주기 위해 생겼으며 도시 생활의 일상적인 압박으로부터 해방되는 평온한 장소로서 기능한다는 내용으로 볼 때, 공원은 도시 거주자들의 필요를 염두에 두고 만들어졌다는 의미의 (b)가 정답이 된다.

오답 분석

도시의 공원은 (a) 단순히 식물을 보존하기 위해서 또는 (c) 친구를 사귀기 위하여 만들어진 것은 아니며, 그것들은 지엽적인 내용에 불과하다. 늘 주제나 제목은 궁극적인 목적에 부합하는 것을 찾아야 한다.

2.

Is life better in a large city? Probably not. There is little space for each person, and this overcrowding causes problems—sickness, traffic, and crime. There isn't enough water, transportation, or housing. And there aren't enough jobs. One-third to one-half of the people who are living in many cities in developing nations cannot find work or can find only part-time jobs. Millions of these people are hungry, homeless, sick, and afraid of the future. This crisis is worsening daily.

Q. What is the best title for the passage?

(a) The Process of Urbanization
(b) The Urban Crisis
(c) The Advantages of City Life
(d) The Population Explosion

오답과 정답 분석

정답 분석

윗글의 첫 부분에 '대도시가 정말 더 살기 좋은가? 아마 아닐 것이다' 라는 문장이 나오고 그 뒤에는 그 문제점에 대해 상술하고 있다. 제목 찾기 문제에서는 늘 전체적인 분위기가 긍정적이냐 부정적이냐 하는 것과 찾은 제목이 너무 포괄적이거나 미시적이지는 않은가라는 문제에 부딪치게 된다. 이 글의 제목으로는 (b) '도시의 위기' 가 글의 부정적인 내용과 나열된 문제점들을 포괄적으로 잘 나타내고 있기에 적합하다.

오답 분석

이러한 유형에서 오답 보기는 아예 언급되지 않았거나 지문과 다른 내용을 담아 수험자를 혼란에 빠뜨린다. (a) 도시화 과정이나 (c) 도시 생활의 이점에 관한 내용은 아예 언급되지 않았다. (d) 인구 팽창은 도시 생활의 위기의 한 원인에 불과하다.

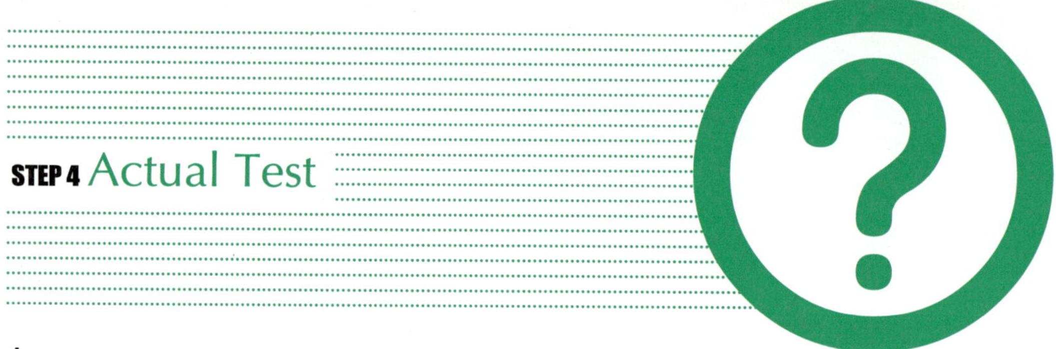

1.

Some geographers say that urbanization is a good thing because it relieves pressure on the land and in many countries there are too many people for the work available. Others consider that urbanization is a bad thing because a city depends very much on food being supplied from the surrounding countryside. In countries where there is a shortage of food supply, this massive increase in the size of towns will place a tremendous strain on the surrounding agricultural areas. Moreover, it is generally the young and active members of population who tend to migrate, leaving the elderly, children, and the infirm to run the farms, which is unlikely to improve the efficiency of the farms. There is thus a decline in rural industries and food supply.

Q. **Which of the following arises from urbanization?**

(a) The agricultural areas surrounding big cities become less productive.
(b) The elderly and children become worse off.
(c) Land becomes less fertile.
(d) Farmers become more inactive.

2.

In many countries, overcrowded cities face a major problem. Unfortunately poor conditions in the urban areas, such as lack of housing, worsening sanitation and unemployment, bring about an increase in poverty, disease and crime. The only long-term solution is to make life in the rural areas more attractive, which would encourage people to stay there. Facilities in the rural areas should be improved to foster a more positive attitude towards rural life. The improvement for a rural lifestyle is undoubtedly important because the cities themselves cannot be developed without the prior development of the rural areas.

Q. **What is the best title for the passage?**

(a) Rural Facilities: Present and Future
(b) Urban Facilities: Present and Future
(c) Rural Education: Problem and Solution
(d) Urban Overcrowding: Problem and Solution

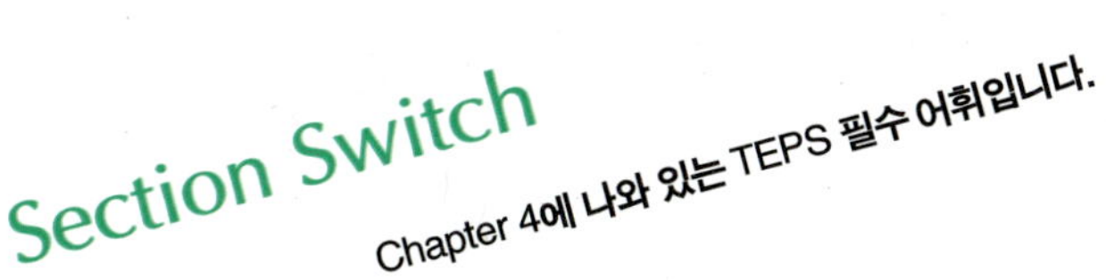

☐ **admirably** 훌륭하게

☐ **aerospace** 항공 우주(의)

☐ **assure** 확인하다, 확신하다

☐ **cognoscenti** (미술, 문예 작품 따위에) 통달한 사람, 감정가

☐ **donor** 기증자

☐ **dreary** 음울한, 황량한

☐ **dub** (이름·명칭을) 붙이다, ~라고 부르다

☐ **expertise** 전문 지식

☐ **fashion-forward** 패션을 선도하는

☐ **file for bankruptcy** 파산 신청을 하다

☐ **fleet** (항공기의) 기단(機團), 비행대

☐ **foster** 촉진하다, 조성하다

☐ **gearbox** 변속 장치

☐ **geographer** 지리학자

☐ **hangar** 격납고

☐ **homeless** 집 없는

☐ **human remains** 유해, 사체

☐ **implementation** 구현, 성취

☐ **infirm** 허약한

☐ **kidney** 신장

☐ **longevity** 수명

☐ **migrate** 이주하다

☐ **overcrowding** 과밀, 혼잡

☐ **owe it to yourself to** 자신에게 ~할 의무가 있다

☐ **populace** 대중, 서민, (한 지역의) 전체 주민

☐ **rarefied** 드문, 일류의

☐ **reap** (성과·이익 등을) 올리다, 거두다

☐ **refuge** 피난처

☐ **sanitation** 공중위생, 위생 설비

☐ **shrink** 축소시키다, 줄이다

☐ **snag** 획득하다, 재빨리 잡다

☐ **sought-after** 수요가 많은

☐ **strain** 큰 부담

☐ **tranquil** 조용한, 평온한

☐ **transmission** (자동차의) 변속기

☐ **tremendous** 거대한

☐ **twice-yearly** 해마다 두 번씩

☐ **unveil** 발표하다, 공개하다

☐ **unwind** (긴장을) 풀다, 편안한 마음을 갖게 하다

☐ **urbanization** 도시화

☐ **vanish** 사라지다, 실종되다

☐ **wreckage** 잔해, 파편

Chapter 5

Chapter 5

STEP 1 Pattern Study

유형별 빠른 풀이법

일치 불일치 문제의 출제 포인트는 주된 내용에서 벗어난 내용을 수험생이 찾아내는가이다.
따라서 수험생의 입장에서는 빠른 시간 내에 해당 지문을 읽고 선택지에서 긍정적이거나 부정적인 내용을 뒷받침하는 부사나 형용사 등을 체크하는 것이 중요하다.

Sample

Wall Street shook off news of a historic decline in house prices last month and followed international markets upward after the Japanese market gained 6% and Hong Kong rose 14% overnight. The Dow Jones industrial average added 4% in the first half hour of trading today. The question is, is the market coming up off a bottom or experiencing what Wall Street sardonically refers to as a 'dead-cat bounce,' a reference to the idea that if you drop a cat on a trampoline, it will go up, once.

Q. **Which of the following is correct about the article?**

(a) House prices moved up slightly last month.

(b) The Japanese stock market suffered from a decline in stock prices last month.

(c) The Dow Jones industrial average went up 4% today.

(d) We can't be sure whether today's upward market is coming up off a bottom or not.

풀이 적용

다음처럼 지문 내용에 대비하여 틀린 점을 찾아 오답 보기를 제거한다.

(a) House prices moved up slightly last month. → slightly는 아니다.

(b) The Japanese stock market suffered from a decline in stock prices last month. → last month가 아니다.

(c) The Dow Jones industrial average went up 4% today. → 개장 초반에 잠깐 올랐다는 내용이 있을 뿐이다.

오답을 모두 제거하고 나면 자연스럽게 (d)가 정답이 된다는 것을 알 수 있다.

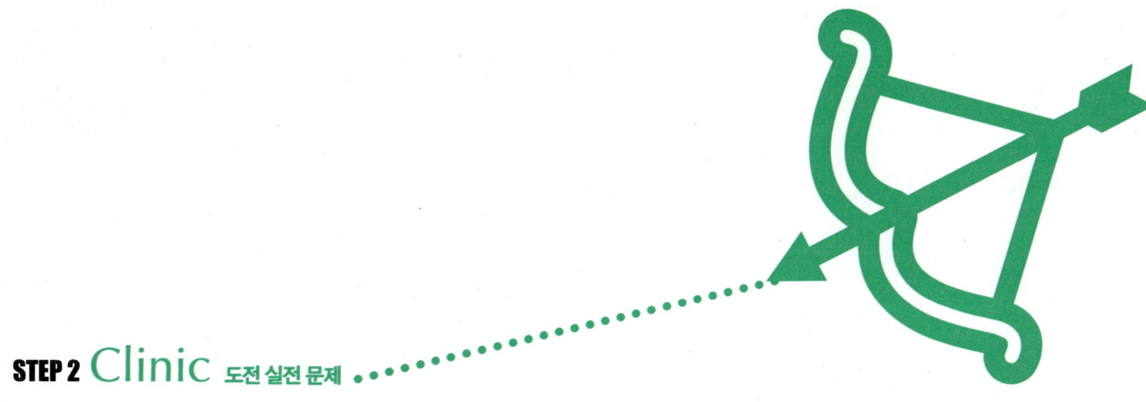

1.

A U.S. university will begin the practice of teaching classes in both Korean and English to enable Korean students with limited English skills to earn a degree. Fairleigh Dickinson University in New Jersey will offer a three-year liberal arts associate degree with classes taught in the two languages. This program is an effort by the university to reach out to the growing Korean population in the state. Korean college graduates already suffer a low standard of English, and it's believed by some educators that the practice of U.S. institutions teaching in Korean will lower the general English competency of the college graduates.

Q. **Which of the following is correct about the article?**
   (a) Most Korean students have sufficient English skills to earn a degree.
   (b) Some experts think teaching in Korean will aggravate the English fluency of the college graduates.
   (c) The number of Koreans in New Jersey has been decreasing for decades.
   (d) To teach in two languages definitely helps Koreans in studying.

2.

Schaumburg-based Motorola Inc. said it is laying off 4,000 workers in 2009, with 3,000 of them in the company's mobile phone development division. The layoffs are expected to begin immediately and come on top of a 3,000 workforce reduction announced during the fourth quarter of 2008. Motorola also announced preliminary fourth-quarter results for 2008, saying it expects a net loss of between $0.07 and $0.08 per share. The company will announce its earnings on Feb. 3.

Q. **Which of the following is correct about the article?**
   (a) Personnel from the Marketing division lost the most amount of workers.
   (b) At least 7,000 workers have left Motorola since 2008 in Schaumburg.
   (c) Restructuring at Motorola will proceed gradually.
   (d) Many stockholders of Motorola suffered heavy losses in the stock market slump.

1.

A U.S. university will begin the practice of teaching classes in both Korean and English to enable Korean students with limited English skills to earn a degree. Fairleigh Dickinson University in New Jersey will offer a three-year liberal arts associate degree with classes taught in the two languages. This program is an effort by the university to reach out to the growing Korean population in the state. Korean college graduates already suffer a low standard of English, and it's believed by some educators that the practice of U.S. institutions teaching in Korean will lower the general English competency of the college graduates.

Q. **Which of the following is correct about the article?**
 (a) Most Korean students have sufficient English skills to earn a degree.
 (b) Some experts think teaching in Korean will aggravate the English fluency of the college graduates.
 (c) The number of Koreans in New Jersey has been decreasing for decades.
 (d) To teach in two languages definitely helps Koreans in studying.

오답과 정답 분석

정답 분석

일치 불일치 문제에서는 다소 치밀하고 깐깐한 읽기가 필요하다. 윗글 후반부에 그 프로그램이 졸업생들의 영어 능력을 저하시킬 것이라고 일부 전문가가 우려하는 내용이 있다. 그것을 정확히 지적한 (b)가 정답이다.

오답 분석

일치 불일치 문제에서 오답을 만드는 데 잘 쓰는 요소는 주로 형용사와 부사이다. (a) 한국인 대학 졸업생들이 영어 능력이 부족해 어려움을 겪고 있다는 내용이 이미 소개되었기에 '충분한'(sufficient)이라는 서술은 오답이다. (d) 두 개의 언어로 가르치는 것에 대한 논란이 있다. 그럼에도 불구하고 '명확하게'의 의미를 가지는 definitely를 사용한 것은 오류가 있다.

2.

Schaumburg-based Motorola Inc. said it is laying off 4,000 workers in 2009, with 3,000 of them in the company's mobile phone development division. The layoffs are expected to begin immediately and come on top of a 3,000 workforce reduction announced during the fourth quarter of 2008. Motorola also announced preliminary fourth-quarter results for 2008, saying it expects a net loss of between $0.07 and $0.08 per share. The company will announce its earnings on Feb. 3.

Q. Which of the following is correct about the article?

(a) Personnel from the Marketing division lost the most amount of workers.

(b) At least 7,000 workers have left Motorola since 2008 in Schaumburg.

(c) Restructuring at Motorola will proceed gradually.

(d) Many stockholders of Motorola suffered heavy losses in the stock market slump.

오답과 정답 분석

정답 분석

(b) 2008년 4분기에 3,000명, 2009년 4,000명, 총 7,000명의 직원이 모토롤라를 떠났거나 떠날 것이다. 이렇게 숫자를 동반한 문제는 단순하게 답이 나오는 경우보다는 한 번 정도의 계산 과정을 수반하는 경우가 많다. 즉 이 문제에서도 3,000 더하기 4,000이라는 계산을 요구하고 있다.

오답 분석

(d) 직원을 해고까지 한 상황이니 주식도 떨어졌을 것이라 예측되기는 하나 지문의 내용만 가지고는 알 수 없다. 일치 불일치 문제에서 가장 많이 내는 오답 보기는 있지 않은 내용을 담는 것이다. 물론 어느 정도 추론은 되지만 지문에 나와 있지 않다면 반드시 오답으로 골라내야 한다.

1.

Michael Jackson's attorney says the singer might be too sick to travel to testify in a case claiming he owes $7 million to an Arab sheikh. The sheikh is calling Jackson a rip-off artist, claiming he took $7 million as an advance on an album and an autobiography but hasn't produced either. Lawyers for the sheikh say the money was given to Jackson while he was short on cash and struggling to revive his career after his child molestation trial. A lawyer for Jackson says there was never a valid agreement and that the money was given freely.

Q. **Which of the following is correct about the article?**
(a) Michael Jackson is in good health right now.
(b) Michael Jackson acknowledged he borrowed $7 million from the Arab sheikh.
(c) Michael Jackson was willing to produce an autobiography for the money.
(d) There hasn't been any consent between the two parties so far.

2.

Nobel Peace Prize winner Muhammad Yunus predicted that world poverty would be cut in half by 2015 and eliminated fifteen years later. King County vowed to end homelessness within a decade. Now, an economy mired in severe recession threatens to throw those goals off track. Some of the biggest givers are determined to maintain their ambitions. However, they are either curbing their planned growth or reducing their donations. The Bill & Melinda Gates Foundation is trimming its growth to ten percent in 2009, compared with a thirty percent expansion last year.

Q. **Which of the following is correct about the article?**
(a) Yunus expected that world poverty would be abolished completely in ten years.
(b) One of the counties promised to terminate homelessness in ten years.
(c) Economic recession has nothing to do with the givers' choice.
(d) The Bill & Melinda Gates Foundation increased its growth up to ten percent.

3.

New York governor Eliot Spitzer has resigned after being linked to a prostitution ring. Flanked by his wife, he told a news conference he could not allow "private failings" to disrupt public work. Spitzer again apologized for not living up to the standards he demanded of others—but he gave no details. The governor had allegedly been identified arranging to meet a prostitute in a Washington hotel. Spitzer made his name as an investigator of organized crime, financial crime and prostitution, and his fall from political grace is being seen as one of the biggest New York has known. At one point he was known as the "Sheriff of Wall Street" for the vigor with which he pursued dirty dealing in high finance.

Q. Which of the following is correct according to the passage?
(a) Eliot Spitzer has resigned due to his suspicion in bribery.
(b) Eliot Spitzer has excused his wrongdoings in detail.
(c) Eliot Spitzer owes his fame to pursuing dirty dealing in high finance.
(d) Eliot Spitzer resisted the press on the prostitution matters.

4.

Screw caps were a sign of cheap wines. But problems with other types of stoppers, most notably cork, have prompted winemakers to rethink screw caps. The Australians are into screw caps in a big way. Even the French, keepers of wine traditions, are making some screw-cap wines. Yes, most expensive, age-able wines are still stoppered with cork. There's a microscopic exchange of oxygen with cork that allows a wine to age over years and decades. Screw caps are better for wines you're not going to keep more than a few years. And screw caps are blissfully easy to open.

Q. Which of the following is correct according to the passage?
(a) All the wines stoppered with cork are expensive.
(b) More and more wine companies are using screw caps as a stopper.
(c) There's a microscopic reciprocation of air that occurs when using screw caps.
(d) Cork stoppers are easier to open than screw caps.

The U.S., a Nation of Immigrants
미국은 이민 국가이자 다민족 국가이다

출제 경향 파악

미국은 전형적인 이민(immigrant) 국가이자 동시에 다민족 국가이다. '이민 오다' 라고 할 때는 im-을 붙여 immigrate라고 하고, '이민 가다' 라고 할 때는 e-를 붙여서 emigrate라고 한다. 미국은 역사가 깊은 나라가 아니라 이민자들에 의해 건설된 나라이기 때문에 그들의 다민족성을 인정하면서도 미국이라는 하나의 국가를 유지하기 위한 단일성을 부각시킨다. 그리고 그 과정에서 빚어지는 갈등 같은 것들이 주로 출제된다. 예를 들어 언어 사용에 있어서 그들 각자의 모국어(mother tongue)를 사용하게 해야 하는가 아닌가 같은 문제 등이 출제 빈도가 높다.

STEP 1 Theme Research

Fill in the blanks with suitable words.

1.

No study to the United States would be complete without a discussion of immi___ants because America is a nation of immigrants. Since 1607, when the first English settlers reached the New World, over 45 million people have mi___ated to the United States. This represents the largest migration of people in all of recorded history.

2.

For 400 years, a nation of over 200 million people has been built by persons who came from all parts of the world and all w___lks of life. Every aspect of American life, from business to athletics, has been influenced in one way or another by immigrants. No one could ever completely understand this "tee___ing nation of nations," as the poet Walt Whitman called it, without first knowing something about the history of m___lting pot.

Translation

1. 미국은 이민자들의 나라이기 때문에 미국에 관한 어떤 연구도 이민자들에 대한 논의를 배제하는 한 완벽해지지 않을 것이다. 최초의 영국 정착민들이 신대륙에 도착했던 1607년 이래 4천 5백만 명 이상의 사람들이 미국으로 이주했다. 이는 역사상 가장 큰 인구 이동을 보여준다.

2. 400년간 전 세계에서 온 온갖 부류의 사람들에 의해 2억이 넘는 인구를 가진 하나의 국가가 건설되었다. 미국인의 모든 삶은 사업에서 운동 경기에 이르기까지 이민자들에 의해 이런저런 방식으로 영향을 받아왔다. 먼저 인종과 문화의 도가니인 미국의 역사에 관해 무엇인가를 배우지 않고서는 아무도 시인 월트 휘트먼이 '여러 나라가 바글바글 섞여 있는 나라'라고 일컬은 이 나라를 완벽하게 이해할 수는 없을 것이다.

STEP 2 Words and Expressions

어구 해설

migration 이동, 이주
represent 나타내다, 의미하다
teeming 바글바글한
walk of life 신분, 계급, 지위

POP Quiz

다음 어휘나 어구의 뜻을 빈칸에 써 넣으시오.

1. immigrant ________________
2. migrate ________________
3. melting pot ________________
4. unity ________________
5. diversity ________________

ANSWERS

STEP 1 1. immigrants / migrated
2. walks of life / teeming nation / melting pot

STEP 2 1. 이민자 2. 이주하다, 이동하다 3. 인종과 문화의 도가니 4. 통일성 5. 다양성

1.

For years, it was thought that the United States was and should be a "melting pot"—in other words, that people from all over the world come and adopt the American culture as their own. More recently, some people have compared the United States to a mosaic—a picture made of many different pieces. America's strength, they argue, lies in its __________ and the contributions made by people of many different cultures. In a homogeneous culture such as that of Iceland, minority problems lack the immediacy they have in the multicultural United States.

Q. Choose the option that best completes the passage.
   (a) unity
   (b) diversity
   (c) variation
   (d) discrimination

오답과 정답 분석

정답 분석

빈칸 앞에서 인종의 도가니, 전 세계 사람들이 미국으로 와 미국 문화를 자신들의 문화로 선택했다는 것, 모자이크 등의 내용이 있는데 그것은 곧 다양성을 뜻한다. 인종적 다양성이 바로 미국을 구성하는 중요한 특징이라면 미국이 이민 국가라는 것을 강조하는 이 지문에서는 당연히 diversity, 즉 '다양성' 이 답으로 처리될 수밖에 없다.

오답 분석

윗글은 인종의 도가니 등의 내용으로 미루어 보아 미국의 다양성에 관한 이야기이다. 다양성은 (a) 단결(unity)과는 반대되는 개념이며, 다양성이 (d) '차별' (discrimination) 또는 (c) '변화' (variation)를 뜻하지도 않는다.

2.

The United States remains an underdeveloped country when it comes to language skills. Immigrants are importing their mother tongues at record rates. Yet the vast majority of Americans remain stubbornly monolingual. Ignorance of other languages and cultures handicaps the United States in dealing with the rest of the world. Today the language policies in the United States address this problem primarily with efforts to teach "foreign" languages to monolingual Americans. Meanwhile, the United States seeks to eliminate these same skills among ethnic minorities by reducing existing bilingual programs, ___________ or haste to force their assimilation. Instead of focusing on immigrants' disabilities in English, why not encourage them to maintain their abilities in their mother tongues while they learn English?

Q. Choose the option that best completes the passage.
  (a) out of misplaced fears of diversity
  (b) by the brightened mind of congeniality
  (c) forming the heart to unity
  (d) through the entire fear for their unhealthiness

오답과 정답 분석

정답 분석

이민자들이 그들의 다양한 모국어를 들여오고 있다는 점과 미국이 서둘러 이민자를 동화시켜려 한다는 점에서 미국이 두려워하는 것은 다양성이고, 그것은 필자의 견해대로 라면 다분히 그릇된 판단에서 비롯된 것임을 알 수 있다. 따라서, 정답은 (a)가 되어야 한다.

오답 분석

윗글에 따르면, 미국인들이 다양성을 부정하려는 태도는 절대 긍정적으로 평가될 수 없을 것이다. 따라서 (b)에서, 동질성에 대한 밝은 마음에 의해서 만들어지는 것은 아니고, (c)처럼 진심으로 일치성을 기원한다는 것은 설득력이 약하다. 또한 (d)는 fear의 서술은 얼핏 타당해 보이기도 하지만, 그 대상이 unhealthiness라면 주제와 거리가 멀기에 답이 될 수 없다.

1.

Compulsory schooling began in the United States in the 19th century as a way of transmitting and maintaining Anglo-American culture and language. Educators believed that proficiency in two languages was not possible, so educational policymakers declared that students should learn English only. Also, the ability to speak English was made a condition for American citizenship in 1906, and in 1915 an English-literacy requirement was added. The justification provided for these measures was a peculiar doctrine about the connection between language and political thought, which held that speaking a foreign language was inimical to grasping the fundamental concepts of a democratic society.

Q. **What's the mood of the article?**
(a) Critical
(b) Horrible
(c) Humorous
(d) Pessimistic

2.

Puerto Rican immigration to the city constituted the largest influx of people since the great waves of European immigration in the 19th century. The islanders soon found out what earlier immigrants had learned. Wages were better but prices were higher; houses were dilapidated; crime was rampant; the weather was cold and damp; and the society at large was strange and different. How to keep one's family together and preserve one's identity were problems faced by every immigrant group, and they are problems faced by New York Puerto Ricans today. Life in the city was not easy, but there was little to return to. Unlike many other non-English-speaking newcomers to the city, Puerto Ricans are American citizens. As Americans, they have the right to come and go as they please. Also unlike previous immigrants, Puerto Ricans did not have to sever their ties to the homeland once they arrived in the city. Thus they could maintain, and even constantly renew, contact with their culture.

Q. **Puerto Ricans faced all the following problems previous immigrant groups faced except for ____________.**
(a) prices outdistancing wages
(b) inadequate housing
(c) poor climate
(d) broken cultural ties

Section Switch

Chapter 5에 나와 있는 TEPS 필수 어휘입니다.

☐ **address** 다루다, 처리하다
☐ **adopt** (자기 것으로) 받아들이다
☐ **advance** 선금
☐ **allegedly** 전해진 바에 따르면
☐ **Anglo-American** 영미(英美)의, 영국계 미국인의
☐ **argue** 논하다, 논의하다
☐ **assimilation** 동화, 융합
☐ **associate degree** 준학사 (2년제 대학 졸업생에게 수여되는 학위)
☐ **autobiography** 자서전
☐ **be flanked by** ~옆에 서다
☐ **bilingual** 2개 국어를 하는
☐ **blissfully** 즐겁게
☐ **citizenship** 시민권
☐ **competency** 능력
☐ **compulsory** 강제적인, 의무적인, 필수의
☐ **constitute** 구성하다, 구성 요소가 되다
☐ **contribution** 기여, 공헌
☐ **curb** 억제하다
☐ **damp** 습한
☐ **dilapidated** 황폐한, 초라한
☐ **doctrine** 주의, 원칙
☐ **earnings** 소득
☐ **eliminate** 제거하다, 없애다
☐ **grasp** 파악하다, 이해하다
☐ **handicap** 불리한 입장에 세우다
☐ **high finance** 거액 융자, 대형 금융 거래[기관]
☐ **homogeneous** 동종의, 단일한
☐ **immediacy** 직접, 즉시(성)
☐ **influx** 유입
☐ **inimical** 해로운
☐ **justification** 정당화
☐ **liberal arts** 교양 과목
☐ **melting pot** 인종과 문화의 도가니

☐ **microscopic** 극히 작은, 미세한
☐ **mired in** ~의 곤경[궁지]에 빠진
☐ **misplaced** 잘못된
☐ **molestation** 희롱, 추행
☐ **monolingual** 1개 국어를 사용하는
☐ **mother tongue** 모국어
☐ **net loss** 순손실
☐ **notably** 그중에서도 특히
☐ **on top of** ~에 더해
☐ **peculiar** 기묘한, 특이한
☐ **policymaker** 정책 입안자
☐ **preliminary** 예비의
☐ **preserve** 유지하다, 보존하다
☐ **prostitution** 매춘
☐ **rampant** 만연하는
☐ **recession** 불경기, 경기 후퇴
☐ **reference** 언급, 가리킴
☐ **ring** 조직, 도당
☐ **rip-off artist** 사기꾼
☐ **sardonically** 냉소적으로
☐ **sever** (인연·관계 등을) 끊다
☐ **sheikh** (이슬람교, 특히 아라비아에서) 가장, 족장
☐ **stopper** 마개; 마개를 막다
☐ **stubbornly** 완고하게
☐ **testify** 증언하다
☐ **ties** 유대, 기반
☐ **transmit** 전하다
☐ **trim** (예산 등을) 깎다, 삭감하다
☐ **underdeveloped** 저개발의, 후진의
☐ **vow** 단언하다, 맹세하다

Chapter 6

Chapter 6

STEP 1 Pattern Study

유형별 빠른 풀이법

이 유형은 일치 불일치 문제의 일종의 변형된 형태라고 보아야 한다. 지문 전체의 개별적인 사실에 대한 이해를 바탕으로 큰 맥락을 잡는 것이 중요하다. 일단 문제에서 물어보는 사실 관계에 충실하면서 내용을 하나씩 파악해가는 데 주력해야 한다.

Sample

A cool-headed pilot maneuvered his crippled jetliner over New York City and ditched it in the frigid Hudson River, and all 155 on board were pulled to safety as the plane slowly sank. It was, the governor said, "a miracle on the Hudson." One victim suffered two broken legs, a paramedic said, but there were no other reports of serious injuries. The Airbus A320 bound for Charlotte, N.C., struck a flock of birds just after takeoff minutes earlier at LaGuardia Airport, apparently disabling the engines.

Q. **What caused the aircraft to experience problems?**

(a) It made an emergency landing on the Hudson River.
(b) There were communication problems between the airport and the plane.
(c) It collided with a flock of birds.
(d) There were mistakes made in the maintenance of the aircraft.

 **풀이 적용**

글을 읽어보면 '고장 → 그럼에도 불구하고 안전하게 구출 → 원인은 새와의 충돌' 식으로 사고 진행 상황을 일목요연하게 설명했다. 따라서 사고의 원인은 (c)라는 것을 알 수 있다.

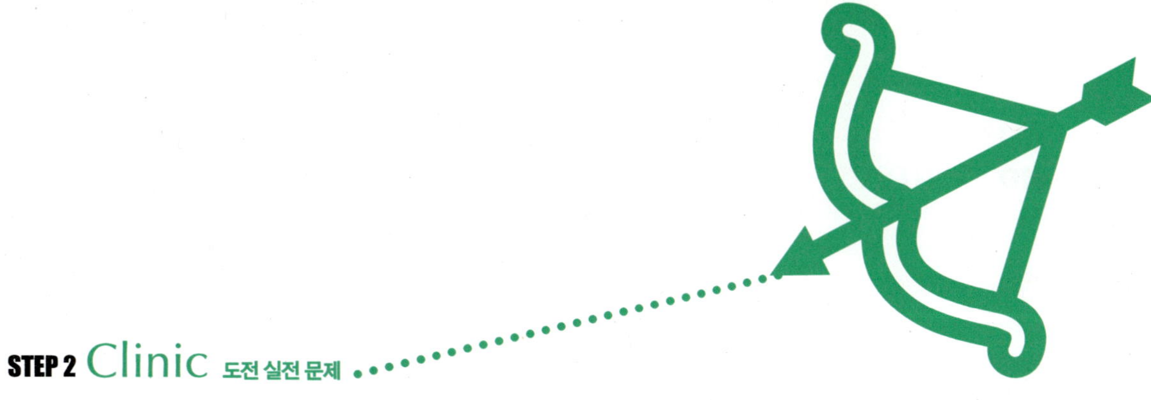

1.

Set against a breathtaking Sonoran Desert backdrop, Scottsdale, Arizona, is a luxury oasis with a sophisticated style. With lavish resorts and spas, world-class shopping, award-winning restaurants and a vibrant nightlife scene, Scottsdale offers something for everyone. And for those who like to vacation where there are always exciting new things to see, Scottsdale is the perfect choice.

Q. **What is this passage advertising?**
(a) A tourist spot
(b) A shopping mall
(c) An oasis
(d) A resort

2.

In the face of our common dangers, in this winter of our hardship, let us remember these timeless words. With hope and virtue, let us brave once more the icy currents, and endure what storms may come. Let it be said by our children's children that when we were tested we refused to let this journey end, that we did not turn back nor did we falter; and with eyes fixed on the horizon and God's grace upon us, we carried forth that great gift of freedom and delivered it safely to future generations. Thank you. God bless you. And God bless the United States of America.

Q. **Where could this passage be used?**
(a) At a graduation ceremony
(b) During a commencement ceremony
(c) During the press conference of a politician
(d) At an inaugural ceremony

1.

Set against a breathtaking Sonoran Desert backdrop, Scottsdale, Arizona, is a luxury oasis with a sophisticated style. With lavish resorts and spas, world-class shopping, award-winning restaurants and a vibrant nightlife scene, Scottsdale offers something for everyone. And for those who like to vacation where there are always exciting new things to see, Scottsdale is the perfect choice.

Q. **What is this passage advertising?**
(a) A tourist spot
(b) A shopping mall
(c) An oasis
(d) A resort

오답과 정답 분석

정답 분석

윗글은 관광지에 대해 광고하는 글이다. (c) An oasis나 (d) A resort도 관광의 대상이 될 수는 있지만 이 문제에서는 포괄적으로 관광의 대상이 되는 (a) A tourist spot에 대해서 이야기하고 있다.

오답 분석

(b), (c), (d) 쇼핑몰, 리조트 등은 그 관광지의 일부일 뿐이다. 대상을 찾는 문제에서 오답을 만드는 방법은 정답과 유사성은 있되 범위가 작은 것을 제시하는 것이다. 이 문제에서도 그러한 식으로 관광지보다 작은 부분들을 오답으로 제시하고 있다.

2.

In the face of our common dangers, in this winter of our hardship, let us remember these timeless words. With hope and virtue, let us brave once more the icy currents, and endure what storms may come. Let it be said by our children's children that when we were tested we refused to let this journey end, that we did not turn back nor did we falter; and with eyes fixed on the horizon and God's grace upon us, we carried forth that great gift of freedom and delivered it safely to future generations. Thank you. God bless you. And God bless the United States of America.

Q. **Where could this passage be used?**
(a) At a graduation ceremony
(b) During a commencement ceremony
(c) During the press conference of a politician
(d) At an inaugural ceremony

오답과 정답 분석

정답 분석

이 글은 2009년 1월 20일 미국 국회 의사당 앞에서 개최된 제44대 미국 대통령 버락 오바마의 취임사 마지막 부분이다. 지문 중에서도 특히 Thank you. God bless you. And God bless the United States of America. 부분은 이 글이 확실하게 연설문임을, 그것도 대통령 취임식에 쓰인 연설문임을 알려주고 있다.

오답 분석

나머지 오답들은 연설문이 쓰일 수 있는 여러 가지 상황들을 예시적으로 만들어서 출제자가 제시한 것이다. 따라서 상황을 빨리 파악해서 어떤 장소에서 이 말들이 쓰이고 있는지를 간파해 답을 찾아내야 한다.

1.

Hundreds of Buddhist monks have marched around Burma's most revered temple, in a third consecutive day of protests against the military government. The monks were allowed into the Shwedagon Pagoda in Rangoon for the first time since their protests began. They walked through the city surrounded by a human chain of civilians holding hands to protect them. They want a government apology for the violent break-up of a recent rally, triggered by protests over price rises.

Q. **Why did the Buddhist monks march around the temple?**
(a) To chant a sutra
(b) To meet their believers
(c) To ask the government for apology
(d) To break up a rally against the government

2.

Should you be buying stocks right now? If you have a $500,000 portfolio, you should download the latest report by Forbes columnist Ken Fisher. In it he tells you where he thinks the stock market is headed, and why. This must-read report includes his latest stock market prediction, plus research and analysis you can use in your portfolio right now. Don't miss it!

Q. **What is this passage advertising?**
(a) Stock
(b) A portfolio of stocks
(c) The outlook of the stock market
(d) A Forbes column

3.

We are making three noticeable changes to our office space. The cubicles you work at will be replaced by desks made of high-quality oak. The change should improve communication in the office and will give the area a more open, comforting atmosphere. And our carpeted floor is being replaced with hardwood floors. This should reduce dust. More importantly, it should improve the working environment of those who suffer from allergies.

Q. What is the benefit of using wood floors according to the passage?
   (a) It makes us feel comfortable.
   (b) It doesn't make any dust.
   (c) It is more state-of-the-art than carpeted floor.
   (d) It can improve the communication among employees.

4.

A nurse found a plastic notch in a Cosco Touriva product while trying to figure out what caused a baby's skull to fracture in a low-speed crash. She warned the company of the potential hazard of a small head hitting the edge of this hard, hidden indentation. Yet the company sold hundreds of thousands of the Touriva seats before removing the notch from all versions of the seat in 2005, five years after the nurse alerted the company. Among those buyers were at least two more families who now allege the notch injured or killed their children during crashes.

Q. What is the Cosco Touriva product?
   (a) A safety seat belt
   (b) An automobile toy
   (c) A wheelchair
   (d) A child car seat

출제 경향 파악

TEPS에서 환경 문제의 출제 경향은 환경이 파괴되고 있는 것을 부각시키는 측면, 즉 대기 · 수질 · 토양 오염의 문제를 부각시키는 측면과 그 대책의 측면으로 나눠진다. 산업 폐기물과 재활용은 각종 오염을 일으키는 산업 폐기물과 그에 대한 대책으로서 재활용을 다루는 전형적인 환경 오염 대책에 대한 문제이다.

STEP 1 Theme Research

Fill in the blanks with suitable words.

1.

Our land, air, and water are slowly being po___oned by the w___te we create. As a result, we are now facing waste problems in proportions beyond imagination. We dispose of our waste by storing, dumping, burying or burning it.

2.

But it does not go away and will most certainly come back to haunt both of us and future generations, whose problems may be greatly magnified because of our failure to handle waste appropriately. The irony of the problem is that the wastes we throw away are val___ble res___rces, for which we all pay the price. The solution, then, lies with all of us to reduce the amount of waste we create, and to rec___le or re___se what remains.

Translation

1. 우리의 땅과 공기, 물이 우리가 만들어내는 쓰레기에 의해 서서히 오염되어 가고 있다. 그 결과 우리는 상상을 초월할 정도의 쓰레기 문제에 직면해 있다. 우리는 쓰레기를 쌓아 놓거나 갖다 버리거나 땅에 파묻거나 소각해버리는 식으로 처리한다.

2. 그러나 쓰레기는 사라지지 않고 분명히 되돌아와 우리와 우리의 미래 세대를 괴롭힐 것이며 우리가 쓰레기를 제대로 처리하지 못하면 미래 세대의 문제는 더욱 심각해질 것이다. 문제의 아이러니는 우리가 버리는 쓰레기들이 귀중한 자원이며 그것을 위하여 우리 모두가 값을 지불한다는 점에 있다. 그렇다면 해결책은 우리가 만드는 쓰레기의 양을 우리 모두가 줄여가고 남는 것은 재활용하거나 재사용하는 데 있다.

STEP 2 Words and Expressions

어구 해설

dispose of ~을 처리하다, 처치[처분]하다
haunt 괴롭히다, 문제를 일으키다
magnify 확대하다
appropriately 적절히

POP Quiz

다음 어휘나 어구의 뜻을 빈칸에 써 넣으시오.

1. waste _______________
2. recycle _______________
3. dump _______________
4. bury _______________
5. emission _______________
6. filler _______________

ANSWERS

STEP 1 1. poisoned / waste
2. valuable resources / recycle or reuse

STEP 2 1. 쓰레기 2. 재활용하다 3. (내)버리다 4. 매립하다 5. 방출, 방사 6. 충전재

1.

In the United States, about 10 million computers are thrown away every year. Because most unwanted computers are sent to a dump, they have caused a problem. The computer industry and the government are working on ways to solve it. They have concluded that there must be changes in the way computers are built. They must be made in ways that will allow their parts to be recycled.

Q. **What can be inferred from the passage?**

(a) The computer industry should reduce the production of computers.

(b) The computer industry should use the parts which can be recycled later.

(c) More computers will be buried in the following decade.

(d) The computer is a hazardous appliance to our mental health.

오답과 정답 분석

정답 분석

지문 마지막에 컴퓨터는 각 부품들이 재활용될 수 있는 방식으로 제조되어야 한다는 내용이 있다. 따라서 (b) 컴퓨터 회사들은 나중에 재활용될 수 있는 부품을 사용해야 한다는 것을 알 수 있다.

오답 분석

(a) 컴퓨터 생산으로 인해 문제가 발생하긴 하지만 생산을 줄이는 것은 현실적으로 불가능한 일이다. (c) 더 많은 컴퓨터가 매립될 것이라는 내용은 없다. (d) 컴퓨터와 정신 건강에 관한 내용 역시 없다.

2.

Automobiles belch out too much noxious exhaust and burn a large amount of nonrenewable gasoline. But perhaps not for much longer, the government plans to pass laws that will force carmakers to curb smog—one way or another. Until now nobody has been able to agree on what that way should be. Utilities think the answer is to run cars on clean-burning natural gas. Farmers like ethanol made from fermented agricultural waste. Oil companies want to stick with gasoline, which could be reformulated to produce fewer emissions. Environmentalists prefer electricity, generated if possible from solar energy. Automakers would like to make cars lighter and more efficient, no matter what the fuel.

Q. **How will the carmakers tackle environmental concerns?**
(a) By using clean energy
(b) By making cars more fuel-efficient
(c) By using ethanol gas cars
(d) By making water-run cars

오답과 정답 분석

정답 분석
지문 마지막에 나오는 '자동차 제조업자들은 연료가 무엇이든 상관없이 자동차를 더 가볍고 효율적으로 만들기를 원한다' 는 내용으로 볼 때 자동차 회사는 환경을 위해 연비가 높은 차를 만들 것이다.

오답 분석
(a) 깨끗한 에너지를 사용하자는 것은 가스 공사의 입장이고, (c) 에탄올 가스를 이용하자는 것은 농부의 입장이다.
(d) 물로 움직이는 자동차는 논의된 바 없다.

1.

In the United States, about 160 million tons of garbage were produced this year alone. Ten percent was recycled, ten percent was burned, and the rest was put into landfills. But finding land for landfills is becoming more difficult. Therefore there is a growing need to recycle the garbage they produce. The US government plans to increase the amount of recycling by ten percent next year. If the total amount of garbage is same, the amount of recycled garbage will be ____________ .

Q. Choose the option that best completes the passage.
(a) 6 million tons
(b) 32 million tons
(c) 48 million tons
(d) 128 million tons

2.

Another solution is to find a new use for the tires. During the Great Depression, shoes with tire soles were very common in the United States. The State of Maine is very cold, and in the winter the ground freezes solid. Large bumps are formed in the roads, and then in the spring, the bumps may turn into holes. Roads must be rebuilt often, at great expense to the state. To prevent this, road workers have started to use old tires broken into small pieces. These tire pieces are spread in a thick layer underneath the surface of a new road. The tires then act ____________ , keeping the ground below from freezing. This way the road surface remains smooth.

Q. Choose the option that best completes the passage.
(a) as a filler
(b) as a softener
(c) as a spring
(d) as a blanket

Section Switch

Chapter 6에 나와 있는 TEPS 필수 어휘입니다.

- [ ] **allege** 강력히 주장하다
- [ ] **backdrop** 배경
- [ ] **belch** 분출하다, 내뿜다
- [ ] **brave** 용감히 맞서다
- [ ] **break-up** 진압, 분쇄
- [ ] **bump** (도로 등의) 턱
- [ ] **consecutive** 연속적인
- [ ] **crippled** 고장난
- [ ] **cubicle** 칸막이 공간
- [ ] **ditch** (비행기를) 불시착시키다
- [ ] **dump** 쓰레기 버리는 곳
- [ ] **emission** 배기, 배출물
- [ ] **exhaust** 배기가스
- [ ] **falter** 머뭇거리다
- [ ] **ferment** 발효시키다
- [ ] **fracture** 부서지다, 부러지다
- [ ] **frigid** 몹시 추운
- [ ] **the Great Depression** 대공황
- [ ] **hardship** 고난
- [ ] **in the face of** ~에도 불구하고
- [ ] **indentation** 톱니 모양, 벤 자국
- [ ] **jetliner** 제트 여객기
- [ ] **landfill** 쓰레기 매립, 매립지
- [ ] **lavish** 풍부한, 화려한
- [ ] **maneuver** 조종하다, (비행기를) 곡예 비행시키다
- [ ] **notch** V자 모양의 홈, 벤 자국
- [ ] **noxious** 유해한, 해로운
- [ ] **paramedic** 구급 요원
- [ ] **portfolio** 투자 자산 구성 (각종 금융 자산의 집합)
- [ ] **rally** 집회, 시위
- [ ] **reformulate** 재처리하다
- [ ] **revere** 존경하다, 숭배하다
- [ ] **sole** (구두 등의) 바닥, 밑창
- [ ] **sophisticated** 세련된

- [ ] **trigger** 일으키다, 유발하다
- [ ] **unwanted** 쓸모없는, 불필요한
- [ ] **utilities** (전기 · 가스 · 상하수도 · 교통 기관 등의) 공익 사업체
- [ ] **vibrant** 활기 넘치는

Chapter 7

Chapter 7

STEP 1 Pattern Study

유형별 빠른 풀이법

추론 문제는 정답이 내용에서 직접 도출되는 것이 아니라 한 번 더 생각해야 알 수 있는 경우가 많다. 지문에 나온 항목들을 중심으로 먼저 사실 관계를 파악한 뒤 선택지를 하나씩 따져봐야 한다.

Sample

A court handed down a death sentence to a man who manufactured a milk additive that caused thousands of Chinese babies to develop kidney stones, some of them fatal. Nearly 0.3 million Chinese babies were sickened and six died after drinking a formula that had been spiked with melamine, a compound used in making plastics that allowed the formula to pass quality tests. The defendant sentenced to death was identified as a technical worker who had manufactured and sold 600 tons of melamine additives under the name of "protein powder" to dairy farmers in Hebei.

Q. **What can be inferred from the passage?**

(a) Many babies developed a stomachache because of the melamine formula.

(b) The technician who made the melamine formula received a life sentence.

(c) Melamine was not originally intended for human consumption.

(d) Melamine additives can increase the fat content of milk.

 **풀이 적용**

지문에 나온 멜라민에 대한 정보는 플라스틱을 만드는 데 사용된다는 것이다. 직접적으로 나오지는 않았지만 한 번 더 생각해 본다면 멜라민은 플라스틱을 만드는 데 사용되는 물질이므로 식용에는 적합하지 않을 것이라는 점을 추론할 수 있다.

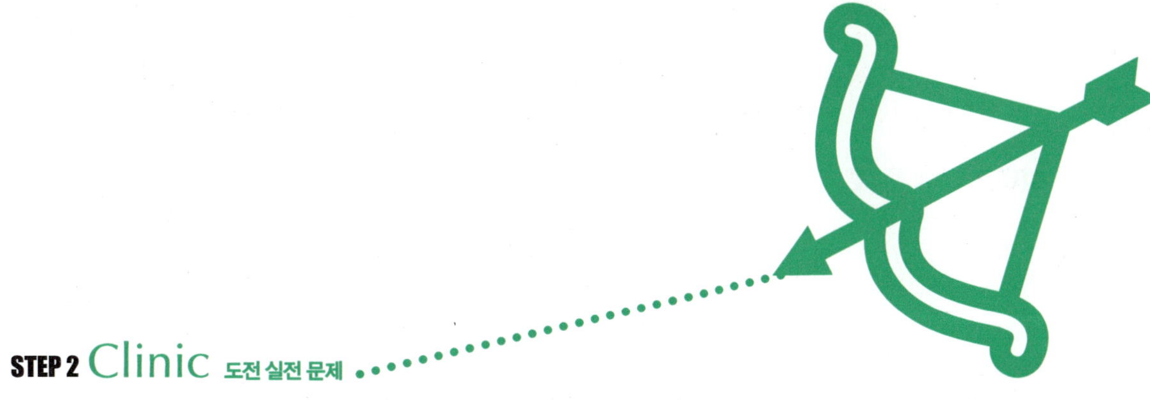

STEP 2 Clinic 도전 실전 문제

1.

The national average price for gas has climbed for the third week in a row, reaching $1.85 a gallon on Thursday. This is the highest price for gas since Nov. 24 and a 6.3-cent-per-gallon jump from last week. Still, compared to a year ago gas is an average of $1.17 cheaper per gallon and it's still down vastly from its summer high of more than $4. Prices are highest on the West Coast, at $2.02 per gallon, and lowest in the Rocky Mountain states, where the regional price hovers around $1.61 per gallon. While the increase is small change, it's something to keep an eye on, especially in the coming months as winter gives out and Americans begin driving more.

Q. **What can be inferred from the passage?**
(a) The price of gas is likely to climb as winter finishes.
(b) The discrepancy in gas prices among states are very stiff.
(c) The price of gas is wholly dependent on the international market.
(d) The price of gasoline depends on the price of crude oil.

2.

Israeli Prime Minster Ehud Olmert defended his country's 22-day offensive in the Gaza Strip and pledged to defend the military against international calls for an investigation of potential war crimes. "The soldiers and commanders who were sent on missions in Gaza must know that they are safe from various tribunals and that the state of Israel will assist them on this issue and defend them," Olmert said before his weekly Cabinet meeting in Jerusalem.

Q. **What can be inferred from the passage?**
(a) Hamas fighters used Palestinian civilians as human shields.
(b) More than 4,000 schoolchildren returned to their schools.
(c) Israeli soldiers went out of their way to avoid civilian casualties.
(d) Global activists and some governments have called for an inquiry into charges of unlawful use of weapons and war crimes.

1.

The national average price for gas has climbed for the third week in a row, reaching $1.85 a gallon on Thursday. This is the highest price for gas since Nov. 24 and a 6.3-cent-per-gallon jump from last week. Still, compared to a year ago gas is an average of $1.17 cheaper per gallon and it's still down vastly from its summer high of more than $4. Prices are highest on the West Coast, at $2.02 per gallon, and lowest in the Rocky Mountain states, where the regional price hovers around $1.61 per gallon. While the increase is small change, it's something to keep an eye on, especially in the coming months as winter gives out and Americans begin driving more.

Q. What can be inferred from the passage?
(a) The price of gas is likely to climb as winter finishes.
(b) The discrepancy in gas prices among states are very stiff.
(c) The price of gas is wholly dependent on the international market.
(d) The price of gasoline depends on the price of crude oil.

오답과 정답 분석

정답 분석
지문 마지막에 '겨울이 끝나면 미국인들이 차를 더욱 많이 몰기 시작한다' 는 내용이 있고 또 중간에 나오는 '휘발유 가격이 $4 이상이었던 지난 여름' 이라는 내용을 볼 때 겨울이 끝나면 휘발유 가격이 오를 것임을 추측할 수 있다.

오답 분석
(b) 각 주의 유가가 조금씩 다르긴 하나, 그것이 터무니없는 정도인지는 알 수 없다. (c) '겨울이 끝나고 미국인들이 더 많이 운전을 하기 시작한다' 는 내용은 international한 문제라기보다는 미국 내부의 문제로 봐야 한다.

2.

Israeli Prime Minster Ehud Olmert defended his country's 22-day offensive in the Gaza Strip and pledged to defend the military against international calls for an investigation of potential war crimes. "The soldiers and commanders who were sent on missions in Gaza must know that they are safe from various tribunals and that the state of Israel will assist them on this issue and defend them," Olmert said before his weekly Cabinet meeting in Jerusalem.

Q. What can be inferred from the passage?

(a) Hamas fighters used Palestinian civilians as human shields.

(b) More than 4,000 schoolchildren returned to their schools.

(c) Israeli soldiers went out of their way to avoid civilian casualties.

(d) Global activists and some governments have called for an inquiry into charges of unlawful use of weapons and war crimes.

오답과 정답 분석

정답 분석

총리가 잠재적인 전쟁 범죄의 조사에 관한 국제적인 요구에 대해 군을 변호할 것이라고 약속했다면 실제로 국제적인 요구가 있었을 거라고 추론할 수 있다.

오답 분석

(a) human shields, 즉 '인간 방패' 에 대한 언급은 없다. (b) schoolchildren에 대한 언급도 없다. 추론 문제는 범위가 광범위해서 풀기 어려운 점이 있기는 하지만 적어도 근거가 되는 언급은 필요하다. 앞서 제시한 오답들은 그러한 근거가 없다.

1.

Judges at the California State Fair Wine Competition scored poorly at giving the same wine an identical rating when they tasted it multiple times in a blind tasting. That was the conclusion of a four-year study of judging decisions at the California State Fair Wine Competition by retired Humboldt State professor Robert Hodgson. "Consumers should have a healthy skepticism about the medals awarded to wines from the various competitions," he said.

Q. What can be inferred from the passage?
(a) Fair officials are considering making changes in the operating of future wine competitions.
(b) Valuable information could be used to improve wine competitions.
(c) Finding ways to evaluate the skills of judges is an important issue for wine competitions.
(d) Wine judges are rather unsteady.

2.

Two men were arrested on the Southwest Side of Chicago and face charges involving an attempted drug deal involving cocaine and heroin worth more than $2.5 million, Chicago police said today. On Thursday night, Narcotics Section officers followed a Dodge pick-up truck and red Honda from a parking lot in the 6800 block of South Pulaski Road to a garage in the 6800 block of South Keeler Avenue, according to Police News Affairs.

Q. Which of the following is most likely to follow this passage?
(a) How the police arrested the suspects
(b) The evil effect of narcotics
(c) The mission of Narcotics Section officers
(d) The amount of the drugs being dealt in Chicago

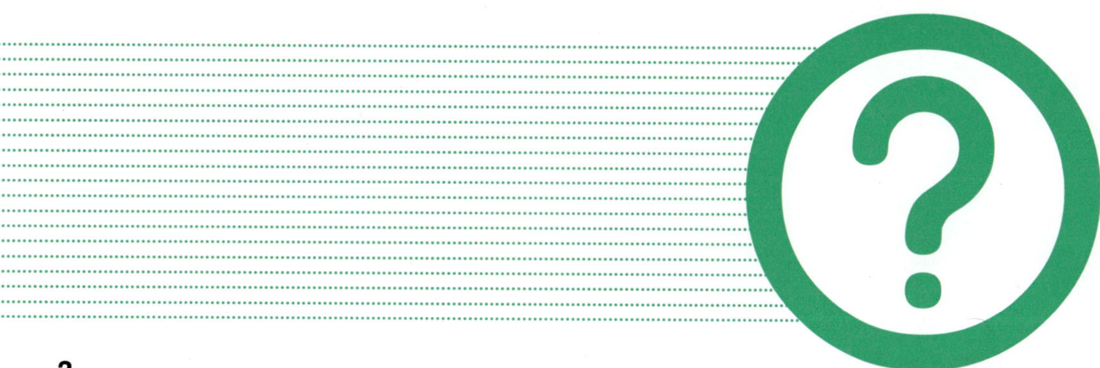

3.

More than 2.5 million Americans lost their jobs in 2008. And at least 2 million jobs are expected to evaporate in 2009. But laid-off employees aren't the only ones who suffer from staff reductions. Employees who remain employed are prone to greater role ambiguity and job demands that can contribute to greater alcohol consumption and depression. In addition, layoff survivors often experience worsening physical health. Those consequences are long-term. The psychological fallout of surviving a layoff lasts six years, according to the study published by the Institute of Behavioral Science. And the effects of surviving multiple layoffs are cumulative.

Q. **What can be inferred from the passage?**
(a) Surviving a layoff can hurt too.
(b) The unemployed and forced laid-off employees suffer from severe depression.
(c) Those who are laid off lose confidence in their employer.
(d) Those who are not laid off may experience feelings of guilt.

4.

A startling development in the recently 2 million dollar rare coin robbery happened last month. A tip given to police resulted in the recovery of the entire cash of stolen coins. Oddly enough, the coins were found in a small travel bag that was hanging on a mannequin on the main floor of a department store. How they got there and how long they have been there is anyone's guess.

Q. **What can be inferred from the passage?**
(a) Coin robbery barely happens.
(b) The police found little money.
(c) The rare coins were found in a travel bag.
(d) Anybody can guess where the money was.

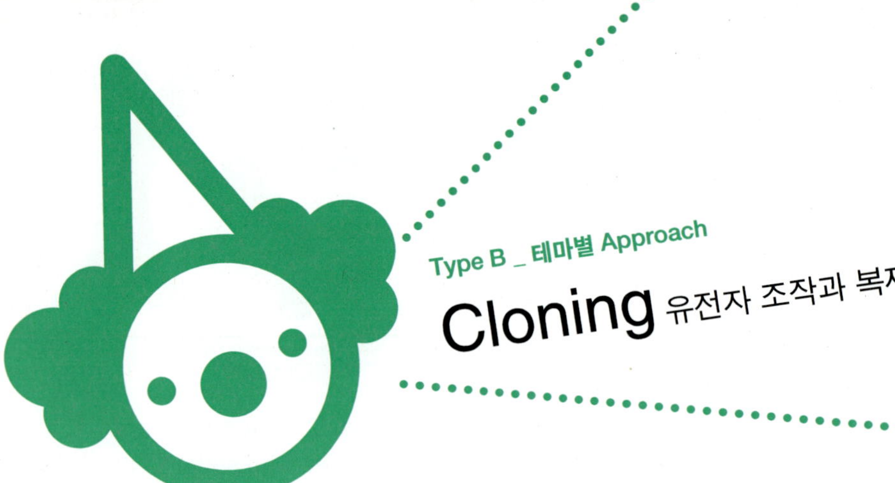

출제 경향 파악

유전 공학의 핵심은 유전자 조작 등의 유전적 형질 변화에 있다. 유전자 형질의 변화로 인한 식품의 안전성과 유전자 형질의 변화, 즉 cloning이 인간에게까지 확대된 human cloning의 허용과 가능 범위가 자주 출제된다. 의료 발달을 위해 cloning이 필요한 부분도 있지만 늘 윤리적 · 종교적 문제를 수반한다는 데에 이 문제의 핵심이 있다.

STEP 1 Theme Research

Fill in the blanks with suitable words.

1.

Scientists began to develop "superplants" in the 1920s. Unlike "na___ral" plants, these plants were developed to withstand pollution, drought, dirty soil, and poor light. Superplants were first created through making chemical changes in the plants, and then with ge___tic changes. Some plants created this way include some new cotton and corn species.

2.

Giant pumpkins, tomatoes, and strawberries are being developed now, as well as new flowers. The techniques have produced plants that re___ist disease, require less special care, and grow larger seeds and fruits on fewer nutrients and less water. So what began as an effort to make stronger plants may end up as a way to increase the yields of farms and garden crops.

Translation

1. 과학자들은 1920년대에 "초식물"을 개발하기 시작했다. "자연적인" 식물과는 달리 이 식물은 공해와 가뭄, 더러운 토양이나 나쁜 일조 상태에서도 잘 견딜 수 있도록 개발되었다. 초식물은 처음에는 식물 내에 화학적 변화를 조성함으로써 만들어졌다가 이후에는 유전자 변형으로 만들어졌다. 새로운 면화나 옥수수 종 같은 식물들은 이러한 방식으로 만들어진 것이다.

2. 거대한 호박과 토마토, 딸기가 신종 화훼류와 함께 현재 개발 중이다. 과학 기술은 질병에 강하고 돌보기 쉬우면서 더 적은 영양분과 물로 더 큰 씨와 열매를 맺는 식물을 만들어냈다. 더 강한 식물을 만들어내기 위해 시작한 이 노력은 마지막에는 농장과 밭의 농작물 생산량을 증가시키는 방법이 될지도 모른다.

STEP 2 Words and Expressions

어구 해설

withstand 저항하다, 견디다
drought 가뭄
nutrient 영양분
yield 생산량, 수확
crop 농작물

POP Quiz

다음 어휘나 어구의 뜻을 빈칸에 써 넣으시오.

1. superplant ______________
2. genetic ______________
3. artificially induced fertility ______________
4. cloning ______________

ANSWERS

STEP 1   1. "natural" plants / genetic changes
2. resist disease

STEP 2   1. 초식물 2. 유전적인 3. 인공 수정 4. (생물) 복제

STEP 3 Clinic 오답 및 정답의 분석 ·······················

1.

Consumer advocates have called for additional testing of crops and mandatory labeling of genetically engineered products. Administration officials say that it is unnecessary, and the food industry has argued that it would unfairly stigmatize biotech food. I think we need an urgent UN-sponsored global summit on biotechnology followed by international agreement. Either we control gene technology today, or gene technology will redesign us by tomorrow.

Q. **Who has taken the strongest standing against genetically engineered products in the passage?**

(a) Consumer advocates
(b) Engineers
(c) Administration officials
(d) People in the food industry

오답과 정답 분석

정답 분석

지문 첫 문장의 '소비자의 대변자들은 곡물의 추가적인 검사와 유전자 가공식품에 대한 의무적인 등급제를 요구한다' 는 내용으로 보아 소비자의 대변자들이 유전자 가공식품에 대해 가장 까다로운 요구를 하고 있다는 것을 알 수 있다.

오답 분석

정부는 유전자 가공식품에 대한 소비자들의 까다로운 요구에 대해 불필요하다는 입장이며, 식품 회사들은 더더욱 정부의 입장을 지지할 것이다. 이 문제처럼 어떤 행위의 당사자를 묻는 문제는 역시 단순하게 그 대상에 대하여 긍정적으로 생각하는 입장과 부정적으로 생각하는 입장을 대치시키면 답이 쉽게 나온다.

2.

Cloning was originally a way of reproducing plants or animals by manipulation of their body cells, to produce exact copies of one parent, either male or female. We must eventually decide if human cloning should be allowed in the near future. This is the most volatile issue within the cloning debate. In fact, there are many of us who argue against cloning itself, ignoring its potentially positive effects. They are concerned that cloning technology will ____________ once the technology becomes capable of accomplishing such tasks.

Q. **Choose the option that best completes the passage.**
(a) be permanently abandoned
(b) not be used with humans
(c) begin to decline gradually
(d) be applied to human beings

오답과 정답 분석

정답 분석
생물 복제를 반대하는 사람들의 궁극적인 반대 이유는 그 복제 기술이 인간에게 적용되는 것을 두려워하기 때문이다. 따라서 (d) be applied to human beings가 정답이다.

오답 분석
인간 복제를 반대하는 사람들이 (a) 인간 복제 기술이 영구적으로 폐기되거나 (b) 인간에게 사용되지 않는 것 또는 (c) 그 기술이 후퇴하기 시작하는 것을 두려워할 이유는 없다. 유전자 복제 문제에서 핵심은 이미 동물 등의 실험체에서는 성공적으로 진행되는 실험의 결과를 인간에게 적용시킬 것인가이다.

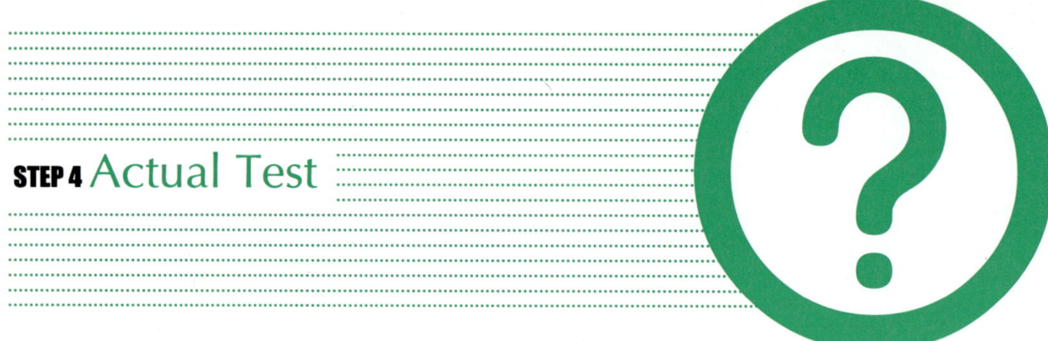

1.

Human cloning has always caught the public imagination. We now have the technology to take a few cells from a modern day Einstein, or a musical genius or a child prodigy and to create hundreds of cloned babies which have the exact same genes. President Clinton announced in May 1997 that human clones should not be born. He was warmly applauded. However, what he went on to say was that the ban was only for 5 years. As a result, it is predicted that human cloning will be made in commercial laboratories in the U.S. or by using U.S. technology, but they will be born elsewhere.

Q. How may President Clinton's comments best be paraphrased?

(a) Human clones may be born in America for the five years starting 1997.

(b) Human clones can be born in America after five years have passed since 1997.

(c) Human clones can be born in America only once between 1997 and 2002.

(d) Human clones may not be born in America after the year 2002.

2.

Some critics may question the policy of using science and technology to aid reproduction. To the parent hoping for a child, these new methods may represent God. But by utilizing such enhanced methods of fertility, we are going against the very basic principles of evolution. If the aim of evolution is to screen out unfit genes from a population and aid the perpetuation of superior genes, artificially induced fertility may bring with it a multitude of unforeseen repercussions. Regardless of how tempting reproductive therapy is, we won't know the negative side effects of this technology until we come to a stage at which we may not be able to do much about it.

Q. Which of the following best expresses the idea of the passage?

(a) People should use these new methods to aid reproduction.

(b) People should realize the importance of enhancing methods of fertility.

(c) People should be cautious of the side effects of these enhanced methods of fertility.

(d) These new methods of fertility should support the principles of evolution.

- ☐ **a multitude of** 다수의, 수많은
- ☐ **additional** 부가적인, 추가의
- ☐ **additive** 첨가제
- ☐ **advocate** 대변자
- ☐ **prone to** ~하기 쉬운
- ☐ **biotech** 생물공학 (=biotechnology)
- ☐ **charge** 혐의
- ☐ **compound** 합성물질
- ☐ **contribute to** ~의 원인이 되다
- ☐ **cumulative** 누적적인, 가중의
- ☐ **develop** (병에) 걸리다
- ☐ **evaporate** 증발하다, 사라지다
- ☐ **evolution** 진화
- ☐ **fallout** 후유증, 악영향
- ☐ **fatal** 죽게 하는
- ☐ **formula** 분유
- ☐ **Gaza Strip** 가자 지구
- ☐ **genetically engineered product** 유전자 가공 식품
- ☐ **give out** 다하다, 바닥나다
- ☐ **hand down** (판결을) 내리다, 언도하다
- ☐ **hover** 맴돌다, 배회하다
- ☐ **identical** 동일한, 똑같은
- ☐ **judge** 감정가, 심사위원
- ☐ **keep an eye on** ~을 지켜보다
- ☐ **kidney stone** 신장 결석
- ☐ **laid-off** 구조 조정 당한, 해고된
- ☐ **mandatory** 강제의, 의무의
- ☐ **manipulation** 조작
- ☐ **narcotics** 마약(류)
- ☐ **offensive** 공격, 공세
- ☐ **perpetuation** 영속화, 영구 보존
- ☐ **pick-up truck** 소형 트럭
- ☐ **pledge** 맹세하다, 약속하다

- ☐ **prodigy** 천재
- ☐ **redesign** 재설계하다
- ☐ **repercussions** 반향, 영향
- ☐ **reproduction** 재생, 번식
- ☐ **screen out** 가려내다
- ☐ **skepticism** 회의론
- ☐ **spike** (음료에) 화학 약품 등을 타다
- ☐ **startling** 깜짝 놀랄 만한
- ☐ **stigmatize** 오명을 씌우다, 비난하다
- ☐ **summit** 정상 회담
- ☐ **tribunal** 법정
- ☐ **volatile** 불안정한, 일촉즉발의

Chapter 8

Chapter 8

STEP 1 Pattern Study

유형별 빠른 풀이법

글의 분위기를 묻는 문제는 주로 결론이 제시되는 마지막 부분을 중점적으로 살펴보아야 한다. 상업적인 광고 지문의 목적을 묻는 문제 등도 이와 유사한 형태로 주로 지문의 뒷부분을 보면 정답이 보인다.

Sample

The real heroes of the fight against drugs are the teenagers who resist the ghetto's fast track—those who live at home, stay in school, and juggle their studies with a low-paying job. The wonder is that there are so many of them. "Most of our youngsters are not involved in drug," says the chief judge of one juvenile court in Michigan. "Most are not running around with guns. Most aren't killing people. Most are doing very well—against great odds." These are the youngsters who fit Jesse Jackson's words: "You were born in the slum, but the slum wasn't born in you."

Q. **The author's attitude toward ghetto teenagers who live at home, stay in school, and work is ___________ .**
(a) hesitant
(b) admiring
(c) neutral
(d) indifferent

 풀이 적용

"여러분은 빈민가에서 태어났지만 빈민가가 여러분에게서 태어난 것은 아닙니다" 라는 마지막 문장에서 알 수 있듯이 필자는 대부분의 빈민가 청소년들을 매우 바람직하게 보고 있다. 따라서 정답은 (b)가 된다.

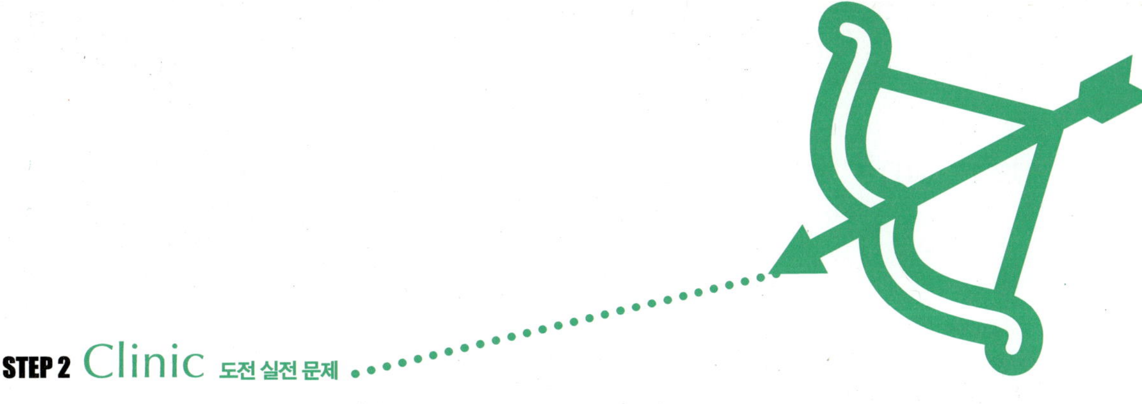

1.

Some people insist on "love at first sight," but I suggest that they calm down and take a second look. There is no such thing as love at first sight. Some of those attractive first-sight qualities may turn out to be genuine and durable, but don't count on the storybook formula. The other saying "love is blind" is far more sensible. The young girl who believes herself to be in love can't see the undesirable qualities in her man because she is not to see them.

Q. **What is the mood of the article?**

(a) Ironic
(b) Critical
(c) Angry
(d) Romantic

2.

Abraham Lincoln, the sixteenth president of the United States, may have received a message about his own death in a dream. One night in 1865, he had a strange dream. He had a dream about being inside the White House. A group of people were standing around a coffin in the East Room of the White House. Many of them were crying. "Who is dead?" he asked. "The president," someone answered. "He was killed by an assassin." A few days after this, on April 14th, Lincoln was shot and killed while he was watching a play at Ford's Theater in Washington, D.C.

Q. **What is the mood of the article?**

(a) Pessimistic
(b) Mysterious
(c) Sarcastic
(d) Sorrowful

STEP 2 Clinic 오답 및 정답의 분석 ●●●●●●●●●●●●●●●●●●●●●●●●●●●●

1.

Some people insist on "love at first sight," but I suggest that they calm down and take a second look. There is no such thing as love at first sight. Some of those attractive first-sight qualities may turn out to be genuine and durable, but don't count on the storybook formula. The other saying "love is blind" is far more sensible. The young girl who believes herself to be in love can't see the undesirable qualities in her man because she is not to see them.

Q. **What is the mood of the article?**
   (a) Ironic
   (b) Critical
   (c) Angry
   (d) Romantic

 오답과 정답 분석

 **정답 분석**

지문의 분위기나 전체적인 의도를 파악하라는 문제에서는 글의 마지막 부분을 체크하는 것이 중요하다. 여기에서는 can't see the undesirable qualities라는 어구를 통해 사람들의 통념에 대한 필자의 부정적 평가를 읽을 수 있다.

오답 분석

(a) Ironic은 이 글의 분위기와는 전혀 맞지 않다. (b) Critical의 정도가 지나치면 (c) Angry해질 수는 있겠지만 이 글만으로는 (c) Angry라고 보기 힘들다. (d) Romantic 역시 지문의 마지막 부분에 나타난 냉소적인 어조를 감안하면 오답임을 알 수 있다. 

2.

Abraham Lincoln, the sixteenth president of the United States, may have received a message about his own death in a dream. One night in 1865, he had a strange dream. He had a dream about being inside the White House. A group of people were standing around a coffin in the East Room of the White House. Many of them were crying. "Who is dead?" he asked. "The president," someone answered. "He was killed by an assassin." A few days after this, on April 14th, Lincoln was shot and killed while he was watching a play at Ford's Theater in Washington, D.C.

Q. **What is the mood of the article?**
(a) Pessimistic
(b) Mysterious
(c) Sarcastic
(d) Sorrowful

오답과 정답 분석

정답 분석

글의 분위기를 파악할 때에는 뒷부분을 중점적으로 살펴봐야 하는데 killed 같은 표현으로 끝이 났기 때문에 다소 슬프거나 비관적인 요소는 있다. 그러나 앞에서 꿈에 관한 이야기가 나왔고, 그것에 이어진 결론이 죽음이므로 전체적인 분위기는 (b) Mysterious하다고 봐야 한다.

오답 분석

(a) Pessimistic이나 (c) Sarcastic, (d) Sorrowful 역시 비극적인 요소를 포함하고 있기는 하지만 정답 분석에서 밝힌 대로 전체적으로는 죽음 전에 나타난 꿈과 관련된 (b) Mysterious한 내용이기 때문에 모두 정답으로 보기는 힘들다.

1.

Although teeth are meant to last a person's lifetime, toothbrushes aren't, says the American Dental Association, and should be tossed out about every four months. So Oral-B Laboratories of Redwood City, California, has introduced the Indicator, the first toothbrush with a replacement alert. When the blue coloring disappears halfway down the bristle, which usually takes about three or four months, it's time to buy a new toothbrush. The cost: $3.

Q.　**What is the purpose of this passage?**
(a) Warning
(b) Advertising
(c) Complaining
(d) Questioning

2.

The town was beyond description. Heaps of mud and sand covered the entire town. Main street could hardly be recognized. Two large streams were running through the middle of the town. Houses were blown down or brought down by the flood. Several dead bodies of unfortunate victims were lying in the streets, while lots of people were searching for their family members and relatives who had disappeared in the ruins.

Q.　**What is the mood of the article?**
(a) Calm
(b) Solemn
(c) Boring
(d) Miserable

3.

If there is anyone to remember it, the 20th century may someday be seen as a time when shades of the prison house fell across much of the earth. This age has brought a fiendish ingenuity in people for what they do or do not believe. George Orwell among others foresaw this development and tried to forestall it with *Nineteen Eighty Four*, one of the most horrific cautionary tales ever written.

Q. **What is the purpose of the passage?**
(a) To persuade people of the writer's remarks
(b) To advise people not to read George Orwell
(c) To foresee the 20th century
(d) To introduce people to the horrible novel

4.

Over the last few hundred years, there have been numerous reports of strange objects falling from the sky. In 1680, hundreds of live rats fell on a village in Norway. Showers of fish, frogs, lizards, and worms have all been documented. In 1977, a couple walking home from church in Bristol in England were rained on by hundreds of hazelnuts falling from a clear blue sky. In 1984, a single house in Lancashire was bombarded with apples, and in 1989, it rained sardines on a small town in Australia. In 1994, a pensioner in France was rained on by enough coins to do her weekly shopping.

Q. **What is the mood of the passage?**
(a) Humorous
(b) Horrible
(c) Religious
(d) Mysterious

아인슈타인은 상대성 이론(the theory of relativity)으로 유명하다. 상대성 이론이란 사물의 절대
적인 위치와 운동이란 존재하지 않고 언제나 상대적인 평가만이 가능하다는 것이다. 상대성 이론
은 발표 당시부터 획기적인 이론으로 받아들여졌다. 아인슈타인에 대한 출제 사항은 주로 상대성
이론이지만 별로 천재라고 인정받지 못했던 그의 특이했던 어린 시절 이야기나 그의 사후 이야
기, 즉 뇌를 연구 대상으로 기증하여 여전히 연구되고 있다는 이야기도 자주 출제된다.

STEP 1 Theme Research

Fill in the blanks with suitable words.

1.

In 1905, Albert Einstein argued that time and distance were not ab___olutes, but could be
shorter or longer depending on the relative motion between the observer and the thing
being observed. In 1927, Werner Heisenberg announced that, in subatomic experiments,
the very act of observation dis___orts reality in such a way that one can determine either
the position or the velocity of a particle, but never both at once. Reality is loosed from its
moorings, and the human observer becomes an agent in determining what's there.

2.

The popular mind was excited by these new departments. So far as Einstein could be
understood, he was saying that it was no longer possible for ordinary people to
comp___ehend the universe, and that what the scientist actually did understand was
strange and unsettling. Time, space, matter, energy—all these dissolved, shifted, blurred.
Everything depended on where the observer was located; rela___ivity replaced fixity;
ultimate things are hidden.

Translation

1. 1905년 알베르트 아인슈타인은 시간과 거리는 절대적인 것이 아니라 관찰자와 관찰 대상 사이의 상대적인 움직임에 따라 더 짧거나 길 수도 있다고 주장했다. 1927년 베르너 하이젠베르크는 소립자 실험에서 관찰 행위 자체가 입자의 위치나 속도 가운데 하나를 결정하는 식으로 실재를 왜곡하지만 결코 그 두 요소를 동시에 왜곡하지는 않는다고 발표했다. 실재는 그 실재를 묶어두고 있는 것에서 느슨해지고 대신 관찰자가 대리인이 되어 그곳에 무엇이 있는가를 결정하게 되는 것이다.

2. 대중들은 이러한 새로운 영역에 흥분했다. 아인슈타인의 이론을 이해하는 한, 그의 말은 일반인들이 우주를 이해하는 것은 더 이상 불가능하며, 그 과학자(아인슈타인)가 이해한 것은 이상하고 확실치 않다는 뜻이었다. 시간, 공간, 사물, 에너지—이 모든 것들이 해체되고 이동하고 모호해졌다. 모든 것은 관찰자가 어디에 있는지에 달려 있었다; 상대성이 고정성을 대체했다. 궁극적인 것들은 보이지 않았다.

STEP 2 Words and Expressions

어구 해설

observer 관찰자
subatomic 소립자의
distort 왜곡하다
velocity 속도
particle 입자
moorings 계류 설비[장치]
agent 대리인

POP Quiz

다음 어휘나 어구의 뜻을 빈칸에 써 넣으시오.

1. the theory of relativity ________________
2. absolute ________________
3. atomic ________________
4. disheveled hair ________________

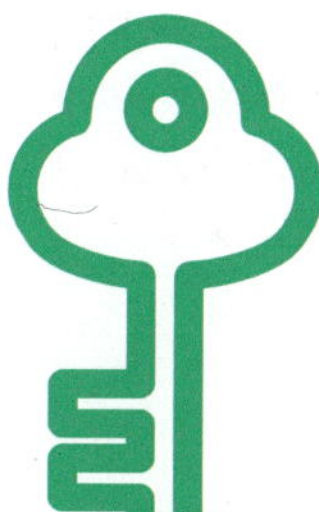

ANSWERS

STEP 1   1. absolutes / distorts reality
   2. comprehend the universe / relativity

STEP 2   1. 상대성 이론 2. 절대적인 3. 원자의 4. 흐트러진 머리

1.

When we think of the public face of scientific genius, we often remember someone with old and graying appearances. For example, we think of Albert Einstein's disheveled hair, Charles Darwin's majestic beard, Isaac Newton's wrinkled visage. Yet the truth is that most of the scientific breakthroughs that have changed our lives are usually made by people who are still in their 30s—and that includes Einstein, Newton and Darwin. Indeed, not surprisingly, younger scientists are less affected by ___________ than their elders. They question authority instinctively. They do not believe it when they are told that a new idea is crazy, so they are free to do the impossible.

Q. **Choose the option that best completes the passage.**
  (a) economic concerns
  (b) innovative experimental data
  (c) individual moral responsibility
  (d) the intellectual dogma of the day

오답과 정답 분석

정답 분석
빈칸 넣기 문제는 거의 항상 빈칸의 앞뒤에 힌트가 있다. 빈칸 뒤의 내용을 보면 젊은 과학자들은 새로운 아이디어를 좋아해서 불가능한 일을 해내는 데 있어 자유롭다고 나와 있다. 따라서 젊은 과학자들은 기존의 지적인 이론에 관해서도 나이 많은 과학자들보다 자유로울 것이라는 점을 추론할 수 있다.

오답 분석
이 글에서는 (a) 경제나 (c) 도덕 문제를 언급하고 있지 않다. 젊은 과학자들은 혁신적인 실험 자료에는 오히려 영향을 더 받을 것이므로 (b)도 정답이 될 수 없다.

2.

Democratic theory is in a condition akin to that of theoretical physics when Einstein began his speculations at the turn of the century. The accepted doctrine at that time was in the main what Newton had ___________ centuries earlier. Fundamental to his thinking was the concept of space and time. Newton had conceived of each as being distinct from the other. Meanwhile, Einstein said they are not separate. Moreover, he added, energy and mass are equivalent and transmutable, which is called Mass-energy equivalence: $E = mc^2$.

Q. **Choose the option that best completes the passage.**
   (a) enunciated
   (b) alleviated
   (c) dispatched
   (d) forwarded

오답과 정답 분석

정답 분석

빈칸 뒤에는 뉴턴의 사상에 대해 설명하고 있기에 빈칸에는 뉴턴이 그의 생각을 발표 · 표방했다는 말이 와야 한다. enunciate는 사상이나 생각을 외부에 '표현하다' 라는 의미를 가지는 동사이다. 아이슈타인의 가장 큰 업적은 뉴턴이 발표한 기존의 물리학적 세계관을 변화시켰다는 것에 있다는 점을 늘 염두에 두고 풀어야 한다.

오답 분석

(b) '뉴턴이 경감했던 것' 은 문맥상 옳지 못하다. (c) '뉴턴이 보냈던 것' 도 문맥상 타당하지 않다. (d)의 forward 는 '앞으로' 의 의미를 가지는 형용사이면서 동사로 쓰이면 '전송하다' 의 의미를 가지게 되어서 역시 문맥에 맞지 않다.

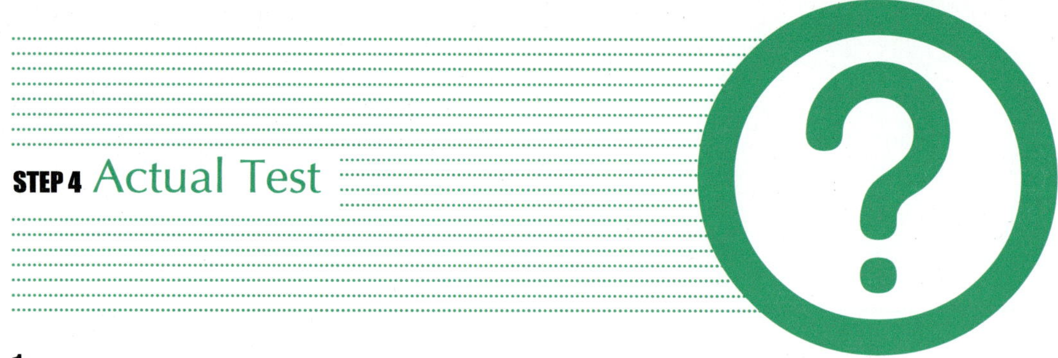

1.

Einstein often invoked God, although his was a rather depersonalized deity. He believed, he said, in God who reveals himself in the harmony of all that exists. His faith in this divine harmony was what caused him to reject the view that the universe is subject to randomness and uncertainty. The Lord God is subtle, but malicious he is not. Searching for God's design, he said, was the source of all true art and science. Although this quest may be a cause for humility, it is also what gives meaning and dignity to our lives.

Q. **Which of the following can be inferred about Einstein from the passage?**

(a) Searching for God's design can often lead to humility.

(b) He should have rejected the theory of divine harmony for all his religion.

(c) His faith in a harmonious universe didn't have a deep impact on his scientific quest.

(d) Randomness and uncertainty is an important question in science.

2.

The brain of Albert Einstein has clear differences from an average person's gray matter, according to a California researcher. But any possible link between these differences and his great intelligence is still unknown, she added. To investigate whether the brain of a genius might show special features, Dr. Dahlia W. Zaidel of the University of California, Los Angeles, examined two slides made from the physicist's brain shortly after his death in 1955 at age 76. The slides contained samples of Einstein's hippocampus, a part of the brain responsible for memory and word associations. Zaidel compared Einstein's brain with tissue from 10 individuals of ordinary intelligence who ranged in age from 22 to 84 at the time of death. The neurons on the left side of the Nobel Prize winner's hippocampus were consistently larger than those on the right. Zaidel said these findings were "markedly different" from those seem in the brains of individuals with normal intelligence. She presented her findings Monday at the Society for Neuroscience's annual meeting in San Diego, California.

Q. **Which of the following is NOT correct according to the passage?**

(a) Einstein's brain is different from other people's.

(b) Dr. Zaidel compared Einstein's brain with tissue from 10 individuals of various age.

(c) Einstein's intelligence is closely related to the texture and hardness of his brain.

(d) Slides of Einstein's brain were made just after his death.

- akin to ~와 유사한
- assassin 암살자
- blow down 불어 넘어뜨리다
- bombard 퍼붓다
- breakthrough (과학 등의) 큰 발전, 약진
- bring down 주저앉다
- bristle (솔 등의) 털
- cautionary tale 경고하는[경각심을 일깨우는] 이야기
- coffin 관
- conceive of A as B A를 B라고 생각하다
- count on 믿다, 의지하다
- deity 신(성)
- depersonalize 비인간화하다
- dignity 존엄, 품위
- disheveled 부스스한, 헝클어진
- divine 신의
- durable 영속성 있는, 오래 가는
- equivalence 등가(성)
- equivalent 동등한, 같은 값의
- fast track 출세 가도
- fiendish 사악한
- forestall 선수를 치다, ~에 앞서다
- formula 방식, 공식
- fundamental 중요한, 기본의
- genuine 진짜의
- ghetto 빈민가
- gray matter 두뇌, 지능
- heap (쌓아 올린) 더미
- hippocampus (뇌의) 해마상 융기
- humility 겸손
- in the main 대체로, 대부분
- indicator (신호) 표시기
- ingenuity 독창성
- introduce (신제품 등을) 발표하다, 출시하다

- invoke 기원하다, 의지하다
- juggle 잘 병행하다
- juvenile 청소년(의)
- majestic 위엄 있는
- malicious 악의 있는
- neuroscience 신경 과학
- odds 가능성
- pensioner 연금 수령자
- rain 비처럼 내리다
- randomness 무작위(성)
- rat 들쥐
- run around 돌아다니다
- sardine 정어리
- shower 쏟아짐
- speculation 사색, 성찰
- subject to ~의 지배를 받는, ~할 수밖에 없는
- subtle 이해하기 어려운, 불가사의한
- theoretical physics 이론 물리학
- toss out (불필요한 것을) 버리다
- transmutable 변형 가능한
- visage 얼굴
- word association 언어 연상

Chapter 9

Type A

Part III 문맥상 어울리지 않는 것 찾기

Type B

Global Warming & the Greenhouse Effect
지구 온난화와 온실 효과

Chapter 9

STEP 1 Pattern Study

유형별 빠른 풀이법

문맥상 어울리지 않는 문장을 찾는 문제는 상당히 난해한 유형이다. 먼저 전체적인 주제를 이해하고 내용을 파악한 다음 대의에서 어긋나는 것을 찾아야 한다. 해당 주제의 큰 흐름에 맞지 않는 선택지를 골라야 한다.

Sample

An aching back is a source of annoyance, misery or even disability for millions of sufferers. (1) Undergoing surgeries is expensive and may not help patients much. (2) Expensive treatments with glossy advertising may not be as good as they sound, says Brook Martin, a health services researcher at the University of Washington in Seattle. (3) Weak muscles can cause problems by forcing the spine to support extra weight. (4) More professionals now argue that doctors need to think more before they resort to the knife.

Q. **Identify the option that does NOT belong.**
(a) (1)
(b) (2)
(c) (3)
(d) (4)

풀이 적용

윗글은 척추 통증에 대한 여러 가지 치료 방법이 크게 도움이 되지 않는다는 것이 주된 내용이다. 약한 근육이 척추로 하여금 더 많은 하중을 지탱하게 함으로써 문제를 유발할 수도 있다는 문장은 전체적인 단락의 맥락에 어긋난다.

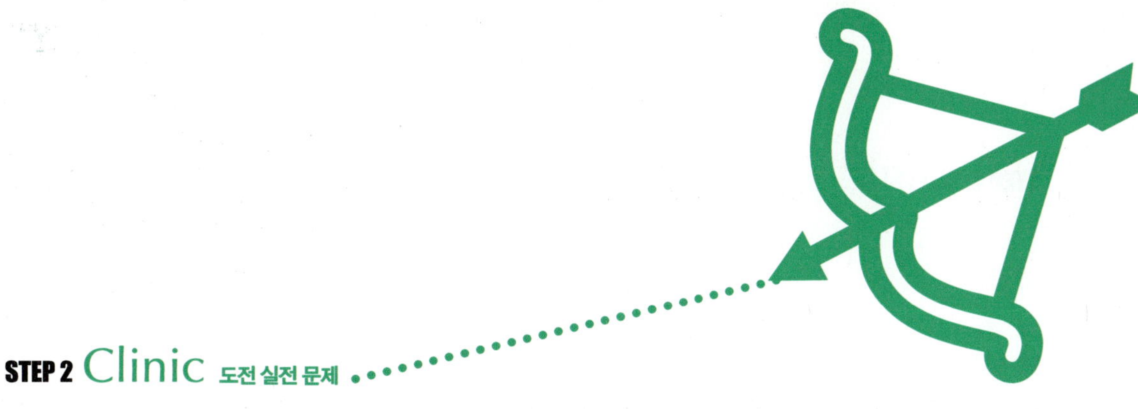

1.

When her husband, Barack Obama, said he wanted to run for president, she wasn't sure if it would be possible. (1) She had questions and wanted them answered. She wanted to know how the campaign would raise money and what the campaign strategy would be. (2) Once those plans were more real and clear, she began to see the possibilities. (3) While working together, Michelle was assigned to mentor Barack while he was a summer associate. (4) Then, she started using her talents to help her husband's campaign.

Q. **Identify the option that does NOT belong.**
  (a) (1)
  (b) (2)
  (c) (3)
  (d) (4)

2.

Russia won't be sending tourists to the international space station after this year because of plans to double the station's crew from three to six people. (1) Since 2001, the lucrative Russian space tourism program has flown six "private spaceflight participants" who paid $20 million. (2) The most recent private citizen to fly aboard a Soyuz craft, computer game designer Richard Garriott, paid a reported $35 million for his trip. (3) Maybe they'll have to spend a few more rubles on a population that still has the lowest life expectancy in the developed world. (4) The space station crew is expanding to six to accommodate Canadian, European and Japanese astronauts who have been waiting years to live aboard the station.

Q. **Identify the option that does NOT belong.**
  (a) (1)
  (b) (2)
  (c) (3)
  (d) (4)

1.

When her husband, Barack Obama, said he wanted to run for president, she wasn't sure if it would be possible. (1) She had questions and wanted them answered. She wanted to know how the campaign would raise money and what the campaign strategy would be. (2) Once those plans were more real and clear, she began to see the possibilities. (3) While working together, Michelle was assigned to mentor Barack while he was a summer associate. (4) Then, she started using her talents to help her husband's campaign.

Q. Identify the option that does NOT belong.

   (a) (1)
   (b) (2)
   (c) (3)
   (d) (4)

오답과 정답 분석

정답 분석

윗글은 미셸이 버락의 선거 운동을 돕게 되는 과정에 관한 것이다. 그러나 시간적으로도 (c)는 미셸이 결혼 후에 버락의 선거 운동을 돕는다는 내용이 아니라 대통령 선거에 뛰어들기 전에 (다른 직장 생활 중에서) 오바마를 지도하는 일을 맡았다는 내용이기에 타당하지 않다.

오답 분석

여름에 잠시 동료로 있는 동안 미셸이 오바마에게 일을 가르친 것은 버락이 법률 회사에서 일할 당시에 관한 내용이기에 지문의 맥락과 맞지 않는다. 흐름상 틀린 것을 골라내는 문제를 만들어내는 출제자들은 글의 전체적인 분위기에 맞지 않는 문장을 제시하는 것도 하나의 방법이고, 시간적으로나 논리적으로 엉뚱한 문장을 중간에 끼워 넣는 방법도 있음을 명심해야 한다.

2.

Russia won't be sending tourists to the international space station after this year because of plans to double the station's crew from three to six people. (1) Since 2001, the lucrative Russian space tourism program has flown six "private spaceflight participants" who paid $20 million. (2) The most recent private citizen to fly aboard a Soyuz craft, computer game designer Richard Garriott, paid a reported $35 million for his trip. (3) Maybe they'll have to spend a few more rubles on a population that still has the lowest life expectancy in the developed world. (4) The space station crew is expanding to six to accommodate Canadian, European and Japanese astronauts who have been waiting years to live aboard the station.

Q. Identify the option that does NOT belong.

(a) (1)
(b) (2)
(c) (3)
(d) (4)

오답과 정답 분석

정답 분석

러시아가 우주 정거장의 승무원을 늘리려는 계획 때문에 민간인을 더 태우지 못하게 되어 민간인을 대상으로 한 우주 관광 계획이 취소되었다는 대의를 파악한다면 (3)이 문맥에 전혀 동떨어진 문장이라는 걸 쉽게 알 수 있다.

오답 분석

러시아가 평균 수명이 짧은 국민들에게 돈을 좀 더 써야 한다는 것과 우주 정거장의 인원 증가 및 우주 관광 프로그램의 취소는 아무런 관련이 없다.

1.

With her gumball pearls and chic dresses, could Michelle Obama be the next Jacqueline Kennedy as a fashion leader? (1) By Inauguration Day, the populace was ready for just about any fashion curve ball Obama could throw. (2) And curve she did, in a lemon-colored coat, paired idiosyncratically with green pumps and green gloves. (3) Women's fashions are always changing, so it's harder to point out if a trend is going to take off. (4) In her first dance with the white-bowtied president that night, she appeared in a white one-shoulder gown that earned less-glowing reviews.

Q. **Identify the option that does NOT belong.**
   (a) (1)
   (b) (2)
   (c) (3)
   (d) (4)

2.

Microsoft employees I spoke with this evening were preparing for a major announcement—possibly news of layoffs—from the company. (1) One person expected to be notified at around 7 a.m. (2) No one I spoke with had details on the size of any job cuts or specific groups that might be affected. (3) Microsoft has grown total worldwide employment more than 340 percent from 20,561 to 91,259 as of June 30. (4) All were looking forward to the prospect of the persistent, with distracting layoff rumors being put to rest.

Q. **Identify the option that does NOT belong.**
   (a) (1)
   (b) (2)
   (c) (3)
   (d) (4)

3.

Scientists had believed that Antarctica has been resisting the global warming trend, but that is not the case. (1) East Antarctica has been cooling recently, but the remainder of the continent is warming at a rate that offsets the cooling. (2) Global-warming skeptics have pointed to the presumed cooling of the continent as evidence that researchers' computer projections of climate change are in error. (3) We now see warming is taking place on all of the Earth's continents in accord with what models predict as a response to greenhouse gases. (4) During the last 50 years temperatures for the entire continent rose an average of 0.2 degree Fahrenheit per decade.

Q. Identify the option that does NOT belong.

    (a) (1)

    (b) (2)

    (c) (3)

    (d) (4)

4.

Every time Qantas lands the Airbus A380 at Los Angeles International Airport, parts of the airport come to a halt. (1) Runways must be closed to airfield trucks, cars and other commercial aircraft as the world's largest passenger plane arrives. (2) The plane is so immense that air traffic controllers give it priority, so it doesn't have to wait for takeoff at the end of the airport's runways in cloudy weather because it can disrupt radio signals from the airport's instrument-landing system. (3) These planes are the future of aviation. (4) More than any other airliner the A380 requires special procedures because Los Angeles International Airport was not built to accommodate a plane of its size.

Q. Identify the option that does NOT belong.

    (a) (1)

    (b) (2)

    (c) (3)

    (d) (4)

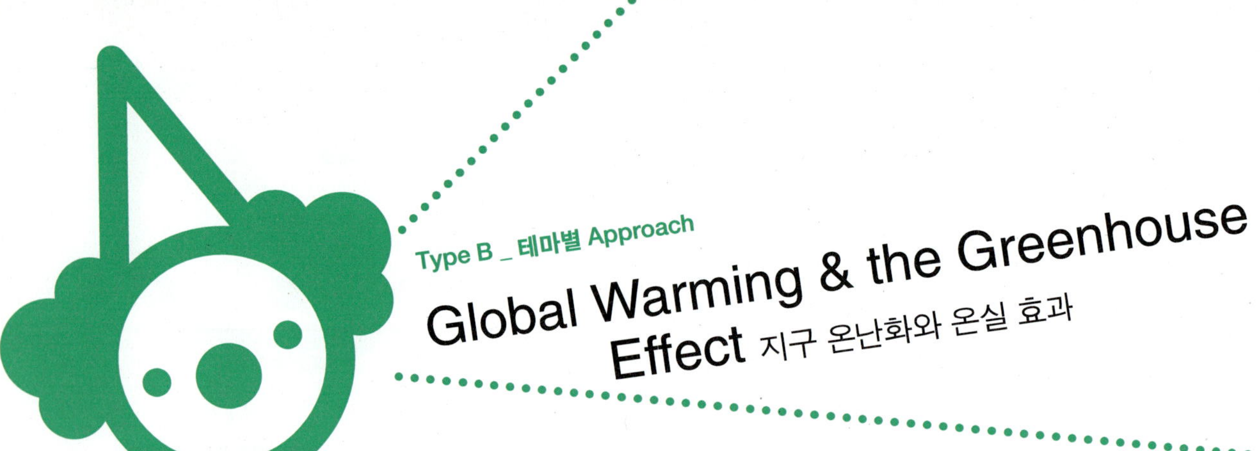

출제 경향 파악

지구 온난화(global warming)나 온실 효과(the greenhouse effect)의 주원인은 자동차 배기가
스(exhaust fumes)와 공장의 매연, 생활 오염 등이다. 특히 환경 문제와 더불어 자동차 배기가스
에 관한 문제가 중요하게 다뤄지고 있다. 부차적인 주제로 오존층 파괴와 관련된 문제도 많이 출
제되는데 현재까지 밝혀진 바로는 지구 온난화와 오존층 파괴는 직접적인 연관성은 없다고 한다.

STEP 1 Theme Research

Fill in the blanks with suitable words.

1.

The automotive industry may be in its worst time. From Detroit to Stuttgart, Tokyo, Paris,
Turin and Seoul, automakers face the terrible problems of global issues that make the
energy crisis of the early 1970's look like a fire drill. Competition among manufactureres has
never been more aggressive; congestion in cities worldwide has never been worse. The
issue of automobile safety looms ever larger. And now that the industry has finally acceded
to emi___ion standards set years ago, the threat of glo___l wa___ing is pointing the finger at
another villain; carbon dioxide, an enemy no catalytic converter can van___ish.

2.

Suspicions that global warming is already af___ecting the seasons and wildlife have been
backed by new research which also suggests that, a century or so from now, spring will
begin almost a month earlier.

Translation

1. 자동차 산업은 최악의 시기를 맞고 있는 것 같다. 디트로이트에서 슈투트가르트, 도쿄, 파리, 토리노, 그리고 서울에 이르기까지 자동차 제조업체들은 1970년대 초의 에너지 위기를 화재 대피 훈련 정도로 보이게 하는 엄청난 전 세계적인 문제들에 직면하고 있다. 제조업체들 간의 경쟁은 과거 어느 때보다도 더 공격적이며, 세계 곳곳의 도시에서 교통 정체는 최악의 상태에 이르렀다. 자동차 안전 문제가 그 어느 때보다 더 부각되고 있다. 또한 이제 자동차업계가 수년 전에 제정된 배기가스 배출 기준에 마침내 동의한 이상 지구 온난화 현상의 위협은 또 다른 범인으로 촉매 변환 장치로도 정복할 수 없는 적인 이산화탄소를 지목하고 있다.

2. 지구 온난화가 이미 계절과 야생 동식물에 영향을 주고 있다는 의심은 앞으로 1세기쯤 후엔 봄이 거의 한 달이나 일찍 시작될 것임을 또한 시사하는 새로운 연구에 의해 뒷받침되고 있다.

STEP 2 Words and Expressions

어구 해설

loom (위험 · 근심 등이) 불안하게 다가오다

accede 동의하다

emission standard (배기가스의) 배출 기준

point the finger at ~을 비난하다

villain 악인, 악역

suspicion 의심, 혐의

global warming 지구 온난화

affect (부정적인) 영향을 주다

wildlife 야생 동식물

POP Quiz

다음 어휘나 어구의 뜻을 빈칸에 써 넣으시오.

1. ozone hole ＿＿＿＿＿＿＿＿＿＿

2. ultraviolet ＿＿＿＿＿＿＿＿＿＿

3. greenhouse effect ＿＿＿＿＿＿＿＿＿＿

4. congestion ＿＿＿＿＿＿＿＿＿＿

5. catalytic converter ＿＿＿＿＿＿＿＿＿＿

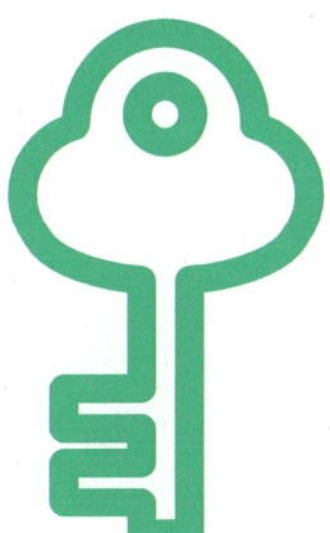

ANSWERS

STEP 1 1.emission standards / global warming / vanquish
2. affecting

STEP 2 1. 오존층 구멍 2. 자외선 3. 온실 효과 4. 교통 정체 5. 촉매 변환 장치

1.

What does the ozone hole have to do with the greenhouse effect? For all practical reasons, nothing. Ozone, naturally occurring from oxygen, is of great concern for another reason. In the upper atmosphere it helps protect us from ultraviolet sunlight, which can cause skin cancer. In 1985, scientists discovered a temporary thinning in the ozone layer over Antarctica, leading to a new concern: if ozone thinning spreads to populated areas, ____________.

Q. **Choose the option that best completes the passage.**
(a) it would result in global warming
(b) it could cause an increase in the disease
(c) it would bring about greenhouse effect
(d) it would help one to tan his skin

오답과 정답 분석

정답 분석
지문 중간에 보면 '오존은 대기권 상층부에서 태양의 자외선으로부터 우리를 보호해 주는데 자외선은 피부암을 유발시킬 수 있다' 는 내용이 나온다. 따라서 오존층이 얇아지는 현상이 인구 거주 지역에까지 퍼지게 된다면 (b) 피부암 등의 질병이 광범위하게 발생할 수 있으리라는 점을 알 수 있다.

오답 분석
(c) 오존층이 얇아지는 것은 온실 효과와는 관계 없다. (d) 오존층에 구멍이 생기거나 얇아지게 되면 피부암을 유발할 수 있다는 것이 이 글의 요지로서 피부를 태우는 데 도움이 된다는 것은 문맥상 맞지 않다.

2.

What are the causes of world pollution? The longer-term issues are centered on __________. The roughly one billion people who live in advanced industrial countries are responsible for the overwhelming majority of the world's environmental problems; whether it's the greenhouse effect on ozone depletion, or even deforestation, we at the top are the problem, and we can't consume our way out of this. We have got to shift our emphasis away from gross consumption of things to a more, maybe, appropriate lifestyle.

Q. **Choose the option that best completes the passage.**
(a) overpopulation
(b) overconsumption
(c) mass production
(d) industrialization

오답과 정답 분석

정답 분석

이 문제는 빈칸을 제외하고는 중심적인 내용이 뒤에 쏠려 있다. 즉 중간 부분은 뒤에 나오는 주제를 뒷받침하고 보강하기 위한 것이다. 특히 중간의 whether it's the greenhouse effect on ozone depletion, or even deforestation 등도 결국에는 과소비를 부각시키기 위한 표현으로 사용되었다.

오답 분석

(a) 인구 과밀, (c) 대량 생산, (d) 산업화의 내용은 윗글에 없다. 특히 마지막 줄에서 We have got to shift our emphasis away from gross consumption of things 라는 표현을 써서 과소비가 환경 문제의 주범이라는 경각심을 불러일으키고 있다.

1.

According to some experts, we are leaving our children and grandchildren a frightening inheritance: an increased accumulation of so-called greenhouse gases in the atmosphere and the potentially disastrous climate changes that this increase may bring about. However, the scientific community ____________. Other scientists claim that the evidence for global warming is inconclusive and argue that predictions based on it are questionable. The scientific debate has been intense. It has also fueled a political controversy about what measures, if any, should be taken to address the possible problem of climate changes.

Q. **Choose the option that best completes the passage.**
(a) is not speaking with one voice
(b) has suggested many practical ideas
(c) is concerned about the climate change
(d) worries about the misuse of scientific discovery

2.

The state of the environment in the latter part of the next century will be determined largely by one factor: human population. If the worst occurs, countless millions will become environmental refugees, swamping the nations that tried to conserve their soil, water and forests. The great-grandchildren of today's young people would have to share the planet with adaptable species dominated by rats, cockroaches, weeds, microbes. The world in which they survived would consist largely of deserts, patches of tropical forests, and eroded mountains.

Q. **What is the mood of the article?**
(a) Romantic
(b) Optimistic
(c) Pessimistic
(d) Indifferent

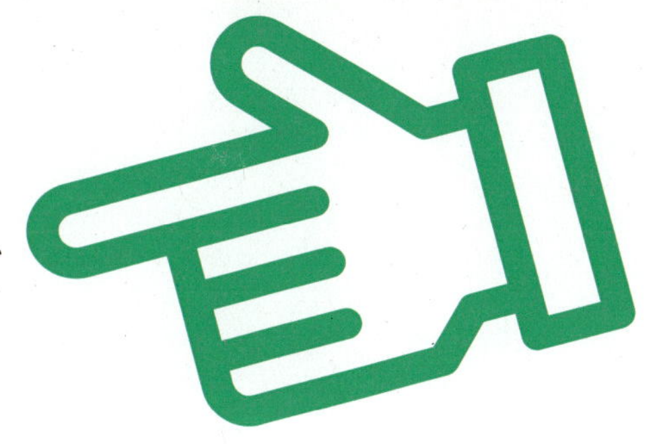

Section Switch

Chapter 9에 나와 있는 TEPS 필수 어휘입니다.

☐ accumulation 축적(물)
☐ air traffic controller 항공 관제사
☐ annoyance 짜증, 불쾌감
☐ Antarctica 남극 대륙
☐ astronaut 우주 비행사
☐ aviation 비행, 항공기 산업
☐ bow tie 나비넥타이
☐ chic 멋진, 세련된
☐ cockroach 바퀴벌레
☐ come to a halt 멈추다, 정지하다
☐ culprit 범인, (문제의) 원인
☐ deforestation 삼림 벌채, 남벌
☐ disability 장애
☐ disrupt 혼란시키다, 불통으로 만들다
☐ distracting 마음을 산란케 하는
☐ fuel 자극하다, 부채질하다
☐ glossy 그럴듯한, 겉만 번지르르한
☐ idiosyncratically 특이하게
☐ immense 거대한
☐ in accord with ~에 맞게, ~와 일치하여
☐ inauguration 취임(식)
☐ inconclusive 결정적이 아닌
☐ inheritance 유산
☐ instrument-landing system 계기 착륙 장치
☐ intense 격렬한
☐ layoff 해고
☐ lucrative 돈이 벌리는
☐ microbe 미생물, 세균
☐ misery 고통
☐ offset 상쇄하다, 벌충하다
☐ ozone depletion 오존 감소
☐ patch 파편, 일부
☐ populace 대중
☐ presumed 추정된
☐ projection 예상, 예측
☐ resort to ~에 의지하다
☐ run for ~에 출마하다
☐ skeptic 회의론자
☐ spaceflight 우주 비행
☐ spine 척추
☐ sufferer 환자
☐ summer associate 여름 인턴십
☐ swamp 궁지에 빠뜨리다
☐ throw ~ a curve ball ~를 놀라게[당혹하게] 하다
☐ ultraviolet 자외선

Final Test

파이널 테스트 01

파이널 테스트 02

Final Test 01

Part 1

1-16. Read the passage. Then choose the option that best completes the passage.

1. Congressional Democrats are drafting legislation that would give the teetering Detroit automakers at least $15 billion in emergency loans early next week and grant the federal government broad authority to manage a massive restructuring of their operations. The proposal, which could be put to a vote in Congress as soon as tomorrow, would establish a seven-member "auto board" of Cabinet officials and a chairman to be appointed by President Bush to oversee both the ___________ and a long-term effort to restore the faltering industry to profitability. If the companies take the cash, they would be accountable to the government for nearly every move, and for every transaction of $25 million or more.

   (a) mid-term loans
   (b) short-term plan
   (c) short-term loans
   (d) long-term execution

2. President-elect Barack Obama warned Sunday that the nation's economic problems were "going to get worse before they get better," pointing to the ___________ and to recent numbers showing the U.S. with its highest unemployment rate in 15 years. He later sought to balance the stark assessment with optimism about the economy's future as he voiced support for a newly proposed government bailout of the nation's carmakers that would be tied to restructuring and a push for greater fuel efficiency.

   (a) fragility of the financial system
   (b) bailout of the nation's carmakers
   (c) confidence in the economy
   (d) tax raise on Americans

3. Now that the petroleum industry has cleaned up its act, __________. The petrol folks are producing diesel fuel with 97 percent less noxious sulfur so diesel-powered vehicles run cleaner. Nine states—including the car-heavy California and New York—had adopted emission regulations so strict they effectively barred diesel sales, a hurdle the cleaner fuel helped the oil burners clear. For 2009, Mercedes-Benz has a trio of 50-state diesel SUVs: the ML, GL and R. Each is called BlueTEC due to the technology which injects a special fluid into the catalytic converter that reduces oxides of nitrogen to the same levels as gasoline.

(a) they reduced oxides of nitrogen
(b) the auto industry has too
(c) they effectively barred diesel sales
(d) the auto industry hasn't, either

4. A songwriter friend of mine once observed that some people can walk around the block and see the whole world while others can go around the world and not see a thing. __________ With the current availability of almost anything from almost anywhere, thanks to the Internet, sometimes it's easy to lose sight of the great products we have right here in Southern California. So this Christmas, why not keep your gift-buying close to home? Concentrate on shopping locally and you might find parts of the area you've never seen before and even meet the producers face to face.

(a) The world can work in a different way.
(b) People can work the same way.
(c) The Internet can work the same way.
(d) Food can work the same way.

5. Director Christopher Nolan raises superhero realism to dizzying heights with *The Dark Knight*, which places Christian Bale's morally conflicted Batman and Heath Ledger's creepy Joker in a Gotham City that looks disturbingly like ___________, not some remote, fantastical movie set. Some of Nolan's "Are heroes and villains really so different?" philosophizing is overcooked, but his impressionistic images hold a lot of power, as does his gutsy choice to use iconic characters to explore his usual themes of identity and lost ideals.

(a) contemporary America
(b) America in the past
(c) America in the future
(d) the modern world

6. Three teenagers accused of kidnapping a 75-year-old woman and keeping her tied up in the back of her station wagon for 26 hours without food or water have pleaded not guilty to torture and other charges. The three entered their pleas Friday in San Diego County Superior Court. She was found severely beaten and bound. She had been abducted from her home late Monday night. The defendants face charges ___________, robbery and kidnapping.

(a) except transporting
(b) including smuggling
(c) except bootlegging
(d) including torture

7. A key witness in O.J. Simpson's Las Vegas trial acknowledged to a Nevada investigator that the former NFL star ___________, the investigator told a judge in Santa Monica this morning. The investigator said the witness admitted that Simpson gave him his Hall of Fame ring in exchange for altering his testimony to help the defense. "I asked what did you get to change your testimony," said Bill Falkner, who worked with prosecutors building the armed robbery and kidnapping case against Simpson.

(a) paid him off
(b) let him down
(c) turned him over
(d) lied to him

8. A Vatican bioethics document condemned artificial fertilization and other techniques used by many couples and also said human cloning, embryonic stem-cell research and "morning-after" drugs were immoral. The long awaited document from the Vatican's doctrinal body marks a major step by the Vatican into biotechnology. The document also condemns new drugs that ___________ from taking hold, such as the morning-after pill, which blocks the action of hormones needed to keep a fertilized egg implanted in the uterus.

(a) block pregnancy
(b) fertilize artificially
(c) make embryonic stem-cell
(d) reduce merely to a group of cells

9. John Travolta's teenage son, Jett, died in the Bahamas after suffering a seizure and hitting his head at his family's vacation home. A house caretaker found Jett unconscious in a bathroom late Friday morning. He was taken by ambulance to a Freeport hospital, where he was pronounced dead. The teenager had last been seen entering the bathroom on Thursday and had ___________, according to the statement. An autopsy is planned.

(a) a history of seizures
(b) symptoms of influenza
(c) records of cerebral concussions
(d) out of vertigos

10. The world's stock markets are off to a strong start in the new year, after the crash of 2008. The Dow Jones industrial average was up 228 points, or 2.6%, to 9,004. It's just too bad that there are so few people working on Wall Street today to enjoy this. Trading is very light, with most investors making a four-day weekend of the New Year's holiday. And that means any significant market move today would be suspect. Better to ___________ to see what the big money really thinks about stocks in 2009.

(a) think about the stock market
(b) wait until Monday
(c) invest more money
(d) analyze recent moves of capital

11. A coffee plantation in Hawaii hopes to perk up profits with a new brew: Barack O
Blend, a smooth medley of Hawaiian, Kenyan and Indonesian beans that honors
the ___________ of President-elect Barack Obama. So far, it seems to be working.
Obama, whose father was Kenyan, was born in Hawaii and lived for several years
in Indonesia. Asked to describe the Barack O Blend, the producer said, "It is very
rich and very easy to drink." For proprietary reasons, he declined to reveal the
exact blend of coffee.

(a) adversities in his life
(b) diversity of his experience
(c) flavor in coffee
(d) multinational roots

12. Protesters turned out in downtown Chicago to protest Israel's recent military action
in the Gaza Strip. The protest was one of many recent demonstrations around the
world in response to Israel's air strikes on the Gaza Strip. The U.N. estimates that
20 to 25 percent of the more than 400 Palestinians killed by Israeli air strikes on
Hamas militants were civilians. Many of the protesters in Chicago decried the
deaths of civilians. "It's just innocent people getting killed," said Hammad Haq who
attended the protest with several classmates. "All we're protesting against is
___________."

(a) Islamic tradition and culture
(b) the killing of innocent people
(c) rocket attacks into southern Israel by Hamas
(d) the war between the two parties

13. Scientists researched the relationship between proximity to alcohol retailers in zones around homes and drinking in children aged under 17. In California, retail licenses are not typically approved within 100 feet of a residence or within 600 feet of schools, but ____________. More attention on the proximity rule is needed and environmental interventions need to curb opportunities for youth to purchase alcohol from commercial sources.

(a) proximity by itself is not sufficient to deny a license
(b) proximity to alcohol outlets is a risk factor for youth
(c) alcohol is more readily available in minority and lower-income areas
(d) living in areas with higher alcohol sales could also mean more exposure to violent crime and drunk driving

14. The snow that fell in the Seattle area Sunday night was expected to turn to rain overnight, making today's commute on main roads a bit messy but ____________. In all, 1 to 3 inches was expected, but as much as 5 inches was recorded, according to the National Weather Service. More snow was reported on the ground in some areas, for instance, 6 inches in North Seattle's Broadview neighborhood.

(a) a little dirty
(b) too high
(c) very chilly
(d) not that slippery

15. Amtrak says one of its trains slammed into a tractor-trailer that blocked the tracks in southern Illinois, injuring nine passengers and a crew member. Amtrak spokesman Marc Magliari says the 10 injured went to hospitals for evaluation __________ none of the injuries are considered to be life-threatening. Macoupin County Sheriff Don Albrecht said the driver of the truck became stuck on the crossing at around 11:15 a.m. on Monday and that the driver left the vehicle when he heard the train, which was traveling to St. Louis from Chicago.

(a) as
(b) but
(c) then
(d) instead

16. When Army Sgt. Ryan Kahlor returned from Iraq last year, he was a walking billboard for virtually every affliction suffered by today's veterans. He was diagnosed with post-traumatic stress disorder and traumatic brain injury. He carried a loaded handgun everywhere. He drank until he passed out and would often cut himself. He also burned his own skin with cigarettes. He bit through his tongue just to watch himself bleed. Pushed hard by his parents, __________, he slowly accepted and then embraced counseling and treatment. Today, he has begun to recover and his parents are still trying.

(a) however
(b) instead
(c) to make matters worse
(d) all the more

Part 2

17-37. Read the passage and the question. Then choose the option that best answers the question.

17. The company that owns the *Los Angeles Times*, the *Chicago Tribune* and Chicago Cubs baseball team is preparing for a possible bankruptcy filing as it attempts to renegotiate $12 billion in debt with banks and other creditors, a Tribune Co. executive said Sunday. The Chicago media conglomerate hired Lazard Ltd. a little more than a week ago for advice on a possible bankruptcy filing, though people familiar with internal talks said the company was exploring several options.

Q. **What is the best title for the passage?**
(a) The Migration of Advertising Revenue to the Internet
(b) Covering Accelerated Debt Payments
(c) Difficult Financial and Economic Environment Around Tribune Co.
(d) Debt-laden Tribune Co. Explores Possible Bankruptcy Filing

18. While traffic officials applaud a new law that makes it illegal for drivers to read, write or send text messages, they admit there is little evidence that last year's ban against talking on a hand-held cellphone has actually prevented accidents. Since holding a phone to your ear was made a traffic violation last July, the California Highway Patrol has written about 48,000 tickets. But just how effective the law has been, no one can say.

Q. **What is the best title for the passage?**
(a) A Paucity of Data on the Role of Cellphones
(b) Necessity of Ban of Cellphone Use While Driving
(c) The Cellphone is a Distraction From Driving
(d) Effectiveness of Drivers' Cellphone Ban is Debatable

19. Long-term trials with more than 50,000 participants offered fresh evidence that vitamin C and vitamin E supplements don't reduce the risk of prostate and lung cancer. Other recent studies have found that over-the-counter vitamins and minerals offer no help in fighting other cancers, stroke or cardiovascular disease. Research has even suggested that, in some circumstances, the supplements can be unsafe. Some physicians now advise their patients not to bother with the pills, and to rely instead on a healthy diet to provide the needed vitamins and minerals.

Q. **What is the main idea of the passage?**
(a) Vitamin supplements prevent cancer, heart disease, stroke and other ailments.
(b) Vitamin supplements don't fight cancer.
(c) Faith in vitamin supplements runs deep.
(d) Scientists remain convinced that vitamins are essential to health.

20. You don't need to cut grocery coupons from the newspaper anymore! Start saving the easy way with online printable grocery coupons. Before you go to the supermarket, simply visit this Printable Grocery Coupons page here at CoolSavings, select your favorite name-brand coupons, and print. Every week the coupons change, and your total savings could be between $50-$100! Be sure to scan through all our coupon pages so you don't miss these.

Q. **What is the passage mainly about?**
(a) Printable coupons
(b) Total savings from free coupons
(c) Favorite name-brand coupons
(d) Grocery coupons from the newspaper

21. This election draws the attention to President Bush. In his weekly radio address, Bush called on the people to go to the polls as an example for emerging democracies around the world. "Young democracies from Georgia and Ukraine to Afghanistan and Iraq can look to the United States for proof that self-government can endure. And nations that still live under tyranny and oppression can find hope and inspiration in our commitment to liberty." Bush has already cast his ballot by absentee. While others are waiting in lines, 30+ states allow early voting ahead of election day. Election experts predict voter turnout could be the highest since the 1960 election.

Q. **What is the best title for the passage?**
(a) Bush Urges Americans to Vote
(b) Early Voting Begins
(c) The Election Day Has Come
(d) Liberty Suffering in Countries like Georgia and Ukraine

22. One of China's coldest cities, Harbin, is celebrating the deep freeze with its annual Ice and Snow Festival. Hundreds of massive sculptures—from Chinese palaces to French cathedrals—are created each January from blocks of ice cut from the city's frozen river. Almost a million people are expected to tour the ice creations this month.

Q. **What is the best title for the article?**
(a) A Cold City of China
(b) Massive Ice Sculpture Show
(c) Chinese City Celebrates the Cold
(d) From Ice to Sculptures

23. Dear Ms. Jenkins,

I've been offered a job promotion that would require me to relocate abroad to Paris from Chicago. The salary for my new position would be much higher than what I'm getting now, and I've always wanted to work in the French branch of our company, but I'm worried that living in Paris could be more expensive than where I live now. If this is the case, perhaps the increase in salary won't make a big difference. Can you tell me anything about the cost of living in Paris?

With lots of love,

Dennis Alice

Q. **What is the purpose of this letter?**
(a) To get some information on relocating to Paris
(b) To get a promotion through relocation abroad
(c) To ask for an increase in salary
(d) To get some tips on the cost of living in Paris

24. Digital photography's flexible format has been a boon to consumers. You can print images at home, upload them to the Internet or e-mail a cute shot from your phone to your mom. You can even use some cameras underwater. But in the digital age, you couldn't print a photo directly from the camera—a technology Polaroid developed more than 60 years ago. That's about to change.

Q. **Which of the following is most likely to follow this passage?**
(a) The technology which Polaroid developed more than 60 years ago
(b) Digital cameras and camera phones
(c) Waterproof digital cameras
(d) Digital cameras with a built-in printer

25. My oldest daughter asked me what was wrong, and I realized that I was just unhappy with my body. I never took that into consideration until that day in the dressing room. I knew something needed to change, but I wasn't sure how I could do it. Losing 25 pounds was easier than I thought it would be. I ended up using a combination of 2 diet supplements that I saw on TV, and I didn't need some trendy diet to lose the weight. In the end all it took was a simple two-step process and it changed my life forever. After one week I had lost 5 pounds and now after one month, I've reached my goal and I feel great.

Q. **When did she decide to lose weight?**
(a) When her oldest daughter asked her what was wrong
(b) When she saw her body in the dressing room
(c) When she saw the ads on TV
(d) When she began a trendy diet to lose the weight

26. Boeing employment in Washington state slipped in the last two months of 2008, according to just-released numbers showing the first job reductions at the airplane maker since mid-2004. Total Boeing employees in Washington declined from 76,869 at the end of October to 76,417 at the end of the year. Boeing has not announced any layoffs and most of the reduction is likely due to letting go of long-term contractors. International Association of Machinists union spokeswoman Connie Kelliher said the cuts are not in the blue-collar sector.

Q. **Which part of the Boeing workforce decreased the most?**
(a) Blue-collar workers
(b) Contract laborers
(c) White-collar workers
(d) Production workers

27. The state Department of Mental Health, facing a more than $9 million cut in its budget, laid off nearly one quarter of the case managers who supervise people with severe mental illness and make sure they get the services they need. About 100 case managers received their pink slips or will get them today. State officials said about 3,000 clients would lose their current case managers. Those clients will be shifted to other case managers among the remaining 350.

Q. **Why will case managers receive their pink slips?**
(a) Case management is not vital anymore.
(b) The number of mentally ill children is decreasing.
(c) The state Department of Mental Health will curtail the budget.
(d) The state Department of Mental Health hired too many case managers.

28. When cholera was the scourge of London in the mid-1800s, people thought the disease was carried by vapors. An early epidemiologist identified cases that didn't fit with what one would predict if the disease traveled by air. The common factor among cholera victims was not living in the most affected neighborhood, but getting water from a particular public well. Cholera is now known to be caused by bacteria, and sanitation in the form of modern plumbing prevents outbreaks in the developed world.

Q. **How was cholera carried from person to person?**
(a) By some sort of microorganisms
(b) By vapors
(c) By living closely to the most affected neighborhood
(d) By air

29. California regulators adopted the nation's first comprehensive plan to slash greenhouse gases. The ambitious blueprint would cut the state's emissions by 15% over the next 12 years, bringing them back down to 1990 levels. Adopted by the state's Air Resources Board in a unanimous vote, it lays out targets for virtually every sector of the economy, from automobiles to buildings, forests and landfills. It would require a third of California's electricity to come from solar energy, wind farms and other renewable sources.

Q. **Which of the following is incorrect according to the passage?**
(a) The plan is a stepping stone to curb greenhouse gases.
(b) California is planning to get more energy from fossil fuels.
(c) The plan is aimed at almost every sector of the economy.
(d) Congress is expected to make its efforts to craft climate legislation.

30. Morris F. Collen is a pioneer in harnessing the vast power of computers to improve healthcare. He is studying the ways that prescription drugs could interact and harm the elderly. He's hard at work on his sixth book. But he just might be even prouder of his brand-new driver's license. "Can I show you something you'll never see again?" Collen asks, reaching for his billfold. He pulls out the rectangle of plastic and points to the date of birth: 11-20-13. He points to the expiration date: 11-20-13. He grins. "One is in the 20th century, the other is in the 21st century. That represents 100 years."

Q. **Which of the following is incorrect about the article?**
(a) He is writing his book these days.
(b) He has lived for 100 years.
(c) He's got his driver's license.
(d) He is studying some sort of medicine.

31. Today's children face noise-induced hearing loss due to personal audio devices. A big concern with portable music is that people often listen too loudly with headphones, which is increasingly leading to hearing loss problems. According to the Academy of Pediatrics, 85dB is considered the threshold for dangerous levels of noise. Also, the length of time one listens to music is a concern, so children should not listen continuously for long stretches, no matter the volume level.

Q. Which of the following is correct according to the passage?
(a) Today's youngsters need to use MP3 players more often.
(b) The new headphones for kids can help prevent some of the damage.
(c) 85dB is deemed the outset for risky levels of noise.
(d) The length of time they use personal audio devices isn't a momentous factor.

32. The Army issued a formal apology to the families of soldiers killed in Iraq and Afghanistan after it sent them letters with the salutation "Dear John Doe." In December, the Army sent out 7,000 letters to the families of the 3,544 soldiers killed in Iraq and Afghanistan since 2001. Although the envelopes were properly addressed, a software problem resulted in an error that printed the salutation "Dear John Doe" at the top of the letters, which were printed by a private contractor. In addition to the apology, Gen. George W. Casey Jr., the Army's chief of staff, is sending the families a new letter explaining the error.

Q. Which of the following is correct about the article?
(a) U.S. military forces issued a formal apology to the soldiers killed in the battlefield.
(b) The Army sent out about 3,500 letters to the soldiers who died in the battlefield.
(c) U.S. military forces sent out the letters to the wrong place.
(d) The Army outsourced printing letters to an individual enterprise.

33. U.S. Secretary of State Condoleezza Rice has held talks with her Israeli counterpart amid fresh diplomatic moves to advance the Mid-East peace process. Rice's meeting with Tzipi Livni came after Israel approved a plan to expand a West Bank settlement, which the U.S. called "not helpful." Livni's visit to Washington follows a lull in fighting between Israel and Palestinians in Hamas-run Gaza. U.S. Vice-President Dick Cheney is also due to visit the region shortly. Before the talks U.S. President George W. Bush said he was still optimistic there would be a Middle East peace deal before he leaves office next January.

Q. **Which of the following is correct according to the passage?**
(a) George Bush expressed his satisfaction about the plan to expand a West Bank settlement.
(b) Before Livni's visit to the U.S. there was a fierce battle between Israel and Hamas.
(c) The U.S. vice president is supposed to visit Jerusalem shortly.
(d) George W. Bush hopes to settle the Middle East peace deal soon.

34. GM has a bigger presence outside the U.S. and it employs more people in other countries than here, and actually makes money selling cars abroad from Sao Paulo to Shanghai. Its U.S. revenue has sunk 24% in the last three full years, but in the rest of the world, GM can boast a 28% increase. Now, as U.S. lawmakers mull whether to provide billions of dollars in loans to keep the Detroit-based company from collapse, GM's global reach has become in many ways its most overlooked asset and a key to its ultimate survival.

Q. **What can be inferred from the passage?**
(a) GM should freeze up their foreign plants.
(b) A major solution for keeping GM out of bankruptcy is the strength of its foreign footprint.
(c) Where GM sells the bulk of its cars has changed dramatically.
(d) GM's struggle in the U.S. has nothing to do with the company worldwide.

35. While Mixed Martial Arts has made significant strides in attracting a growing audience and adopting safety rules that have put the sport under regulation in states including Nevada, California, Illinois and New Jersey, there remains lingering criticism of the sport's violent edges. John McCain's home state, Arizona, didn't permit professional MMA fights until September, and New York still bans the sport. "When I see stuff like that, it looks like nothing more than a tough man contest," said Todd duBoef, president of boxing promotion company Top Rank.

Q. **What can be inferred from the passage?**
(a) Punches don't cause much damage in MMA fights.
(b) There have been criticism about the MMA in the United States.
(c) Arizona won't be permitting professional MMA fights.
(d) In a certain way, it's safer than boxing.

36. A recent discovery of microscopic diamonds in North America reveals that a comet caused a cataclysm of fire, flood and devastation nearly 13,000 years ago that extinguished mammoths, scientists said. The nano-diamonds are thought to be remnants of that comet, which would have hit about 65 million years after the much larger collision that wiped out the dinosaurs. According to the theory, as the comet broke apart, it rained fire over the entire continent, igniting the plains and the forests and creating choking clouds of smoke.

Q. **What can be inferred from the passage?**
(a) The nano-diamonds were made from the remainder of dinosaurs.
(b) The comet caused the dinosaurs to become extinct.
(c) Molten glaciers triggered changes in Atlantic Ocean currents.
(d) Such an impact between the comet and the earth would be the most likely
    source of the nano-diamonds.

37. The American League champion Tampa Bay Rays are one team that has expressed an interest, Griffey's agent Brian Goldberg told SI.com. A friend of Griffey's said last year that the future Hall of Famer would love to play for Tampa Bay, which is less than two hours from his Orlando home. While Griffey is on the Rays' list, a couple of younger hitters, such as Bobby Abreu and Pat Burrell, may be higher on it. Another possible destination for Griffey could be Seattle, where he started his big-league career. While the Mariners are rebuilding, they could view Griffey as an aid to their young players and a draw for fans.

Q. **What can be inferred from the passage?**
(a) Griffey is the Hall of Famer now.
(b) Griffey hopes to play for the team which is close to his home.
(c) Griffey is on the top of Tampa Ray's scout list.
(d) Griffey started his career in Tampa.

38-40. Read the passage. Then identify the option that does NOT belong.

38. As the plane lifted off the carrier deck, the pilot quickly knew he was in trouble, possibly with a malfunction in one of the plane's engines. (a) He radioed the air controller at Marine Corps Air Station Miramar, who ordered an emergency landing attempt. (b) As the plane crossed over land at Torrey Pines en route to Miramar, more problems struck, including a possible "flame out" of a second engine. (c) More than 100 firefighters were on the scene within minutes, along with crash specialists from the Marine Corps. (d) Within seconds, the plane nosed downward and smashed into a Cather Avenue home where a mother, a grandmother and two children lived.

39. More than a million homes across the Northeast spent a whole day without power after a bitterly cold storm swept across the region, coating roads with thick sheets of ice and weighing down power lines. (a) In some places, snow had even begun to melt. (b) The storm, which began gusting through the region last night, closed schools and public offices and interrupted travel across Maine and Massachusetts. (c) Entire communities had lost power. (d) Residents spent the day indoors preparing for a frigid, dark weekend of burning candles and firewood, while others scrambled to gas stations to load up on fuel for home generators.

40. That flat-screen television has a big drawback: It's an energy hog. (a) State regulators are getting ready to curb the growing power gluttony of TV sets by requiring retailers to sell only the most energy-efficient models. (b) The consumer electronics industry opposes the regulations and claims that they could remove some TVs from store shelves and slightly boost sticker prices. (c) But the California Energy Commission is looking for ways to relieve the strain on the power grid. (d) It would kill dealerships because people would buy on Amazon and have them shipped in and possibly avoid paying sales tax.

Final Test 02

1-16. Read the passage. Then choose the option that best completes the passage.

1. There are no free lunches in life, but one could always count on free beer at Anheuser-Busch theme parks. Until now. The brewer has __________ in hospitality centers at its SeaWorld theme parks in Orlando, San Antonio and San Diego. Anheuser-Busch Adventure Parks spokesman Fred Jacobs says the free beer had a narrow appeal among park customers. The brewer plans to build more restaurants geared toward families with children. Customers can still buy beer at some of the parks.

(a) stopped giving free beer
(b) started new marketing strategies
(c) built more restaurants
(d) started to attract more customers

2. If you received a new cell phone for Christmas, find out where you can drop off your old one. The U.S. Environmental Protection Agency is targeting phone recycling in a series of ads on buses because __________. Phones are made from precious metals, copper and plastics. Recycling just a million cell phones reduces greenhouse gas emissions equal to taking 1,368 cars off the road for a year, according to the EPA.

(a) The EPA plans to donate the old recycled phones to the poor
(b) more people are encouraged to use a product for its entire life
(c) more people are beginning to recycle their old cell phones
(d) fewer than 20 percent of phone are recycled each year

3. Eleven gay bars in San Francisco were sent letters threatening ricin attacks. The anonymous letters say, "I have in my possession approximately 67 grams of ricin with which I will indiscriminately target at least five of your clients. I expect them to die painfully while in hospital." The San Francisco Police Department said ___________. It has seized the letters and is processing them and is coordinating efforts with the FBI and other federal agencies. The U.S. Centers for Disease Control and Prevention says ricin is a poison that can be deadly if ingested or inhaled.

(a) it takes the threat seriously
(b) the letters were designed to ruin business for gay bars
(c) bars should close their shop temporarily
(d) it warned bar patrons not to leave their drinks unattended

4. The snow came up to his knees, and it was difficult to walk even a few steps. The wind threatened his balance and the blowing snow suffocated him. He waded forward, digging through the snow, fighting his way down the hill. His whole body was so cold. His feet seemed like they belonged to someone else. Down below, he could see ___________. Snow had covered everything. He remembered that the Outside Mall was at the bottom of the hill, but all he could see was snow.

(a) the headlights
(b) the road through the hill
(c) outside of the Mall
(d) nothing but white land

5. The United States has accused North Korea of helping Syria build a nuclear reactor that "was not intended for peaceful purposes." The site, said to be like one in North Korea, was bombed by Israel in 2007. Syria must ___________ about its secret nuclear program, the White House said in a statement after CIA officials briefed members of Congress.

(a) investigate thoroughly
(b) come clean
(c) go forward
(d) negotiate with North Korea

6. The International Committee of the Red Cross said that it had found at least 15 dead bodies in a row of shattered houses in the Gaza Strip and accused the Israeli military of ___________. Red Cross officials said rescue crews had received specific reports of casualties in the houses and had been trying to send ambulances to the area. They said the Israeli military did not grant permission. In an unusual public statement issued by its Geneva headquarters, the Red Cross called the episode "unacceptable" and said the Israeli military had "failed to meet its obligation under international humanitarian law to care for and evacuate the wounded."

(a) killing civilians in the Gaza Strip
(b) preventing ambulances from reaching the site
(c) risking injury in order to assist innocent civilians
(d) chasing rescue workers away from the site

7. Stocks are tumbling, and credit markets remain tight. This is because of news of an unexpected rise in new unemployment claims due to a drop in factory orders. All this is highlighting the troubles facing the economy, even if the House follows the Senate in passing a reworked bailout bill. Economist Mark Lansey says the economic stress is really straining the job market. "The financial crisis panic undermined confidence among business people and they're now laying off workers, and we're going to see hundreds of thousands of ___________ over the course of the remainder of this year into early next."

    (a) severe depressions
    (b) taking out loans for living expenses
    (c) voluntary resignations
    (d) job losses

8. The U.S. economy ___________ since Barack Obama won the November 4th election, with higher unemployment, plunging consumer spending, and further readings of negative growth. With that retrogression comes a question. Will the worsening conditions force the incoming president to jettison the economic strategy he laid out during the campaign and formulate a new one?

    (a) has recovered slowly
    (b) has come to a deadlock
    (c) has deteriorated significantly
    (d) has hit the bottom

9. In his weekly radio address, President Bush said he doesn't see most of the $700 billion being used in the financial bailout as ___________. "Many of the assets that the government will be purchasing still have significant underlying value. As time passes, they will likely go up in price, and this means that the government should eventually be able to recoup much, if not all, of the original expenditure." Bush signed the bill, after it was passed by the House.

(a) big expenditure
(b) great benefit
(c) lost money
(d) underlying value

10. A widely used class of antipsychotic drugs that includes bestsellers Zyprexa, Risperdal and Seroquel is likely to cause a fatal heart attack, researchers reported. The findings, which ___________ a long-standing belief, add to a growing drumbeat of criticism about this class of drugs. Zyprexa, Risperdal and Seroquel are among the 10 most commonly prescribed medications in the world, with annual sales estimated at $14.5 billion.

(a) cite according to
(b) run contrary to
(c) is in compliance with
(d) come to a conclusion of

11. People who slept less than eight hours a night were almost three times as likely to
_____________ as those who slept eight hours or more, according to a new study.
Quality of sleep counted even more than quantity, the study found. Those who
spent as little as 25 minutes tossing and turning faced more than five times the risk
of sniffling and sneezing. The age-old advice to get a good night's sleep is well-
supported by medical research.

(a) come down with a cold
(b) get up late in the morning
(c) be exposed to a bacteria
(d) resist or fight off infection well

12. The Guns N' Roses singer says Dr. Pepper is profiting from his band and their new
album. The soft-drink maker said months ago that it would give a free drink to
everyone in America if the band finally released their long-overdue album this year.
A Lawyer for Guns N' Roses says while the band _____________, Dr. Pepper didn't.
The soda maker's website crashed during the 24 hours it offered a free beverage to
consumers on Sunday, the same day, *Chinese Democracy* was released. So far, Dr.
Pepper hasn't addressed the rock band's complaint.

(a) made good on their promise
(b) gave a free beverage at the concert
(c) featured at their rock concert
(d) had an ax to grind

13. General Motors President Fritz Henderson says they are taking steps needed to stay in business, ____________. "We have to work with the environment we're dealt, if you will, and as part of that, therefore, we need to size our company much differently to address this kind of difficult economic environment." Henderson tells CBS Early Show that even with all the changes, GM will still need billions of dollars just to stay in business. And on Wall Street in early trading, the Dow is down 172 points.

(a) including cutting the size of the company
(b) funding more money to invest in R&D
(c) living to tell the tale
(d) hiring some experts in accounting

14. President-Elect Barack Obama is said to be ready to name former Democratic rival Hillary Clinton to be his Secretary of State. A big hurdle, former President Bill Clinton's International Foundation, ____________. The former President had long refused to disclose the identities of contributors to his Foundation, saying many gave money on the condition that they not be identified. He's now agreed to do so, and has volunteered to step away from day-to-day management of the Foundation while his wife serves in the Obama Administration.

(a) has been cleared
(b) remained unsolved
(c) has been doubled
(d) has been identified

15. Russia's natural gas monopoly dramatically cut flows to Europe through Ukraine, sharpening fears of fuel shortages during the bitter days of winter. __________ warnings from the European Union, a tense pricing dispute between Gazprom and Ukraine showed no signs of letting up even as gas flows dwindled. As the two sides traded accusations and blame, negotiations remained frozen for the sixth day.

(a) Despite
(b) However
(c) As of
(d) Besides

16. Satellite TV in cars has been pretty much a disaster so far, with the picture and sound freezing every time so much as a light pole blocks the signal. To duplicate the effect at home, hit the pause button on your TV about 20 times a minute. __________ a new system by AT&T CruiseCast is a huge improvement. On view in a test vehicle, it managed to play live cable channels almost seamlessly while riding through Las Vegas neighborhoods. The system uses a buffer regimen, similar to packet switching on the Internet, to keep the channel playing even when momentarily blocked.

(a) Finally
(b) But
(c) And
(d) While

Part 2

17-37. Read the passage and the question. Then choose the option that best answers the question.

17. There are rumors that the Big 3 could become the Big 2. General Motors and Chrysler have held preliminary talks about a merger or making a deal in which GM buys Chrysler. Automotive analyst Lincoln Merrihew says whatever the deal is, it is going to cost a lot of money. "Things like uh, possibly closing factories, it costs money to do that; possibly downsizing the workforce, it may take money to do that; you may have to buy people out. Uh, taking out brands, taking out dealerships; all of this costs money."

Q. **What is the best title for the passage?**
(a) Cost in Merger between the Two Companies
(b) GM, Chrysler Discuss Merger
(c) Chrysler Closes Factories
(d) Cost-cutting Measures in Restructuring the Organization

18. Actual premium will vary based on amount of insurance purchased and other factors. $30,000 is a rounded national estimate of personal property value for a standard 2 room apartment. Actual values will vary. Insurance subjects to availability, qualifications and policy terms, including limitations or exclusions of coverage for certain types of losses and personal possessions. Please read your policy for more details.

Q. **What is the purpose of this paragraph?**
(a) To explain an insurance policy
(b) To explain premium and its coverage
(c) To give information on insurance deduction and policy
(d) To show how the premium is fixed in certain conditions

19. Dear Sirs,

It has been a difficult journey for me to get to this point, as I truly believed in my service to the people, but it was less than my best. I want to make things right in my heart even though I cannot undo my blunders, I hope I can restore faith in your hearts by opening up and sharing these thoughts. And even though it took time for me to come to this place, in the end my goal is to do the right thing, no matter how tardy, I hope that my words might help in the healing process of restoring the people's faith in their government and others.

Sincerely yours,

John Fitzgerald

Q. **What is the purpose of this letter?**
(a) To serve the customer
(b) To excuse the tardiness of service
(c) To apologize for his mistakes
(d) To explain his faith in the government

20. We want you to enjoy every visit to DunkinDonuts.com, whether you're here to order coffee, or to tell us about your last trip to one of our shops. So rest assured, any information you share with us, from your email address to your favorite donut, will be carefully guarded through our use of industry-standard security software to encrypt your credit card number and other ordering and shipping information. Dunkin' Donuts reserves the right to change this privacy policy at any time. Be sure to check this page periodically for updates.

Q. **What is the purpose of this passage?**
(a) To give information about their online shopping
(b) To invite customers to DunkinDonuts.com
(c) To inform customers of the privacy policy of DunkinDonuts.com
(d) To show customers the industry-standard security software

21. You must book 3 nights accommodation in Northern Territory with Qantas Vacations to purchase this special "Outback Airpass" offer. The Outback Airpass includes a minimum of 1 sector to the following Outback Regions: Darwin, Ayers Rock or Alice Springs. Seats are strictly limited. Complimentary Adult Entry Tickets to Alice Springs Desert Park or Darwin's Wildlife Park are part of the Outback Airpass promotion and available for the first 100 bookings. Entry Tickets are valid until 31st August 2009. Choice of Wildlife Park tickets are limited and will be serviced on a first-come basis. Please call for our current prices.

Q. **What's the purpose of this passage?**
(a) To inform customers of merit about the Outback Airpass
(b) To attract customers to Australia
(c) To inform customers of terms and conditions about the trip
(d) To inform customers of the offer will end

22. Human skin cells have been reprogrammed by two groups of scientists to mimic embryonic stem cells with the potential to become any tissue in the body. The breakthrough promises a plentiful new source of cells for use in research into new treatments for many diseases. Crucially, it could mean that such research is no longer dependent on using cells from human embryos, which has proved highly controversial.

Q. **What can be inferred from the passage?**
(a) Researchers have made embryonic stem cells from human embryos so far.
(b) The government has prohibited the use of cells from human embryos.
(c) It has been relatively easy to obtain cells from human embryos.
(d) There have been little contentions on using cells of embryos.

23. The latest report, coming from South Korea's Yonhap news agency, quotes someone it calls "a well-informed source," as saying North Korea's Leader Kim Jong Il has chosen the youngest of his three sons, Kim Jong Un, to eventually take control of North Korea. Just two days earlier, a Japanese daily newspaper reported that a collective government will be formed with Kim Jong Nam, the eldest son of the leader Kim Jong Il, as head of state in name only. With North Korea being one of the world's most secretive states, there is no way to verify these reports. And analysts who monitor Pyongyang's official propaganda have not noticed any changes that indicate a successor has been chosen.

Q. **What can be inferred from the passage?**
(a) South Korea's Yonhap news is called an unreliable source.
(b) The successor of North Korea has already been chosen.
(c) The collective government chose Kim Jong Nam as the successor.
(d) No one knows exactly about the succssion matters of North Korea right now.

24. On the first week of a fitness program, people are likely realizing that making resolutions is much easier than keeping them. Many are already faltering on their fitness goals, finding it difficult to brave the morning or evening chill. On this second week of a four-part series on starting a fitness program, we've got help from David Brinton, a former Olympian and currently an elite USA Cycling coach. He explains how to work out like a pro and avoid beginner burnout, and he suggests some tools that make the process easier.

Q. **Which of the following is most likely to follow this passage?**
(a) How to ride the bicycle
(b) How to lose weight from fitness
(c) How to make it easier to rise in the morning
(d) How to plan and start a fitness program

25. The guy at the gas station getting my car ready for winter told me I needed new tires and that they'd cost maybe $500 and he'd be happy to go ahead and do the job. I didn't have an extra $500. And, if I did have any spare money, the most unsatisfying purchase is an auto part. If I hate to spend money on tires, I bet you do, too. So I will do all the homework to help make this miserable experience as painless and cost-effective for you as possible.

Q. **Which of the following is most likely to follow this passage?**
(a) How to replace tires by oneself
(b) Some tips on buying tires wisely
(c) How to find a local gas station
(d) The advertisement of Goodyear tires

26. In the past, when there were not many doctors or hospitals, people used folk remedies to ease illnesses. This week, let's learn some of the most popular folk remedies. A folk remedy is a traditional way of treating an illness at home. A long time ago, when someone had a slight ache or a minor cold, mothers used old remedies to ease the health problems. Folk remedies have been handed down from generation to generation. You may think they are not effective. But many home remedies really work! Why don't you try them yourself next time?

Q. **Which of the following is most likely to follow this passage?**
(a) Effective ways to become fit
(b) How to lose weight
(c) Some tips on physical therapy
(d) Popular folk treatments

27. Thousands of Aborigines who were removed from their families as children will receive no compensation, the Australian government has said. Campaigners had asked for a reparation fund of almost $870m as part of a promised official apology. But indigenous affairs minister Jenny Macklin says money will instead be put into health and education schemes. Many Aboriginal children were handed to white families from 1915 to 1969. They were brought up by white people in an attempt by the government to assimilate the white and Aboriginal populations.

Q. **Why did tons of Aborigines leave their families as children?**
(a) The government wanted Aborigines to study in the cities.
(b) Aborigines have problems with health and education.
(c) Aborigines hoped to make money from the government.
(d) The Australian government wanted to assimilate white and Aboriginal people.

28. A coalition of environmentalists, scientists and actors—including two-time Oscar winner Emma Thompson—is determined to scupper plans by the British government to build a new runway for Heathrow Airport. The motley crew has bought a small plot of land in the heart of the development area where an extra runway would be situated. The group vows to subdivide the property into thousands of smaller parcels and sell them off to environmental activists around the world, in an effort to bog down the government if it tries to buy up or seize the land. They argue that the economic benefits for a third runway are overstated and that the environmental and human costs are too great.

Q. **Why did Emma Thompson take part in buying the small plot of land?**
(a) To construct the road to her house
(b) To protect her own property
(c) To resist the government in building a new runway
(d) To get some economic benefits by selling the plot

29. The hot spring at Salish Lodge is trying to seduce you with their Early Bird Special. The early bird gets a spa treatment for $40 between the hours of 8 and 9 a.m. every Monday through Friday. Seem a little early for a drive up to Snoqualmie? Why not make a getaway out of your home and spend the night before at the Lodge? Sounds wonderful! Call 1-800-272-5474 for details. This ad is valid until the next Friday.

Q. **What is this passage advertising?**
(a) A lodge attached to a resort
(b) The spa's reduced admission fees for the morning
(c) A hotel with a good birdcage
(d) An amusement park with spa

30. The U.S. wars in Iraq and Afghanistan are costing nearly double the amount previously thought, according to a report by Democrats in the U.S. Congress. They say "hidden costs" have pushed the total to about $1.5 trillion—nearly twice the requested $804 billion. Higher oil prices, treating wounded veterans, and the cost to the economy of pulling reservists away from their jobs have been taken into account. The White House has called the report politically motivated.

Q. **How much is the hidden cost?**
(a) $1.5 trillion
(b) $996 billion
(c) $804 billion
(d) $696 billion

31. Inflation in China hit an 11-year high in January after rising price pressures were exaggerated by fierce snow storms. Soaring food prices were largely blamed for pushing consumer inflation up to 7.1% last month, from 6.5% in December. Inflation in China continues to rise despite higher interest rates and other measures by Beijing to keep the economy from overheating. The worst winter for decades hit food supplies, sending food costs up 18%. Massive snowfalls wrecked crops and killed millions of livestock. But analysts cautioned that the severe weather was not the only factor behind rising food costs, and warned that prices could still increase further.

Q. **What is the main reason for consumer inflation?**
(a) Massive snowfalls
(b) Sudden rise in food prices
(c) Death of livestock
(d) Higher interest rates

32. Santa Catalina Island's veterinary clinic has sailed across the ocean by barge and been trucked to its new home in Avalon, where it will serve about 2,400 clients a year. An open house is scheduled for Valentine's Day, when visitors will be able to explore the facility, which is handicapped-accessible and features a surgery suite and a 32-by-14-foot waiting room. Denny, the island's only veterinarian, will continue working in his 310-square-foot office.

Q. **What is Denny's job in Avalon?**
(a) Protecting the environment of the island
(b) Hunting wildlife
(c) Providing medical treatments to people in Avalon
(d) Tending to the health of pets and animals

33. In November of 1963 the Beatles performed in front of the Queen of England. That was an incredible honor for the band. By the end of 1963 the Beatles were the biggest music group in England. The Beatles came to New York City for the first time in 1964, and they were an instant success. A couple of weeks later after their New York appearance, the five best selling records were by the Beatles. They became world-famous by the end of 1964. Also in 1964, the song "I Want to Hold Your Hand" marked the beginning of Beatlemania.

Q. **Which of the following is incorrect according to the passage?**
(a) The Beatles performed in front of the Queen of England in November of 1963.
(b) Performing in front of the Queen of England was an incredible honor for the band.
(c) It was by the end of 1963 that the Beatles were the biggest music group in England.
(d) The Beatles became world-famous by the end of 1960.

34. The debate in Washington has turned to federal funding of stem cell research, with President Bush moving to veto legislation passed by Congress. On one side, those who support the President's veto tend to argue against embryonic stem cell research, pointing to the individual rights of the embryo being discarded for use in research. On the other hand are those who argue the embryo will be discarded anyway, and the research may provide valuable cures for people suffering from terrible illnesses. But neither side in this battle seems to consider the morality surrounding the rights of federal taxpayers.

Q. **Which of the following is correct according to the passage?**
(a) President Bush was against the veto on stem cell research.
(b) Supporters of President Bush's veto are for stem cell research.
(c) Congress opposed stem cell research.
(d) Neither side in this debate regards the rights of federal taxpayers.

35. Lunar scientists have learned a lot about the moon since then. They've found that one of the biggest challenges to lunar settlement is how to live with mantlerock that covers virtually the entire lunar surface from a depth of 7 feet to perhaps 100 feet or more. It includes everything from huge boulders to particles only a few nanometers in diameter, but most of it is a puree created by uncountable high-speed micrometeorites that have been crashing into the moon unimpeded by atmosphere for more than 3 billion years.

Q. **Which of the following is correct according to the passage?**
(a) Lunar settlement has been relatively easy.
(b) Actually, dust covers the entire lunar surface.
(c) Scientists have found the solution to live on the lunar surface.
(d) Dust on the lunar surface has been made by several crashes.

36. The 1750-1850 period was a watershed in the history of workplace and white-collar crime. Appropriations previously legitimated by notions of "customary right" were now increasingly regarded as "pilfering." During the same period, opportunities for employee theft were magnified by changes in the commercial world that opened up the work arena to new vulnerabilities. This epoch witnessed the widespread and unprecedented emergence of financial offences—such as fraud and embezzlement —frequently perpetrated by respectable middle-class offenders.

Q. **Which of the following is correct according to the passage?**
(a) The 1750-1850 period was a watershed in the history of manual worker crime.
(b) Appropriation was regarded as criminal in the past.
(c) Opportunities for employee theft increased in the 1750-1850 period.
(d) These days financial offences have been gradually decreasing.

37. The Suez Canal runs for approximately two hundred kilometers from the port of Suez, on the Gulf of Suez, to Port Said, on the Mediterranean Sea. Some sections of the canal are very narrow, so two ships cannot pass there at the same time. One ship must wait in a special place or in one of the lakes until the canal is passable again. A French engineer, Ferdinand de Lesseps, was the director of the construction of the Suez Canal. Work began in 1859 and continued until 1869. In honor of the completion of the Suez Canal, a famous Italian composer named Giuseppe Verdi wrote a special opera. This opera, *Aida*, is one of the most famous operas ever written.

Q. **Which of the following is correct according to the passage?**
(a) Some sections of the Suez Canal are very deep.
(b) The Suez Canal's length is almost a hundred miles.
(c) The construction of the Suez Canal was directed by a French engineer.
(d) Giuseppe Verdi drew plans for the construction of the Suez Canal.

38-40. Read the passage. Then identify the option that does NOT belong.

38. Hyundai Motor America said that people who purchase a new Hyundai during the next 12 months could return the car if they "experience an involuntary loss of income" within one year of the purchase date. (a) Hyundai said it would absorb as much as $7,500 in negative equity for buyers who opt to walk away from their loans. (b) Many automakers and dealers are already offering a raft of incentives like no-interest financing. (c) Depreciation can reduce a new car's value by about 25% more during the first year of ownership. (d) But since Hyundai's lineup skews toward low-and moderately-priced cars, the $7,500 should be enough to cover the lost value on most Hyundai vehicles.

39. Clean out your medicine cabinet at least once a year, recommends the American College of Emergency Physicians. (a) And while you're at it, consider moving medications out of the bathroom altogether and on to a high shelf in the closet. (b) A year's worth of showers and baths create heat and humidity that can cause some drugs to lose potency. (c) It's good to get rid of them because if a pill loses potency, you may not be getting the necessary dosage of medication. (d) Some locations, such as Arlington Heights, only accept drugs on the first Thursday of each month from 11 a.m. to 1 p.m.

40. Samsung stepped up to the CES plate with a new line of LCD televisions that use LED for back-lighting. (a) The LED back-lighting allows for LCD TVs that are brighter, more environmentally friendly and ultra-slim. (b) Samsung will feature sets only about an inch thick, including the tuner. There will be three models coming out in the spring. (c) Samsung plans to deliver in conjunction with Yahoo for news, stocks, entertainment and other content. (d) No prices were disclosed, but Samsung said they would probably cost at least "several hundred" dollars more than the company's current LED back-lit sets.

정답 및 해설

Chapter 1

Type A _ 유형별 Approach
Part I 빈칸 넣기: 지문의 앞부분에 밑줄이 있는 형태

STEP 1 Pattern Study

Sample

해석_ 피지는 9명의 목숨을 앗아가고 수천 명이 침수된 집을 떠나게 했으며 외국 관광객들을 옴짝달싹 못하게 만들었던 최악의 홍수 이후 최소한 사흘 이상 폭풍우를 맞고 있다. 이 남태평양 국가의 서쪽 가장자리에 있는 수많은 리조트에 묵었던 여행객들은 실내에 머물도록 경고 받았으며 최소한 한 개의 주요 항공사의 추가 항공편이 사람들을 피신시킬 예정이다. 비상사태가 비티레부 섬의 서쪽에서 계속되었는데 그곳은 관광 산업의 본거지이다. 호주 국적기인 Qantas는 나디에서 시드니로 관광객들을 실어 나를 특별기 편을 준비했다.

해설_ 9명의 목숨을 앗아갈 정도의 홍수가 닥쳤다면 (a)와 같이 서둘러 침수된 집을 떠나 피신해야만 할 것이다.

오답 피하기_ (c), (d) 홍수의 와중에 강을 건너거나 그곳으로 뛰어들지는 않을 것이다.

어휘_ strand 오도 가도 못하게 하다
swamp 물에 잠기게 하다
airlift 항공기로 대피시키다
swollen 물이 불어난

정답_ (a)

STEP 2 Clinic

1.

해석_ 애플의 역동적인 경영자 스티브 잡스는 병가를 얻을 것이라고 말했는데 그 결정은 많은 투자자들에게는 회사의 경영 승계 계획에 대해 의문을 갖게 하는 동시에 회사의 창의적인 사고에 대한 잠재적인 타격으로 여겨졌다. 주가가 단기적으로 하락할 것이라는 분석가들의 예견 때문에 애플의 주가는 폐장 후 거래에서 7%나 폭락했는데 스티브 잡스의 건강 문제가 불거질 때마다 언제나 그래왔던 것이다. 그는 2004년 췌장암 발병이 있었으며 좀 더 최근에는 체중 감소의 원인이 된 호르몬 불균형을 겪었다고 말했다.

해설_ 지문을 보면 스티브 잡스의 건강 문제가 불거질 때마다 애플의 주가가 떨어졌다는 내용이 있으므로 이번에도 주가가 떨어진 것(7% 하락)을 보면 그의 건강 문제가 또다시 발생했다는 내용이 빈칸에 와야 한다. 따라서 병가를 얻는다는 의미의 (d)가 가장 적절하다.

어휘_ blow 타격
tumble (가격이) 폭락하다
after-hours trading 시간 외 거래 (폐장 이후의 거래)
suffer 손해를 입다, 나빠지다

much as ~와 같은 정도로
bout 발병, 발작
pancreatic cancer 췌장암

정답_ (d)

2.

해석_ 올해 말이면 밴드를 시작한 지 28주년이 되는 메탈리카는 그 동안 헤비메탈 그룹의 모습을 벗어나 수많은 논란과 비극들 그리고 거의 해체될 뻔한 경험 등 심한 굴곡을 경험해왔다. 80년대를 통틀어 메탈리카의 난폭하고 시끄러운 스피드 메탈 음악은 언더그라운드를 통해 분출되었으며 (그들은) 주류 음악계의 스타가 되었다. 90년대에 다양한 종류의 덜 광포한 음악을 실험해보기 시작하면서 그들은 자신들의 마력을 잠시 잃었었다. 하지만 그 밴드는 자신들의 엄격한 80년대 음악의 정신을 가진 'Death Magnetic' 앨범으로 돌아왔다. 그 기준에 꼭 맞지는 않지만 그 4인조 밴드는 여전히 거칠게 연주하고 있다.

해설_ 빈칸 뒤에 오는 '수많은 논란과 비극들 그리고 거의 해체될 뻔한 경험' 등이 힌트가 된다.

어휘_ transcend 초월하다, 능가하다
brutal 난폭한, 사나운
brazen 시끄러운
frenzied 열광적인, 광포한
mojo 마력, 힘
hard-and-fast (규칙 등이) 엄격한
quartet 4인조
ferociously 사납게, 맹렬하게

정답_ (a)

STEP 3 Actual Test

1.

해석_ 오바마의 대통령 재임 기간은 조지 W. 부시의 재임기와는 철저히 다른 모습을 보여줄 것이다. 새로운 대통령은 그들의 차이점을 부각시키는 데 주저하지 않았다. 오바마는 이라크전에서의 변화와 "국가 안보와 이상 사이에서의 잘못된 선택"에 대해 이야기했다. 그 말들은 시민의 자유와 가혹한 심문 기법에 관한 전 행정부의 입장을 겨냥한 것이었다. 해외에서 부시의 나쁜 평판을 감안하면 가장 놀라운 말은 "우리는 다시 세계를 이끌어갈 준비가 되어 있다"고 세계에 천명한 오바마의 선언이었다.

해설_ 윗글은 오바마 대통령이 부시 전 대통령과는 정책상 분명히 차별화할 것이라는 내용에 관한 것이다.

오답 피하기_ (b) 두려움을 떨치고 희망을 얘기하는 것은 모든 신임 대통령들이 하는 일이다. (d) 최근 미국 경제가 문제이긴 하지만 지문에 경제 이야기는 없다.

어휘_ presidency 대통령의 지위[임기]

harsh 가혹한

interrogation 심문

정답_ (a)

2.

해석_ 자동차와 관련된 사고로 사망한 대부분의 사람들은 누구나 예상할 수 있는 방식, 즉 공공도로에서 주행하던 중 다른 차나 견고한 물체에 충돌함으로써 죽는다. 그와 같은 단순한 시나리오에 따라 2007년에 미국에서 41,000명 이상이 죽고 250만 명 이상이 부상을 입었다. 그러나 사망과 장애 사고에 흔히 그렇듯이, 그리고 절망스럽게도 이게 전부가 아니다. 새로운 연구 결과에 따르면 자동차와 관련되었지만 공공도로에서 일어난 교통사고로 분류되지 않는 사고로 2007년 미국에서는 1,700명 이상이 목숨을 잃었고 추가로 841,000명이 부상을 입었다.

해설_ 빈칸 뒤의 내용인 '도로에서 주행 중 다른 차나 견고한 물체와의 충돌'은 일상적인 교통사고의 사례이다. 따라서 (b) '누구나 예상할 수 있는 방식'이 적합하다.

오답 피하기_ (a) 빈칸 뒤에 나오는 일반적인 사례를 특이한 다른 상황으로 보기는 힘들다. (c) 비접촉 사고에 관한 내용은 없다. (d) 빈칸 뒤의 내용은 냉각기의 과열 같은 차체의 결함과 관계가 없다.

어휘_ unyielding 단단한, 견고한

maim 불구로 만들다

mishap 사고, 재난

claim a life 목숨을 빼앗다

정답_ (b)

3.

해석_ 스플래시토피아는 사막에 있는 어느 휴양지보다 가장 최신의, 믿을 수 없을 만큼 놀라운 물놀이 시설입니다. 규모만도 거의 2에이커에 이르고 재미있고 짜릿한 물놀이를 즐길 수 있습니다. 425피트 길이의 유유히 흐르는 강물에 몸을 맡겨 보세요. 두 개의 100피트 길이의 물 미끄럼틀도 타고 내려가 보시고 완만하게 경사진 강변을 따라 강에 바로 들어가시기 전에 광활한 모래사장에서 모래성도 쌓으면서 즐거운 시간을 보내시기 바랍니다. 스플래시토피아는 분수와 스프링클러, 당사 소유의 산에서 떨어지는 세찬 폭포와 더불어 산기슭에 자리잡은 거품 목욕탕과 거대한 수영장 등 독특한 물놀이 구역

을 갖추고 있습니다.

해설_ 지문 전체의 문맥으로 보아 빈칸에는 '믿을 수 없을 만큼 놀라운 물놀이 시설' 따위의 내용이 들어가야 한다.

어휘_ encompassing 아우르는

lazy (유속이) 느린

zero entry 해변처럼 수심이 완만히 깊어지는 것

raging 맹렬한, 거센

mountainside 산기슭

정답_ (a)

4.

해석_ 텍사스에서 일부다처제를 추종하는 단체의 일원 3명이 추가적으로 기소되었다. 사건은 4월에 엘도라도 인근에 위치한 그 단체의 공동 주거지를 급습하면서 비롯되었다. 슐라이커 카운티 대배심은 두 명을 중혼 혐의로, 다른 한 명은 미성년자와의 불법 혼인 혐의로 기소했다. 피고인들의 이름은 아직 알려지지 않았다. 대배심은 또한 제프스를 가중 성폭행 혐의로 추가 기소했다. 그는 이미 텍사스에서 중혼죄와 어린이에 대한 가중 성폭행 혐의로 기소된 상태이다.

해설_ 그들이 기소된 죄목이 중혼죄라는 것이 지문 중간에 나오고 지문 마지막에 중혼죄에 대해 또다시 언급되어 있다.

어휘_ indict 기소하다, 고발하다

compound 구내, 주택군

raid 급습, 불시 단속

grand jury 대배심

bigamy 중혼(죄), 이중 결혼

defendant 피고

aggravated sexual assault 가중 성폭행

정답_ (b)

Type B _ 테마별 Approach
Whale 고래

STEP 3 Clinic

1.

해석_ 향유고래는 거의 전적으로 오징어를 먹고 산다. 이 재빠른 먹이를 잡기 위해 고래는 깊이 잠수해 들어가 오랫동안 머무는데 이것은 그 종의 독특한 특징이다. 향유고래의 사냥 전략은 적극적인 추격보다는 물속에 조용히 떠 있다가 오징어 떼가 지나갈 때 갑자기 습격하는 것이다. 빛이 거의 스며들지 않거나 아예 없는 심해에서 사냥을

하지만 고래가 잡아먹는 오징어의 대부분은 발광성이다. 그 재빠른 무척추동물을 잡기 위한 노력으로 정적이고 조용한 고래가 수영을 하는 동물보다 유리한 것도 어쩌면 당연하다.

해설_ 잠복해서 먹이를 잡는 향유고래의 습성에 의거해 정답은 심해에서 먹이를 잡는다는 (c)가 되어야 한다.

어휘_ sperm whale 향유고래

squid 오징어

swift 재빠른, 신속한

trait 특징

hover 맴돌다, 어슬렁거리다

pounce 갑자기 달려들기, 급습

shoal 떼, 무리

luminescent 발광성의

invertebrate 무척추동물

정답_ (c)

2.

해석_ 그 관련성에 대한 증거는 일각돌고래의 뾰족한 이가 유니콘의 신화에 나오는 뿔과 현저하게 닮았다는 사실과, 그리하여 북유럽의 어부들이 마력이 있다고 평판이 나 있던 일각돌고래의 뾰족한 이를 15세기에 약제사들에게 판매했다는 사실이다.

해설_ 빈칸 앞과 뒤의 내용이 순접 관계이기 때문에 (c) thus가 가장 적합하다.

어휘_ narwhale 일각돌고래

tusk 입 밖으로 튀어나온 길고 뾰족한 이

property 특성, 속성

apothecary 약제사

정답_ (c)

STEP 4 Actual Test

1.

해석_ 가장 진귀한 음악 앨범 중 하나는 고래에 의해 만들어진 것이다. 이 앨범은 재능 있는 55톤 무게의 고래가 바닷속에서 부른 노래들을 담고 있다. 이 노래를 들었던 사람들에 따르면 노래는 아름다운 동시에 슬프다고 한다. 고래의 수는 지난 10년간에 걸쳐 빠르게 감소했으며 우리는 그들을 보호하기 위한 조치를 취할 필요가 있다. 녹음은 버뮤다 해안에서 떨어진 바닷속에서 이루어졌다.

해설_ 윗글은 고래의 노래에 관한 내용이므로 고래 수의 감소와는 관련이 없다. 따라서 정답은 (c)가 된다.

정답_ (c)

2.

해석_ 스리랑카 해안에서 떨어진 수면에 잠수함처럼 어렴풋이 떠오르는 어린 흰긴수염고래는 길이가 약 45피트 정도이다. 최대 길이가 거의 100피트나 되는 흰긴수염고래는 일찍이 지구상에 살았던 가장 큰 동물로서 공룡을 쉽게 능가한다. 그 고래는 크기와 속도 때문에 증기선과 폭약을 장착한 작살을 발사하는 총이 1800년대 말에 도입될 때까지는 많이 잡히지 않았다. 그후 고래 학살은 1931년에 절정에 달했으며 그 해에 30,000마리가 학살되었다.

해설_ 지문을 보면 길이가 거의 100피트나 되는 흰긴수염고래가 공룡의 크기를 쉽게 능가한다는 내용이 있다.

오답 피하기_ 흰긴수염고래가 공룡보다 더 크기 때문에 (b) 공룡이 제일 컸다는 것은 사실과 다르다. (c) 수영 속도에 관한 내용과 (d) 몸 무게에 관한 내용은 지문에 나오지 않는다.

어휘_ loom 어렴풋이 나타나다

blue whale 흰긴수염고래

outstrip 능가하다

steam-powered ship 증기선

harpoon 작살

subsequent 그후의

slaughter 도살, 학살

정답_ (a)

Chapter 2

Type A _ 유형별 Approach
Part I 빈칸 넣기: 지문의 중간이나 끝에 밑줄이 있는 형태

STEP 1 Pattern Study

Sample

해석_ 티베트 승려들이 외국 언론인들의 라사 방문 중 돌발 시위를 벌였다. 그들은 2주 전 시위가 시작된 이래 처음으로 티베트 재방문이 허락된 최초의 언론인들이었다. 약 30여 명의 승려들은 취재진이 조캉 사원을 방문하고 있던 중 친티베트 구호를 외치며 달라이 라마를 옹호했다. 중국은 달라이 라마가 이번 시위를 주모했다고 비난했으나 미국은 중국에게 망명 중인 티베트의 정신적 지도자와의 대화를 촉구했다. 외국 취재진은 불안이 최고조에 달했을 때 티베트에서 추방되었으나 중국은 20여 명의 기자들이 경호 하에 3일간 라사를 방문하는 것을 허가했다.

해설_ but 앞에 중국이 시위대에 대해 비난하는 내용이 나왔기 때문에 but 뒤의 빈칸에는 반대되는 사실, 즉 미국이 중국에게 유화 정책을 촉구했다는 내용이 나와야 한다.

어휘_ disrupt (일시적으로) 혼란시키다

  erupt (폭동 등이) 발발하다

  mastermind 주모자로서 지휘하다

  expel 내쫓다, 추방하다

  unrest 불안

정답_ (a)

STEP 2 Clinic

1.

해석_ 많은 제품들이 가늘어지고 빠지는 머리카락을 복원할 수 있다고 약속한다. 한 가지 흥미로운 선택은 모낭을 재생한다고 하는 레이저 기구인 헤어맥스 레이저 빗이다. TV 뉴스 프로그램에서 '대머리 치료' 로 각광을 받았던 그 기구는 2007년에 FDA의 승인을 받았다. 의약품과는 달리 대부분의 의료 기구는 엄격한 테스트 없이 승인될 수 있다. 회사는 단지 FDA에게 그 새로운 기구가 이미 시장에 출시된 다른 상품들과 "실질적으로 동등하다" 는 것만 설득하면 되는 것이다.

해설_ 빈칸 뒤의 내용을 통해서 의료 기구에 대한 규제가 약하다는 유추가 가능하다. 따라서 (c) without rigorous testing이 정답이다.

어휘_ intriguing 흥미를 자아내는

  hair follicle 모낭(毛囊)

  hail 환호하여 맞이하다

  clearance 인가, 허가

  equivalent 동등한

정답_ (c)

2.

해석_ 힐러리 클린턴은 미국의 대외 정책에서 외교의 임무를 부활시킬 생각이라고 말하며, 중동에서 "스마트 파워" 라는 전략의 필요성을 강조했다. 대통령 당선자에 의해 마 국무부 장관으로 선택된 그녀는 인사청문회에서 논쟁의 여지가 없는 일련의 질문들에 대해 자연스럽게 대처했다. 그녀는 외교 정책에 대한 그녀의 기본적인 비전에 대한 어떠한 도전도 받지 않았다. 의회에서 인준을 받으면 상원 의원직을 사퇴할 예정인 클린턴은 세계에서 미국의 리더십을 부활시키고 외교력을 강화하기 위한 오바마의 계획에 대해 자신 있게 이야기했다.

해설_ 빈칸 뒤의 내용이 앞으로 그녀의 직위 변화와 관련이 있다는 암시가 된다. 따라서 인준 확정 후에 상원의원직의 사퇴가 타당하다.

어휘_ revitalize 부활시키다

  confirmation hearing 인사청문회

  president-elect (취임 전의) 대통령 당선자

  sail through 무사히 치르다, 통과하다

  an array of 일련의, 연이은

  noncontentious 논쟁[논의]의 여지가 없는

  encounter 마주치다, (위험 · 곤란 등에) 부닥치다

  Senate 상원

정답_ (b)

STEP 3 Actual Test

1.

해석_ 전문 유통업체인 코스트 플러스 사는 힘겨운 유통 시장 환경에 대응하기 위해 26개의 매장을 닫고 8곳의 중개 시장에서 탈퇴할 것이라고 말했다. 회사는 또한 일부 직원 감축과 같은 비용 절감 조치들을 취할 것이다. 코스트 플러스는 문을 닫을 매장의 위치를 지정하지는 않았다. 회사는 현재 33개 주에서 296개의 매장을 운영하고 있다. 이 체인점은 주로 가구와 침구류, 양초 같은 가정용 실내 장식품을 취급하고 있다.

해설_ 빈칸 뒤를 보면 일부 직원 감축에 관한 내용이 있으므로 빈칸에는 '비용 절감 조치' 가 오는 것이 적합하다.

오답 피하기_ 직원 감축은 주로 비용 절감 차원에서 이루어지는 것이기 때문에 (a), (c)의 판매 촉진이나 마케팅 전략 등은 모두 상관없는 항목이다.

어휘_ retailer 유통업체, 소매점

media market 중개 시장

in response to ~에 대응하여

implement 실행[실시]하다

lay off 해고하다

정답 (b)

2.

해석 북한이 원조와 외교적 혜택에 대한 보답으로 핵 프로그램을 끝내겠다고 약속했던 6자 회담은 북한이 지난 6월에 한 핵 신고에 대한 검증 계획을 북한이 받아들이지 않음으로써 교착 상태에 빠졌다. 북한은 미국이 북한과의 관계를 정상화하고 이 공산국가에 대한 이른바 "적대적"인 정책을 포기할 때까지 자신의 작은 핵무기고를 유지할 것이라고 밝혔다.

해설 빈칸 앞뒤의 흐름으로 보아 until 뒤의 조건에 부합할 때까지는 북한이 핵무기고를 유지할 것이라는 내용이 와야 적합하다.

오답 피하기 문맥상 미국이 북한에 적대적인 정책을 철회하기 전까지는 북한이 그들의 핵무기고를 (b), (c) 폐기한다거나 (d) 전 세계에 공개한다는 것은 불가능한 이야기이다.

어휘 six-party talks 6자 회담

in return for ~에 대한 보답으로

stall 오도가도 못하게 하다

arsenal 무기고

hostile 적대적인

정답 (a)

3.

해석 보험은 보험 설계사나 여행사, 그리고 관광업체를 통해 구매할 수 있다. 인터넷은 보험을 탐색하고 구매하는 것을 쉽게 해줬다. Insuremytrip.com, Squaremouth.com 그리고 Totaltravel insurance.com과 같은 사이트들은 가격을 포함하여 비교하는 기능을 제공한다. 해외여행을 가기 전에 여행자들은 어떤 것이 (보험) 보장이 되는지 그들의 의료 약관을 체크해야 한다. 미국 의료보험 사업자들은 해외에서 발생한 비용을 보상하지 않을 수 있다. 노인 의료보험은 추가 구매를 하지 않는 한 일반적으로 보험 적용이 불가능하다.

해설 윗글은 주로 보험의 보장 범위에 관한 이야기를 하고 있다.

어휘 embark on ~에 나서다, 착수하다

coverage 보상

supplement 추가, 보충

정답 (c)

4.

해석 이브라힘 감바리 유엔 미얀마 특사는 최근 미얀마 방문에서 탄 슈웨 군부 지도자와 만나지 못했다. 그는 구금 중인 아웅산 수치 야당 지도자를 만났으나 고위 장성들과의 회담 요청은 거절되었다. 감바리는 미얀마 당국에 정치 개혁을 압박했으나 가시적인 진전은 거의 없었다. 미얀마는 개헌을 위한 국민 투표를 감시할 독립적인 참관인을 두라는 그의 요청을 거절했다. 미얀마는 또한 아웅산 수치가 선거에 참가할 수 있도록 헌법을 수정하는 것 역시 거절했다.

해설 빈칸 앞에는 UN의 미얀마에 대한 개혁 압박이 소개돼 있고 빈칸 뒤에는 미얀마가 그러한 여러 요청을 모두 거절했다는 내용이 있기에 빈칸에는 (a) 진전이 없었다는 내용이 와야 한다.

어휘 envoy (외교) 사절, 특사(特使)

referendum 국민 투표

정답 (a)

Type B _ 테마별 Approach
Stop-smoking 금연

STEP 3 Clinic

1.

해석 구직자들은 흡연이 그들의 경력에 해를 끼칠 수도 있다는 사실을 깨닫고 있다. 신문의 구인 광고란에서는 비흡연 구직자만을 찾는 광고를 흔히 볼 수 있다. 워싱턴의 레드몬드에 있는 뱅가드 일렉트로닉 툴에서 구직자들이 받게 되는 첫 번째 질문 중 하나는 "담배 피우세요?"이다. 만약 당신이 "그렇습니다"라고 대답한다면 면접은 그것으로 끝난다. 그것은 완벽하게 합법적인 조치이다.

해설 흡연을 하게 되면 면접은 그것으로 끝이라는 의미는 더 이상 면접이 의미가 없다는, 즉 채용하지 않겠다는 의미가 된다. 따라서 지원할 필요가 없다는 것이 추론 가능하다.

어휘 classified advertisement 구인 광고, 3행 광고

정답 (d)

2.

해석 불행히도 모든 이들이 다 그녀 같은 의지력을 갖고 있는 것은 아니다. 어떤 이들은 자신이 사랑하는 사람들을 위해서나 자신의 건강을 위해 끊고 싶어 하기도 하지만 니코틴 중독의 힘은 너무도 크다. 또 다른 이들은 흡연의 즐거움을 주장하며 담배를 끊을 생각이 전혀 없다. 만일 당신이 금연을 할 수 없거나 하길 원하지 않는다 해도 여전히 주위 사람들을 보호하기 위해 당신이 할 수 있는 일은 많다. 그 누구도 당신의 가정이나 자동차 내에서 흡연하게 하지 말라.

아이들이 없을 때도. 사람들에게 내 의지와 상관없이 흡연하지 않을 권리를 존중해줄 것을 설명하라. 비록 당신이 눈으로 볼 수 없거나 냄새를 맡지 못한다 해도 독성은 공기 중에 오래 머문다. 만일 당신이 흡연자라면 실외에서 흡연하거나 환기 장치가 당신 가정의 환기 장치와는 분리된 지역에서 흡연하라.

해설_ 단순히 (a)와 같이 금연 방법을 말하는 것이 아니라 간접흡연을 막는 법에 대하여 논하고 있다.

어휘_ willpower 의지력, 정신력

safeguard 보호하다

toxin 독성, 독소

linger 남아 있다, 좀처럼 사라지지 않다

ventilation 통풍, 환기

정답_ (b)

STEP 4 Actual Test

1.

해석_ 아시아는 오랫동안 골수 흡연자들의 본거지였다. 담배는 그들 수백만 명에게 일상적인 사회적 교제물이다. 어떤 것도 담배 없이는 이루어지지 않는다. 어떤 직무도 보상받지 못하며 어떤 식사도 끝나지 않는다. 아시아가 많은 사람들이 지속적으로 폐암, 심혈관 질병, 폐기종 그리고 다른 흡연 관련 질병의 위험에 노출되어 있는 곳, 담배 산업의 마지막 주요 전선이라는 사실을 누구나 알고 있다. 그럼에도 불구하고 아시아의 금연 운동은 전 지역에 걸쳐 조용하지만 굳건하게 힘을 모아가고 있다. 그것은 아직 크진 않지만 예상치 못했던 곳에서의 신선한 법적 승리에서부터 공공장소의 흡연에 대한 강력한 금지에 이르기까지 극적인 충격을 주기 시작하고 있다. 세계 보건 기구에 의해 후원 받는 담배 규제 기본 협약이 첫 번째로 이 조약을 비준한 40개국에서 2월 27일 구속력 있는 법이 되었다. 이 국가들 중 3분의 1이 아시아에 있으며 너 많은 아시아 국가들이 향후 수개월에 걸쳐 이 조약의 강력한 금연 조항을 채택할 것으로 예상된다.

해설_ 지문 중간의 And yet 뒤의 내용에서 아시아 국가들이 금연 운동을 펼쳐가고 있다는 것을 알 수 있다.

어휘_ inveterate 뿌리 깊은, 만성적인

intercourse 교제, 왕래

cardiovascular 심장 혈관의

emphysema 폐기종

inexorably 움직일 수 없이, 엄연히

quarter 지역

binding 구속력 있는

ratify 비준하다

정답_ (d)

2.

해석_ 담배를 피우는 것은 흡연자의 건강에 해가 된다고 오래전부터 알려져 왔다. 그러나 최근의 테스트는 간접흡연이 비흡연자들에게 위험하다는 사실을 명백하게 밝혀냈다. 간접흡연은 식당 같은 실내에서 특히 메스껍다. 그곳에서 죄 없는 사람들은 남을 배려할 줄 모르는 흡연자들이 뿜어내는 해로운 니코틴 연기 속에 휩싸인 채 식사를 하지 않을 수 없다. 많은 사람들은 금연 구역 설정을 위한 법이 도입되기를 바란다. 국회의원들은 왜 그렇게 시간이 오래 걸리는 것인가?

해설_ 윗글은 흡연의 해악에 대처하는 법안을 촉구하는 내용이다.

어휘_ hazard 위험

secondary smoking 간접흡연

disgusting 메스꺼운

envelop in ~으로 싸다

inconsiderate 남을 배려할 줄 모르는, 무관심한

정답_ (d)

Chapter 3

Type A _ 유형별 Approach
Part I 빈칸 넣기: 연결사 찾기

STEP 1 Pattern Study
Sample

해석_ 강한 두뇌 자극을 받은 파킨슨병 환자들이 약물 치료를 받은 환자들보다 6개월 뒤 행동과 삶의 질에 있어 더 큰 진전을 보여주었음을 새로운 연구는 보여준다. 하지만 강한 두뇌 자극을 받은 환자들은 우울증이나 감염, 졸도 또는 심장 문제와 같은 심각한 부작용을 일으킬 위험이 거의 4배나 더 높았다. 대부분의 부작용은 치료될 수 있는 것이었지만 한 환자는 뇌출혈을 일으켜 사망했다.

해설_ 빈칸의 앞뒤 내용이 상반되기 때문에 빈칸에는 역접의 접속사가 들어가야 한다.

어휘_ stimulation 자극
　　　　medication 약물 치료
　　　　depression 우울증
　　　　infection 감염
　　　　hemorrhage 출혈

정답_ (b)

STEP 2 Clinic

1.

해석_ 아홉 명의 미국인과 한 명의 러시아인이 내일 국제 우주 정거장에서 함께 추수감사절을 기념하게 됩니다. 음식은 방사선 처리되고 냉동 건조되어 진공 포장된 상태겠지만 엔데버 호의 우주비행사 스티브 보웬은 메뉴는 더할 나위 없이 현실적이라고 말합니다. 미국 항공 우주국은 우주 왕복선 승무원들만이 충분히 먹을 수 있는 양의 추수감사절 음식을 보냈지만 우주비행사들은 다른 국제 우주 정거장 동료들을 위한 전통 음식까지 마련하기 위해 우주 정거장의 식료품 저장실을 뒤졌습니다.

해설_ 빈칸 뒤의 내용인 메뉴가 현실적이라는 풍성한 이미지에 비해 앞의 내용, 즉 냉동 건조, 진공 포장 등은 왠지 제한적이다. 그래서 역접의 접속사를 쓴다.

어휘_ irradiate 방사선 처리하다
　　　　down-to-earth 현실적인
　　　　raid 급습하다, 쳐들어가다
　　　　pantry 식료품 저장실
　　　　come up with ~을 마련하다

정답_ (c)

2.

해석_ 어떤 이들에게 크리스마스가 다가오고 있다는 신호는 쇼핑몰의 연휴 장식이 아닌 붉은색과 녹색의 또 다른 무엇이다. 수백만 명의 커피 애호가들에게 비공식적으로 연휴의 시작을 알리는 메뉴가 스타벅스에 다시 돌아왔다. 시애틀에 본거지를 둔 이 커피 체인점은 진저스냅 라떼와 페퍼민트 모카 트위스트 같은 연휴를 테마로 한 음료를 어제부터 제공하기 시작했다. 스타벅스 측은 연휴 쇼핑 기간이 연중 가장 바쁜 시기라고 말한다. 그러나 어제의 무료 제공과는 달리 오늘부터는 이들 화려한 크리스마스 음료를 유료로 구입해야 한다.

해설_ 빈칸 앞뒤 내용의 상반성을 보아도, 그리고 Unlike yesterday's freebies라는 빈칸 바로 앞 표현을 참고해도 빈칸에는 역접의 접속사가 들어가야 한다.

어휘_ freebie 공짜

정답_ (d)

STEP 3 Actual Test

1.

해석_ 아프가니스탄 관리들은 탈레반의 학살을 비난했다. 아프가니스탄 정부는 무장 단체가 정지시킨 버스에 타고 있던 50명의 민간인 중 31명이 사살되었다고 밝혔다. 탈레반은 이 나라의 남부 지방에서 이동 중이던 27명의 아프가니스탄 병사들을 사살했다고 주장하고 있다. 그러나 아프가니스탄 국방부는 버스에 병사는 단 한 명도 타고 있지 않았으며 살해된 사람들은 모두 민간인이라고 밝혔다.

해설_ 앞 문장과 상반되는 내용이 뒤 문장에 나오기에 however를 써야 한다.

어휘_ accuse 비난하다, 고발하다
　　　　massacre 대량 학살
　　　　militant group 무장 단체

정답_ (a)

2.

해석_ 만약 파이프가 터졌을 때 당신이 집에 있고 땜납과 용매제 그리고 프로판 토치가 공구 박스에 있다면 파이프 누수를 수리하는 것은 어렵지 않다. 그것은 동 파이프일 경우이다. 플라스틱의 경우는 더욱 쉽다. 하지만 새벽 3시에 분출하는 소리를 찾아 지하실 계단을 더듬어 내려가서 발목까지 차는 물속에 들어가야 하는 상황이라면 문제는 훨씬 더 고약해질 수 있다. 그때는 아마 파이프 근처의 공기 유출이 고여 있는 물을 단단한 얼음으로 만드는 추운 밤일 것이다.

해설_ 상황이 고약해지는 새벽 3시의 상황을 좀 더 상세하게 부연 설명하기 위해서 '정말로'의 의미를 가지는 indeed를 써야 한다.

어휘_ leak 누출
　　　　solder 땜납

flux 용매제

torch 발염(發炎) 방사 장치

stumble 비틀거리며 걷다

gushing 분출하는, 넘쳐흐르는

standing 고여 있는

정답_ (b)

3.

해석_ 조셉 프리차드는 8살이고 그는 축구하는 것을 매우 좋아한다. 그는 매일 친구들과 축구를 한다. 사실, 그는 뛰어난 축구 선수이다. 그의 꿈은 영국 프리미어 리그에서 골키퍼가 되는 것이다. 하지만 약간의 문제가 있다. 그렇다면 문제가 무엇일까? 조셉은 각 손에 3개씩, 6개의 손가락만 갖고 태어났다. 하지만 걱정할 필요 없다. 그는 매우 건강하고 골키퍼로서 특별한 재능을 가지고 있다. 하지만 그의 손에 꼭 맞는 골키퍼용 장갑을 찾기란 어려웠다. 장갑이 계속 벗겨졌다. 그래서 그의 아버지는 그를 위해 특별한 장갑 한 켤레를 사주기로 결심했다.

해설_ 빈칸의 앞과 뒤를 보았을 때, 빈칸 뒤의 내용이 빈칸 앞의 내용을 부연 설명하므로 보기 중에서는 (a) In fact가 가장 적합하다.

어휘_ come off 벗겨지다

정답_ (a)

4.

해석_ 나는 당신의 문제점을 완전히 이해합니다. 나는 소매점에서 정규직으로 일을 잠깐 해봤었고, 당신은 편안한 신발이 얼마나 중요한지를 8시간 이상 동안 그것을 신고 서 있기 전까지 모릅니다. 대부분의 사무 직종은 일하는 시간 중 대부분을 앉아 있기 때문에 신발이 중요하지 않습니다. 나는 에어로졸스를 좋아하며 신발의 대부분을 거기서 삽니다. 그들은 다양한 굽 높이의 신발을 가지고 있으며, 그것들의 밑창은 신축성 있고 쿠션도 좋으며 매우 멋집니다.

해설_ 문맥상 8시간 동안 신고 서 있어 보기 전까지는 모른다는 내용이기에 until이 와야 한다.

어휘_ sole (신발의) 바닥, 밑창

정답_ (b)

Type B _ 테마별 Approach
Darwin 다원과 진화론 vs. 창조론

STEP 3 Clinic

1.

해석_ 고대 이래로 철학자들은 높은 정신적 능력, 즉 사고와 언어가 인간을 다른 종들과 구분해 주는 큰 분수령이 되는 것으로 주장해 왔다. 1637년 르네 데카르트가 주장했듯이 보다 작은 생물들은 자동 장치에 불과하여 일말의 자기 인식도 없이 몽유병처럼 생을 살아가고 있다는 것이다. 이 프랑스 철학자는 동물이 "말이나 신호를 사용하고 우리처럼 그것들을 조합하는" 능력을 가질 수 있다는 것은 상상할 수도 없다고 생각했다. 찰스 다윈은 1세기 전에 인간은 공동의 조상에 의해 동물 왕국의 다른 종들과 연결되어 있다고 강력하게 주장함으로써 이 학설을 뒤흔드는 반격을 가했다.

해설_ 동물들의 지능에 대한 고대로부터 내려오던 관념을 다소 바꿀 필요가 있다는 취지의 글이기에 정답은 (c)이다.

어휘_ antiquity 고대, 태고

    divide 분수령, 분계

    contend (강력히) 주장하다, 논쟁하다

    automaton 자동 장치, 로봇

    mote 티끌, (한 점의) 먼지

    inconceivable 상상할 수도 없는

    deliver (타격 · 공격 등을) 주다, 가하다

    unsettling 동요시키는

    assert 단언하다, 강력히 주장하다

정답_ (c)

2.

해석_ 다윈의 자연 선택 이론은 부적합한 자가 죽고 적합한 자가 더 오래 살아남는다는 개념에 기초를 두고 있는 것이 아니라 차별적 번식력이라는 개념에 기초를 두고 있다. 차별적 번식력이란 보다 적합한 자가 모든 세대에 있어 부적합한 자들보다 좀 더 많은 자손을 남긴다는 주장이다. 다윈주의는 미래의 세대들에게 다음과 같은 일련의 애타는 질문을 제기했던 것이다. 만일 다른 척추동물들이 피와 뼈로 이루어졌다는 점에서 인간과 유사하다면 그것들은 지능을 포함하여 인간의 다른 특성들도 갖고 있지 않겠는가?

해설_ 자연 선택의 핵심은 적자생존이다. 이 지문 역시 적자생존을 다루고 있는데 여기에서는 특히 차별적 번식력(differential fertility)에 주안점을 두고 있다. 즉 the fit이 the unfit보다 번식력에서 우월하다는 내용이 나와야 한다.

어휘_ natural selection 자연 선택

    unfit 부적당한

    longevity 장수

    fertility 번식력

    offspring 자손

    tantalizing 애타게 하는

    vertebrate 척추동물

정답_ (c)

STEP 4 Actual Test

1.

해석_ 환경은 어떤 종이 살아남을 것인지를 궁극적으로 결정하는 요소이다. 환경에 적응하는 것은 생명의 기본적인 필요조건이다. 이에 실패한 생명체는 비록 그 자신만의 방식으로 남긴 하겠지만 반드시 사라지게 된다. 하지만 이에 부합한 생명체는 번성하게 되고 마침내는 어떤 종의 주류가 된다.

해설_ 빈칸 주위의 문맥을 살펴보면 '~하긴 하겠지만 ~한다' 는 내용이기에 빈칸에는 양보의 접속사가 들어가야 한다.

어휘_ ultimately 궁극적으로

    adaptation 적응

    bound to 반드시 ~하게 되어 있는

    perish 사멸하다, 사라지다

    in sync with ~와 조화를 이루는

정답_ (a)

2.

해석_ 대중은 마음속으로 다윈의 진화론에 대한 도전이라고 하면 인간이 원숭이에서 진화했다고 배우고 있는 교실에서 주기적으로 자신의 아이들을 데리고 나오는, 성서에 기초한 창조주의자들과 관련지어 생각한다. 대부분의 사람들이 잘 모르고 있는 것은 금세기의 상당 기간에 걸쳐, 그리고 특히 근래 들어 과학자들이 다윈과 그의 사상에 대해 그들끼리 논쟁을 벌여왔다는 사실이다.

해설_ 교실에서는 진화론을 가르치는데, 그 내용에 따르면 인간은 원숭이에서 진화했다.

어휘_ theory of evolution 진화론

    biblical 성서의, 성서와 관련된

    periodically 주기적으로, 정기적으로

정답_ (c)

Type A _ 유형별 Approach
Part II 제목이나 대의 찾기

STEP 1 Pattern Study

Sample

해석_ 1년을 끌어온 의문의 사건이 해결되려 하고 있습니다. 관계자들은 캘리포니아 동부의 한 지역에서 발견된 것들이 스티브 포셋의 비행기 잔해인 것으로 확인했습니다. 마데라 카운티의 존 앤더슨 보안관이 유류품들을 확인했는데, 이 확인은 시에라 네바다 산맥에서 한 등산객이 발견한 조종사 면허증과 다른 소지품들을 발견한 후 나왔습니다. 관계자들은 사체는 발견되지 않았다고 밝혔습니다. 백만장자이자 모험가인 포셋은 1년도 더 전에 임대한 비행기로 네바다에서 이륙한 후 단독 비행에 나섰다가 실종되었습니다.

해설_ 윗글은 한 백만장자가 탔다가 실종된 비행기 잔해의 발견에 관한 글이다.

어휘_ wreckage 잔해, 파편

    assure 확인하다, 확신하다

    human remains 유해, 사체

    vanish 사라지다, 실종되다

정답_ (b)

STEP 2 Clinic

1.

해석_ 포드 사는 연비와 성능을 향상시키고 유지비를 줄이는 새로운 변속기를 발표했다. 'PowerShift' 라는 명칭이 붙은 새로운 6단 자동 변속기는 북미에서 포드 사의 첫 번째 2중 클러치, 즉 자동화된 수동 변속기가 될 것이다. 포드 사는 PowerShift 변속기가 기존의 4단 자동 변속기에 비해 연비를 9% 향상시키고 무게는 30파운드 더 적을 것으로 기대하고 있다. 포드 사는 2010년까지 소형차에 그 변속기를 장착하기를 원하고 있다.

해설_ 윗글은 포드 사의 새로운 변속기에 대해 소개하는 내용이다.

어휘_ unveil 발표하다, 공개하다

    transmission (자동차의) 변속기

    dub (이름 · 명칭을) 붙이다, ~라고 부르다

    implementation 구현, 성취

    gearbox 변속 장치

정답_ (c)

2.

해석_ 실험용 비행기의 첫 번째 비행. 당신이 설계한 시스템이 기단에 합류하는 것을 보는 것. 이러한 성공 스토리가 왜 노드롭 그루먼이 항공 우주 산업과 방위 산업, 기술 산업의 리더인지를 보여주는

것입니다. 만약 당신이 위대한 업적의 한 부분이 될 수 있는 직업을 찾으신다면 우리가 제공해야 하는 모든 것들을 살펴보십시오. 지난 수십 년 동안 노드롭 그루먼 통합 시스템은 정부에 항공기와 시스템을 공급해 왔으며 엔지니어와 전문 경영인들에게 많은 기회를 보장해왔습니다.

해설_ If you're searching for a career라는 구절에서도 볼 수 있다 시피 직원 채용을 위한 회사 소개문이다.

어휘_ fleet (항공기의) 기단(機團), 비행대
aerospace 항공 우주(의)

정답_ (a)

STEP 3 Actual Test

1.

해석_ 신장 기증자는 이제 기증이 그들의 건강이나 수명에 미치는 장기적인 영향에 대해 걱정하지 않아도 된다. 신장 기증자에 대한 장기간의 연구는 타인에게 신장을 기증한 사람은 정상적인 수명을 누릴 뿐 아니라 보통 사람보다 신장 질환이 더 적다는 것을 밝혀냈다. "우리는 신장 기증이 안전하다는 것에 대해 줄곧 의심해 왔지만 미국에서 많은 수의 환자를 대상으로 장기간 연구를 한 사례는 지금까지 없었다" 라고 연구를 주도했던 미네소타 의과 대학의 핫산 N. 이브라힘 박사는 말했다.

해설_ 윗글은 신장 기증자도 다른 사람들과 마찬가지로 정상적인 삶을 산다는 내용이다.

오답 피하기_ (b) 일반적으로 신장이 가장 이식이 잦은 장기 중 하나라는 것은 사실이나 본문에는 그러한 내용이 없다. (c) 신장 이식이 인기가 있는지에 관한 내용 역시 본문에는 없다. (d) 기증자가 일반인에 비해 신장 질환이 적다는 이야기가 있긴 하지만 기증자 자신이 훨씬 더 좋다고 느낀다고는 할 수 없다.

어휘_ kidney 신장
donor 기증자
longevity 수명

정답_ (a)

2.

해석_ 로스앤젤레스 타임즈는 300명의 인원을 감축하고 데일리 섹션의 수를 5꼭지에서 4꼭지로 줄인다. 신문의 발행인인 에디 하튼스타인은 직원들에게 공지를 통해 (그 사실을) 알렸다. 편집장 러스 스탠튼은 두 번째 공지에서 이번 감축에는 향후 수 주간 편집부에서 이루어질 70여 명의 감축도 포함돼 있다고 밝혔다. 하튼스타인은 섹션 수 축소 조처는 운영, 제작 및 배급에 있어서 효율성을 얻기 위한 것

이라고 밝혔다. 로스앤젤레스 타임즈는 파산 신청을 한 시카고 소재의 트리뷴사가 소유하고 있다.

해설_ 윗글은 로스앤젤레스 타임즈의 인원 감축에 관한 기사이다.

오답 피하기_ (a) 트리뷴사에서 감축되는 직원의 수나 (c) 해고의 영향에 관한 내용은 지문에 없으며 (d) 파산 신청을 한 트리뷴사에 관한 부분은 지엽적인 내용이다.

어휘_ shrink 축소시키다, 줄이다
reap (성과 · 이익 등을) 올리다, 거두다
file for bankruptcy 파산 신청을 하다

정답_ (b)

3.

해석_ 당신이 만약 직장이나 미래에 대해 걱정하고 있다면, 당신에겐 확고한 수입을 올릴 비(非) 전통적인 방법을 최대한 많이 배워야 할 의무가 생기게 되는 것입니다. 기억하세요. 당신과 같은 평범한 수많은 사람들이 인터넷으로 돈을 벌고 있다는 것을. 수익을 창출하기 위해 알타비스타를 사용함에 있어 그리 고급 지식이 요구되는 것이 아닙니다. 우리 제품은 돈을 벌기 위해 알타비스타를 사용하는 것이 얼마나 쉬운 일인지 보여줄 것입니다. 현재 당신의 직장이 안전하더라도 퇴직에 대비하여 저축을 하거나 공과금을 처리하는 데 필요한 여분의 돈을 모을 수 있다는 것은 멋진 일이 아니겠습니까? 바로 이 점 때문에 수백만 명의 미국인들이 돈을 벌기 위해 알타비스타와 같은 재택근무가 가능한 시스템을 애용하고 있는 것입니다.

해설_ 알타비스타 제품의 구입을 유도하기 위해 그것의 특색을 쭉 서술하고 있다.

어휘_ owe it to yourself to 자신에게 ~할 의무가 있다
expertise 전문 지식

정답_ (b)

4.

해석_ 오늘 천 명 이상의 쇼핑 매니아들이 쓸 만한 거울도 안 좋고 탈의실도 없는 산타모니카의 한 비행장 격납고에 떼지어 모여들었습니다. 싼값에 패션 보물을 얻을 수 있다는 희망을 안고 말이죠. 오늘이 바로 남부 캘리포니아의 패션 감정가들을 이 의아한 장소로 이끄는 바니스 창고 대방출의 첫날입니다. 매년 두 번씩 열리는 이 행사의 참가자들은 비싸고 패션을 선도하는 드레스, 신발, 남성 정장, 기타 인기있는 상품들을 특가로 구입할 수 있다는 기대를 안고 옵니다. 여기 바커 격납고에 모아 놓은 상품들은 한때 전국의 바니스 뉴욕 매장을 수놓았던 상품들입니다. 12일간의 행사는 2월 16일까지 진행됩니다.

해설_ 바니스 창고 대방출 행사의 현장 소식을 전하고 있다.

어휘_ hangar 격납고

snag 획득하다, 재빨리 잡다

twice-yearly 해마다 두 번씩

cognoscenti (미술, 문예 작품 따위에) 통달한 사람, 감정가

fashion-forward 패션을 선도하는

sought-after 수요가 많은

rarefied 드문, 일류의

정답_ (a)

Type B _ 테마별 Approach
Urbanization 도시화

STEP 3 Clinic

1.

해석_ 도시의 공원은 원래 지역 주민들에게 북적대고 혼란스러운 주위 환경으로부터 편리한 피난처를 제공해주기 위해 생긴 것이었다. 최근까지 이러한 공원들은 그런 목적을 훌륭하게 수행해왔다. 도시의 공원은 도시 생활의 일상적인 압박으로부터 해방되는 평온한 장소였다. 그곳은 사람들이 소풍이나 스포츠 경기를 하려고 친구들을 만나는 곳이었으며 강철과 유리, 콘크리트 건물들이 끝없이 이어지는 어둡고 황량한 환경 한가운데에서 약간의 햇빛과 신선한 공기를 얻을 수 있는 곳이었다.

해설_ convenient refuge를 제공하기 위해서였다는 내용처럼 마음에 안식을 주는 것이 주목적이므로 (b)가 정답이고, 나머지 선택지는 지엽적이거나 지문에 나오지 않은 내용이다.

어휘_ populace 대중, 서민, (한 지역의) 전체 주민

refuge 피난처

admirably 훌륭하게

tranquil 조용한, 평온한

unwind (긴장을) 풀다, 편안한 마음을 갖게 하다

dreary 음울한, 황량한

정답_ (b)

2.

해석_ 대도시가 정말 더 살기 좋은가? 아마 아닐 것이다. 개인이 차지할 수 있는 공간이 작으며 이런 인구 과밀 현상은 여러 가지 문제들, 즉 질병, 교통, 범죄 문제 등을 초래한다. 물도 교통수단도 주택도 충분하지 않다. 그리고 일자리도 모자란다. 개발도상국의 많은 도시에서 살고 있는 주민들의 3분의 1에서 2분의 1은 일자리를 찾지 못

하거나 시간제 일자리만 구할 수 있을 뿐이다. 이들 가운데 수백만 명은 굶주리고 있으며 집이 없거나 질병에 시달리고 있고 미래를 두려워한다. 이런 위기 상황은 날이 갈수록 악화되고 있다.

해설_ 전체적으로 도시 생활의 병폐들이 나열되고 있기에 '도시의 위기'라는 의미의 (b)가 타당하다.

어휘_ overcrowding 과밀, 혼잡

homeless 집 없는

정답_ (b)

STEP 4 Actual Test

1.

해석_ 일부 지리학자들은 토지 자원에 대한 압력을 덜고 많은 시골 지방의 경우 일에 비해 사람이 너무 많기 때문에 도시화가 바람직하다고 말한다. 다른 지리학자들은 도시가 주변의 농촌에서 공급되는 식량에 너무 많이 의존하기 때문에 도시화는 나쁜 것이라고 생각한다. 이미 심각한 식량 공급 문제를 겪고 있는 국가들에서 이와 같은 도시 크기의 대규모적인 확대는 부근 농업 지역에 엄청난 부담을 주게 될 것이다. 더욱이 노인들과 아이들 그리고 허약한 사람들에게 농장 운영을 맡기고 (도시로) 이주하는 사람들은 일반적으로 젊고 활동적인 사람들이며 이로 인해 농장의 능률은 향상되기 어려워진다. 그리하여 농업과 식량 공급의 몰락을 가져오게 된다.

해설_ 노동력의 변화 등을 통해 대도시 주변 농촌 지역의 생산성은 더욱 떨어지게 된다.

오답 피하기_ (b) 구성이 노인과 아이들이 농촌에 많아지는 것이지 이들이 worse off, 즉 궁색해지는 것은 아니다. (c) 땅의 비옥도와는 무관한 문제이다. (d) 농부들의 구성이 나이든 이들과 아이들로 바뀌는 것이지 이들 자체가 더욱더 비활동적이 된다고 볼 수는 없다.

어휘_ geographer 지리학자

urbanization 도시화

tremendous 거대한

strain 큰 부담

migrate 이주하다

infirm 허약한

정답_ (a)

2.

해석_ 많은 나라에서 인구 과밀 도시들은 큰 문제에 직면해 있다. 불행히도 주택 부족, 위생 악화, 실업 같은 도시 지역의 악조건은 빈곤, 질병, 범죄의 증가를 가져온다. 장기적으로 유일한 해결책은 농촌 지역의 생활을 더욱 매력적으로 만들어서 사람들이 그곳에 머물도록

유도하는 것이다. 농촌 생활에 대해 보다 긍정적인 태도가 조성되도록 농촌의 편의 시설이 향상되어야만 한다. 농촌 지역의 선행적인 발전 없이는 도시 자체가 발전할 수 없기 때문에 농촌 생활의 개선이 중요하다는 것은 의심의 여지가 없다.

해설_ 도시에 사람이 많이 몰리면서 생기는 문제와 그 해결책을 제시하고 있다.

어휘_ sanitation 공중위생, 위생 설비

　　　　foster 촉진하다, 조성하다

정답_ (d)

Chapter 5

Type A _ 유형별 Approach
Part II 일치 불일치 찾기

STEP 1 Pattern Study

Sample

해석_ 월가는 지난달의 기록적인 주택 가격 급락 소식의 충격을 털어내고 하룻밤 사이 일본 시장이 6%, 홍콩이 14% 상승한 뒤 국제 주식 시장의 오름세를 따라갔다. 오늘 다우존스 공업 평균 지수는 거래 초 30분간 4% 상승했다. 문제는 과연 시장이 바닥을 치고 올라오는 중인지 아니면 월가에서 냉소적으로 말하는 소위 '데드 캣 바운스 현상'인가 하는 점이다. 데드 캣 바운스 현상이란 고양이를 트램펄린 위에 떨어뜨리면 한 번은 튀어 오르는 것에 비유한 것이다.

해설_ 오늘 있었던 소폭의 주식 상승이 상승세의 시작인지 아닌지는 알 수 없다는 내용이 지문의 후반부에 나온다.

어휘_ sardonically 냉소적으로

　　　　reference 언급, 가리킴

정답_ (d)

STEP 2 Clinic

1.

해석_ 한 미국 대학이 영어가 부족한 한국 학생들이 학위를 취득할 수 있도록 한국어와 영어 모두로 진행하는 수업을 실시할 예정이다. 뉴저지의 페어레이 디킨슨 대학은 이 두 가지 언어로 수업이 진행되는 3년짜리 교양 과목의 준학사 학위 과정을 개설하기로 했다. 이 프로그램은 이 대학이 주 내에 점차 증가하는 한국인 인구에게 다가가기 위한 노력의 일환이다. 한국인 대학 졸업생들은 이미 영어 실력이 부족해 어려움을 겪고 있으며 일부 교육 전문가들은 한국어로 수업을 진행하는 미국 교육 기관들의 이와 같은 정책이 대학 졸업생들의 전반적인 영어 능력을 저하시키게 될 것으로 생각하고 있다.

해설_ ~ lower the general English competency ~를 통해 한국어 병행 교육이 영어 능력 저하를 가져올 것이라는 일부 전문가들의 견해를 소개하고 있다.

어휘_ liberal arts 교양과목

　　　　associate degree 준학사 (2년제 대학 졸업생에게 수여되는 학위)

　　　　competency 능력

정답_ (b)

2.

해석_ 샤움버그에 본사를 두고 있는 모토롤라는 2009년 4,000명의 직원을 감축할 것이라고 밝혔는데 그중 3,000명은 회사의 휴대폰 개발 부서 직원들이다. 감축은 즉시 시행될 것으로 예상되며 2008년 4

분기에 이미 3,000명의 인력을 감축하기로 발표한 기존의 조치에 추가되는 것이다. 모토롤라는 또한 2008년도 4분기의 예상 실적을 발표했는데 주당 순손실이 0.07에서 0.08 달러 사이일 것이라고 한다. 회사는 수입을 2월 3일 발표한다.

해설_ 2008년 이래로, 즉 2008년과 2009년에 걸쳐서 7,000명의 인원이 모토롤라에서 해고되었다.

어휘_ on top of ~에 더해
preliminary 예비의
net loss 순손실
earnings 소득

정답_ (b)

STEP 3 Actual Test

1.

해석_ 마이클 잭슨의 변호사는 잭슨이 한 아랍 족장에게 7백만 달러를 빚지고 있다는 사건에 증언하러 가기에는 건강이 좋지 않다고 말했다. 족장은 잭슨을 사기꾼이라고 부르며 그가 음반과 자서전 발간을 위해 7백만 달러의 선금을 가져갔으나 어느 것도 제작하지 않았다고 주장하고 있다. 족장의 변호사들은 잭슨이 자금난에 허덕이고 아동 성추행 재판 이후 재기하기 위해 애쓸 때 그 돈을 지불했다고 말한다. 잭슨 측 변호사는 유효한 계약은 없었으며 돈은 대가성 없이 주어진 것이라고 말했다.

해설_ 유효한 계약은 없었고 돈은 공짜로 준 것이라는 마지막 문장에서 현재까지 어떠한 합의도 없다고 보아야 한다.

오답 피하기_ (a) 마이클 잭슨은 건강이 좋지 않다고 했으며, (b) 그는 아랍 족장에게서 돈을 빌렸다는 것을 인정하고 있지 않다.

어휘_ testify 증언하다
autobiography 자서전
sheikh (이슬람교, 특히 아라비아에서) 가장, 족장
rip-off artist 사기꾼, 도둑
advance 선금
molestation 희롱, 추행

정답_ (d)

2.

해석_ 노벨 평화상 수상자인 무하마드 유누스는 세계의 기아가 2015년이면 반으로 줄어들고 그로부터 15년 후에는 완전히 없어질 것으로 예상했다. 킹 카운티는 10년 내에 노숙자를 없애겠다고 단언했다. 현재 심각한 경기 후퇴를 겪고 있는 경제는 그런 목표를 달성하는 데 위협이 되고 있다. 일부 손 큰 기부자들은 그들의 큰 뜻을 계

속 유지하기로 결심한다. 그럼에도 불구하고 그들은 자신들이 당초 계획했던 증액을 억제하거나 기부액을 줄이고 있다. 빌 & 멜린다 게이츠 재단은 2009년 기부금 증액률을 10%로 깎았는데 지난해의 30% 증액률과 비교된다.

해설_ 지문의 두 번째 문장을 보면 킹 카운티는 10년 안에 노숙자를 없애겠다고 약속했다는 내용이 나온다.

오답 피하기_ (a) 유누스는 세계의 기아가 2015년이면 반으로 줄고 15년 후에는 완전히 없어질 것으로 예상했다.

어휘_ eliminate 제거하다, 없애다
vow 단언하다, 맹세하다
mired in ~의 곤경[궁지]에 빠진
recession 불경기, 경기 후퇴
curb 억제하다
trim (예산 등을) 깎다, 삭감하다

정답_ (b)

3.

해석_ 엘리엇 스피처 뉴욕 주지사가 매춘 사실이 드러난 후 사임했다. 아내가 옆에 있는 가운데, 그는 기자 회견에서 "개인적인 흠" 때문에 공무를 담당할 수 없다고 말했다. 스피처는 그가 다른 사람들에게 요구한 기준에 따라 살지 않은 것에 대해 다시 한번 사과했지만 자세한 내용은 말하지 않았다. 보도에 의하면 스피처 주지사는 워싱턴의 한 호텔에서 매춘부와 만나기로 약속한 것으로 확인되었다. 스피처는 조직 범죄, 금융 범죄 및 매춘 검사로 명성을 얻었으며, 정치적 영예에서의 그의 몰락은 뉴욕 역사상 가장 큰 일 중 하나로 간주되고 있다. 한때 그는 대형 금융 기관의 불법 거래를 정력적으로 추적하여 "월스트리트 보안관"으로 알려지기도 했다.

해설_ 마지막 문장을 통해 그가 금융 비리를 추적해서(pursue) 명성을 얻은 검사 출신이라는 것을 알 수 있기에 정답은 (c)가 된다.

오답 피하기_ (a) 뇌물 이야기는 없다. (b) 자신의 잘못에 대해 자세히 이야기하지 않았다. (d) 그는 매춘 문제로 언론과 저항한 사실이 없다.

어휘_ prostitution 매춘
ring 조직, 도당
be flanked by ~옆에 서다
allegedly 전해진 바에 따르면
high finance 거액 융자, 대형 금융 거래[기관]

정답_ (c)

4.

해석_ 돌려 따는 마개는 저렴한 와인의 표시였다. 하지만 주로 코르

크 마개와 같은 다른 유형의 마개들이 가지고 있던 문제점은 와인 생
산자들이 돌려 따는 마개에 대해 다시 생각하게 하였다. 호주인들이
돌려 따는 마개를 대대적으로 선호한다. 와인 전통의 수호자인 프랑
스인들까지도 돌려 따는 마개를 사용한 와인을 일부 생산하고 있다.
물론 대부분의 비싸고 숙성이 가능한 와인들은 여전히 코르크 마개를
쓰고 있다. 코르크는 미세하게 산소가 순환되어 와인이 몇 년 몇 십
년에 걸쳐 숙성하게 해준다. 수년 이상 보관하지 않을 거면 돌려 따는
마개가 더 낫다. 그리고 돌려 따는 마개는 고맙게도 열기가 편하다.

해설_ (a) 코르크 마개를 씌운 와인이 모두 비싸다는 이야기는 없다.
(b) 예전에는 돌려 따는 마개를 잘 안 썼지만 코르크 마개의 문제점
이 불거져 점점 돌려 따는 마개를 사용하는 회사들이 늘어나고 있다.

어휘_ stopper 마개; 마개를 막다

microscopic 극히 작은, 미세한

notably 그중에서도 특히

blissfully 기쁘게도

정답_ (b)

Type B _ 테마별 Approach
The U.S., a Nation of Immigrants 미국은 이민 국가이자 다민족 국가이다

STEP 3 Clinic

1.

해석_ 오랫동안 미국은 "인종과 문화의 도가니", 즉 달리 말해 전 세
계에서 사람들이 와 미국 문화를 자신들의 것으로 받아들이는 (인종
의) 도가니였으며 또 그래야 한다고 생각되었다. 더욱 최근에 일부
사람들은 미국을 모자이크, 즉 여러 개의 다른 조각들로 구성된 그림
에 비유하기도 한다. 그들은 주장하기를 미국의 힘은 다양성과 각기
다른 문화의 사람들에 의해 이루어진 기여에 있다는 것이다. 아이슬
랜드와 같은 단일 문화 국가는 다문화 국가인 미국이 직면한 소수자
의 문제가 없다.

해설_ and로 연결된 관계라면 뒷부분의 내용으로 판단이 가능한데,
뒷부분이 다양한(different) 배경에서 나오는 사람들의 공적을 말하
고 있기에 다양성이 정답이 된다.

어휘_ melting pot 인종과 문화의 도가니

adopt (자기 것으로) 받아들이다

argue 논하다, 논의하다

contribution 기여, 공헌

homogeneous 동종의, 단일한

immediacy 직접, 즉시(성)

정답_ (b)

2.

해석_ 언어 능력에 대해서라면 미국은 후진국 수준에 머물러 있다.
이민자들은 매우 빠른 속도로 그들의 모국어를 들여오고 있다. 하지
만 절대 다수의 미국인들은 완고하게 단일 언어를 고집하고 있다. 다
른 언어와 문화를 무시하는 것은 미국이 다른 나라들과 관계를 유지
하는 데 있어 장애가 되고 있다. 오늘날 미국의 언어 정책은 주로 이
문제를 1개 언어만 사용하는 미국인들에게 외국어를 가르치려고 노
력함으로써 해결하려고 한다. 한편 미국은 다양성에 대한 잘못된 두
려움이나 소수 민족들의 동화를 빨리 이끌어내려는 조급한 마음에
기존의 2개 국어 프로그램을 줄임으로써 소수 민족들 사이의 이 능
력을 없애려고 애쓰고 있다. 이민자들이 영어를 잘 못하는 데 초점을
맞추는 대신 이민자들이 한편으로 영어를 배우면서 자신들의 모국어
능력을 유지할 수 있도록 왜 장려하지 않는 걸까?

해설_ 다양성에 대한 잘못된 두려움에 의해서, 또는 그들의 동화를
강제적으로 이루어내려는 조급함에 의해서, 소수 민족들의 2개 국어
습득 기회를 없애려고 하고 있다는 내용이 문맥에 맞다. 따라서 정답
은 (a)이다.

어휘_ underdeveloped 저개발의, 후진의

mother tongue 모국어

stubbornly 완고하게

monolingual 1개 국어를 사용하는

handicap 불리한 입장에 세우다

address 다루다, 처리하다

bilingual 2개 국어를 하는

misplaced 잘못된

assimilation 동화, 융합

정답_ (a)

STEP 4 Actual Test

1.

해석_ 의무 교육은 19세기 미국에서 영미 문화와 언어를 전파하고
유지하는 방법의 일환으로 시작되었다. 교육학자들은 두 가지 언어
에 유창한 것은 불가능하다고 믿었으며, 그래서 교육 정책 입안자들
은 학생들은 오직 영어만 배워야 한다고 선언했다. 또한 1906년 영
어를 구사하는 능력은 미국 시민권을 얻기 위한 하나의 조건이 되었
고, 1915년에는 영문학이 필수 과목으로 추가되었다. 이 같은 조치
들을 정당화시킨 것은 언어와 정치적 신념 사이에 관한 기묘한 원칙

이었는데 그것은 외국어를 하는 것은 민주 사회의 기본 개념을 이해하는 데 해롭다는 것이었다.

해설_ peculiar doctrine, 즉 '기묘한 원칙'이라고 단정한 것으로 보아 글쓴이의 태도가 굉장히 비판적이라는 것을 알 수 있다.

어휘_ compulsory 강제적인, 의무적인, 필수의

　　　Anglo-American 영미(英美)의, 영국계 미국인의

　　　transmit 전하다

　　　policymaker 정책 입안자

　　　citizenship 시민권

　　　justification 정당화

　　　peculiar 기묘한, 특이한

　　　doctrine 주의, 원칙

　　　inimical 해로운

　　　grasp 파악하다, 이해하다

정답_ (a)

2.

해석_ 19세기에 있었던 유럽 이민자들의 대규모 유입 이래 푸에르토리코인들의 이민이 이 도시에 대한 가장 큰 유입이 되었다. 이 섬나라 사람들은 초기 이민자들이 무엇을 배웠는지 곧 알게 되었다. 임금은 더 높았지만 물가도 더 비쌌고 집은 초라했으며 범죄는 만연해 있었고 날씨는 춥고 습한데다 지역 사회는 대체로 낯설고 고향과 달랐다. 모든 이민자들이 직면한 문제는 어떻게 함께 가족을 지키고 그들의 정체성을 유지할 것인가 하는 것이었으며, 그 문제는 뉴욕에 정착한 오늘날의 푸에르토리코인들이 직면한 문제이다. 도시에서의 삶은 쉽지 않았지만 돌아갈 곳은 거의 없었다. 많은 다른 비영어권 이민자들과는 달리 푸에르토리코인들은 미국 시민이다. 미국 국적이기 때문에 그들은 원한다면 언제든지 입국할 수도 있고 출국할 수도 있다. 또한 이전 이민자들과는 달리 푸에르토리코인들은 일단 이 도시에 정착하면 모국과의 유대를 끊을 필요도 없었다. 그리하여 그들은 자신들의 문화를 유지할 수 있었으며 심지어는 끊임없이 새롭게 할 수도, 접할 수도 있었던 것이다.

해설_ 푸에르토리코인들은 문화적인 유대를 끊지 않고도 잘 정착했다는 내용이기에 정답은 (d)가 된다.

어휘_ constitute 구성하다, 구성 요소가 되다

　　　influx 유입

　　　dilapidated 황폐한, 초라한

　　　rampant 만연하는

　　　damp 습한

　　　preserve 유지하다, 보존하다

　　　ties 유대, 기반

정답_ (d)

Chapter 6

Type A _ 유형별 Approach
Part II 질문 직접 제시형

STEP 1 Pattern Study

Sample

해석_ 냉철한 조종사는 고장난 제트 여객기를 뉴욕 시 상공으로 몰아 혹한의 허드슨 강에 불시착시켰으며 155명의 승객들은 모두 비행기가 천천히 가라앉았을 때 안전하게 구출되었다. 그것은 주지사의 말에 의하면 "허드슨 강의 기적"이었다. 한 피해자는 두 다리가 부러졌지만 다른 심각한 부상 소식은 없다고 한 구급 요원은 말했다. 노스캐롤라이나 주의 샬로트로 향하던 에어버스 A320은 라구아디아 공항을 이륙한 지 불과 수분 뒤에 한 무리의 새들과 부딪쳐 엔진이 고장난 것으로 보인다.

해설_ 지문 마지막을 보면 비행기가 한 무리의 새들과 부딪쳐 엔진이 고장난 것으로 보인다는 내용이 나온다.

어휘_ maneuver 조종하다, (비행기를) 곡예 비행시키다

　　　crippled 고장난

　　　jetliner 제트 여객기

　　　ditch (비행기를) 불시착시키다

　　　frigid 몹시 추운

　　　paramedic 구급 요원

정답_ (c)

STEP 2 Clinic

1.

해석_ 숨막히는 경치를 보여주는 소노란 사막을 배경으로 하고 있는 아리조나 주의 스코츠데일은 세련된 스타일의 호화로운 오아시스입니다. 호화로운 리조트와 스파, 세계적인 수준의 쇼핑가, 수상 경력을 가진 식당 그리고 활기찬 야경이 있는 스코츠데일은 모든 이들에게 즐거움을 선사합니다. 또한 언제나 재미있고 새로운 볼거리가 있는 곳에서 휴가를 보내길 원하시는 분들에게 스코츠데일은 완벽한 선택입니다.

해설_ 이 글은 스코츠데일이라는 관광지에 대해 광고하는 글이다.

어휘_ backdrop 배경

　　　sophisticated 세련된

　　　lavish 풍부한, 화려한

　　　vibrant 활기 넘치는

정답_ (a)

2.

해석_ 이러한 고난의 겨울에 공동의 위험에도 불구하고 이 불멸의 구절들을 기억하도록 합시다. 희망과 고귀한 마음을 갖고 다시 한 번

살을 에는 듯이 차가운 흐름에 용감히 맞섭시다. 그리고 어떤 폭풍우가 다가오더라도 참고 견딥시다. 우리가 시험에 들게 되었을 때 우리는 이 여정을 끝내기를 거절했다고, 결코 등을 돌리거나 머뭇거리지 않았다고 우리 아이들의 아이들이 말할 수 있게 합시다. 그리고 신의 은총과 함께 지평선을 꿋꿋이 응시하면서 전진해 나갔기에 자유라는 위대한 선물을 미래 세대들에게 안전하게 전해 줄 수 있었다고 말할 수 있게 합시다. 감사합니다. 여러분과 미합중국에 신의 가호가 있기를 빕니다.

해설_ 마지막 문장에서 미합중국과 신의 가호를 말했기에 이는 대통령 취임사의 일부임을 알 수 있다.

어휘_ in the face of ~에도 불구하고

brave 용감히 맞서다

hardship 고난

falter 머뭇거리다

정답_ (d)

STEP 3 Actual Test

1.

해석_ 수백 명의 불교 승려들이 군부 정권에 대한 항거 3일째에 버마에서 가장 신성시되는 사원 주위를 행진했다. 승려들은 항거를 시작한 이후 처음으로 랑군에 위치한 쉐다곤 파고다에 들어갈 수 있도록 허용되었다. 승려들은 그들을 보호하기 위해 손에 손을 잡고 둘러싼 시민들의 인간 사슬에 둘러싸여 도시를 가로질러 걸었다. 그들은 최근 물가 인상에 대한 항의로 촉발된 시위를 폭력적으로 진압한 데 대한 정부 측 사과를 원한다.

해설_ 지문의 마지막 문장에 힌트가 있다.

어휘_ revere 존경하다, 숭배하다

consecutive 연속적인

break-up 진압, 분쇄

rally 집회, 시위

trigger 일으키다, 유발하다

정답_ (c)

2.

해석_ 지금 주식을 사려고 하십니까? 만약 당신이 50만 달러 규모의 투자 계획을 운영하고 있다면 당신은 포브스의 칼럼니스트 켄 피셔의 최신 보고서를 다운로드 받아야 합니다. 거기에서 그는 주식 시장이 흘러가는 방향과 그 이유에 대해 당신에게 이야기해 드립니다. 반드시 읽어 봐야 하는 이 보고서에는 주식 시장에 대한 그의 최신 예측과 지금 당장 투자 계획을 짤 때 이용할 수 있는 연구와 분석을 담

고 있습니다. 놓치지 마세요!

해설_ 이 글은 주식 시장의 전망, 포트폴리오 구성 등에 대한 분석 자료를 광고하는 글이다.

어휘_ portfolio 투자 자산 구성 (각종 금융 자산의 집합)

정답_ (b)

3.

해석_ 우리는 사무실 공간에 3개의 큰 변화를 주려고 한다. 당신이 일하는 칸막이 공간은 고급 오크로 만든 책상으로 대체될 것이다. 그 변화는 사무실 내에서 의사소통을 향상시키고 그 장소를 공개되고 편안한 분위기로 만들어 줄 것이다. 그리고 카펫이 깔려 있던 바닥은 단단한 나무 마루로 대체될 예정이다. 이것은 먼지를 줄여 줄 것이다. 더 중요한 것은 그것이 알레르기로 고생하는 직원들의 근무 환경을 향상시켜 줄 것이라는 점이다.

해설_ 전체적으로는 세 가지 변화 중에서 두 가지가 우선 제시되어 있다. 따라서 책상과 바닥의 교체 효과를 나눠서 평가해야 한다. 특히 (b) 어떠한 먼지도 발생하지 않는다는 것은 타당하지 않다.

어휘_ cubicle 칸막이 공간

정답_ (a)

4.

해석_ 한 간호사가 저속 충돌 사고로 아기의 두개골이 골절된 원인을 찾으려 노력하던 중에 코스코 투어리바 제품에서 플라스틱이 V자로 파인 홈을 발견했다. 그녀는 그 회사에게 이 단단하고 숨겨진 홈의 가장자리에 작은 머리가 부딪칠 수 있는 잠재적 위험에 대해 경고했다. 그러나 그 회사는 그 간호사가 회사에게 경고한 5년 후인 2005년에 결국 모든 종류의 시트에서 홈을 제거할 때까지 이미 수십만 개의 투어리바 시트를 팔았다. 그것을 구매했던 소비자 중에는 현재 충돌 때 그 홈 때문에 아이들이 다치거나 죽었다고 주장하는 가족이 최소한 둘 이상 있다.

해설_ '충돌', '시트' 등의 표현이 나오며, 전체 문맥을 살펴보면 아이들을 위한 카시트의 결함에 관한 것이다.

어휘_ notch V자 모양의 홈, 벤 자국

fracture 부서지다, 부러지다

indentation 톱니 모양, 벤 자국

allege 강력히 주장하다

정답_ (d)

Type B _ 테마별 Approach
Recycling 산업 폐기물과 재활용

STEP 3 Clinic

1.

해석_ 미국에서는 매년 약 천만 대의 컴퓨터가 버려진다. 대부분의 쓸모없는 컴퓨터들은 쓰레기 하치장으로 보내지기 때문에 문제를 야기한다. 컴퓨터업계와 정부는 그 문제를 해결하기 위한 방안을 모색하고 있다. 그들은 컴퓨터가 생산되는 방법에 변화가 있어야 한다고 결론을 내렸다. 컴퓨터는 각 부품들이 재활용될 수 있는 방식으로 생산되어야 한다.

해설_ 정부와 업계는 컴퓨터가 생산되는 방법에 변화가 있어야 한다고 결론을 내렸고 그 중 하나가 재활용될 수 있는 방식으로 생산되어야 한다고 했으므로 재활용이 되는 부품을 사용해야 한다는 것이 유추 가능하다.

어휘_ unwanted 쓸모없는, 불필요한
　　　 dump 쓰레기 버리는 곳

정답_ (b)

2.

해석_ 자동차는 너무 많은 유독 배기가스를 내뿜고 재활용이 불가능한 휘발유를 너무 많이 연소시킨다. 그러나 머지않아 정부는 자동차 제조업자들에게 한 가지 어떻게든 매연을 억제하도록 강제하게 될 법들을 통과시킬 계획이다. 지금까지는 아무도 그 방법이 어떠해야 하는지에 대해 합의할 수 없었다. 가스 공사는 자동차에 매연이 없는 천연가스를 이용하는 것이 해결책이라고 생각한다. 농부들은 발효시킨 농업 폐기물로 만든 에탄올을 선호한다. 석유 회사들은 매연을 더 적게 발생시키게 재처리될 수 있는 휘발유에 집착한다. 환경론자들은 가능하다면 태양 에너지로 만드는 전기를 선호한다. 자동차 제조업자들은 연료가 무엇이든 상관없이 자동차를 더 가볍고 효율적으로 만들기를 원한다.

해설_ 마지막 부분에서 자동차 제조업자들은 연료에 상관없이 자동차를 더 가볍게 만드는 것을 원한다고 했으므로 특정 연료의 사용에 집착하는 것은 아니다.

어휘_ belch 분출하다, 내뿜다
　　　 noxious 유해한, 해로운
　　　 exhaust 배기가스
　　　 utilities (전기 · 가스 · 상하수도 · 교통 기관 등의) 공익 사업체
　　　 ferment 발효시키다
　　　 reformulate 재처리하다

　　　 emission 배기, 배출물

정답_ (b)

STEP 4 Actual Test

1.

해석_ 미국에서는 올해에만 1억 6천만 톤의 쓰레기가 발생했다. 10%는 재활용되었고 10%는 소각되었으며 나머지는 매립되었다. 하지만 매립지를 찾는 것은 점점 더 힘들어지고 있다. 그래서 발생하는 쓰레기를 재활용해야만 할 필요성이 더 커지고 있다. 미국 정부는 내년에는 재활용 비율을 10% 늘리기로 계획하고 있다. 만약 쓰레기의 총량이 같다면 재활용되는 쓰레기의 양은 3,200만 톤이 될 것이다.

해설_ 현재 1억 6천만 톤 가운데 10%, 즉 1,600만 톤이 재활용되는데 미국 정부는 내년에 재활용 비율을 10% 더 늘릴 계획을 세우고 있다. 따라서 앞으로는 재활용 쓰레기가 1억 6천만 톤의 20%, 즉 3,200만 톤이 될 것이다.

어휘_ landfill 쓰레기 매립, 매립지

정답_ (b)

2.

해석_ 또 다른 해결책은 타이어의 새로운 용도를 찾아내는 것이다. 대공황 당시 미국에서는 타이어로 만든 밑창이 달린 신발들이 매우 흔했다. 메인 주는 굉장히 춥고 겨울에는 땅이 딱딱하게 얼어붙는다. 도로에는 큰 턱이 생기고 봄에는 그 턱이 구덩이로 변하곤 한다. 도로는 자주 보수해야만 했고 주에는 많은 비용이 부담되었다. 이를 방지하기 위해 도로를 보수하는 사람들은 낡은 타이어를 작은 조각으로 쪼개어 쓰기 시작했다. 이 타이어 조각들은 새 도로의 표면 아래 두터운 층으로 뿌려졌다. 타이어들은 담요 같은 역할을 해서 아래에 있는 땅이 어는 것을 막아주었다. 이러한 방법으로 노면은 고르게 유지되었다.

해설_ '타이어들은 아래에 있는 땅이 어는 것을 막아주었다' 고 했으므로 일종의 담요와 같은 역할이라고 보아야 한다.

어휘_ the Great Depression 대공황
　　　 sole (구두 등의) 바닥, 밑창
　　　 bump (도로 등의) 턱

정답_ (d)

Chapter 7

Type A _ 유형별 Approach
Part II 추론과 다음에 이어질 내용 질문

STEP 1 Pattern Study
Sample

해석_ 법원은 수천 명의 중국 아기들을 신장 결석에 걸리게 하고 일부를 사망하게 한 우유 첨가제를 제조한 남자에게 사형을 언도했다. 거의 30만 명의 중국 아기들이 멜라민이 첨가된 분유를 먹은 뒤 병을 앓았고 6명이 사망했는데, 멜라민은 플라스틱을 만드는 데 사용되는 합성물질로 해당 분유가 품질 테스트를 통과할 수 있도록 하기 위해 사용되었다. 사형이 언도된 피고는 허베이의 낙농업자들에게 '단백질 분말' 이라는 이름으로 600톤에 달하는 멜라민 첨가제를 제조·판매한 기술자로 밝혀졌다.

해설_ 지문 가운데 '멜라민은 플라스틱을 만드는 데 사용되는 합성물질' 이라는 내용이 나온다.

어휘_ hand down (판결을) 내리다, 언도하다
    additive 첨가제
    develop (병에) 걸리다
    kidney stone 신장 결석
    fatal 죽게 하는
    formula 분유
    spike (음료에) 화학 약품 등을 타다
    compound 합성물질

정답_ (c)

STEP 2 Clinic

1.

해석_ 전국 평균 휘발유 가격이 3주 연속으로 상승하여 목요일에는 갤런당 $1.85까지 올랐다. 이것은 11월 24일 이후 최고가이며 지난 주에 비해 갤런당 6.3센트가 오른 가격이다. 하지만 1년 전에 비하면 휘발유는 여전히 갤런당 평균 $1.17가 싸고 $4 이상이었던 지난 여름보다는 훨씬 싸다. 가격은 갤런당 $2.02인 서부 해안지역이 가장 비쌌으며, 가장 싼 곳은 로키 산맥 주변의 여러 주로서 갤런당 $1.61 근처를 맴돌고 있다. 상승폭의 변화가 작긴 하지만 계속 지켜볼 필요가 있는데 특히 몇 달 후에 겨울이 끝나면 미국인들이 차를 더욱 많이 몰기 시작하기 때문이다.

해설_ 지문의 처음부터 휘발유 가격의 인상에 대하여 이야기하고 있고, 마지막에도 가격 인상의 예상 요인에 대하여 이야기하고 있다.

어휘_ hover 맴돌다, 배회하다
    keep an eye on ~을 지켜보다
    give out 다하다, 바닥나다

정답_ (a)

2.

해석_ 이스라엘 총리 에후드 올메르트는 가자 지구에서 벌인 22일간의 공격을 옹호하며 잠재적인 전쟁 범죄의 조사에 관한 국제적인 요구에 대해 군을 변호할 것이라고 약속했다. "임무를 수행하기 위해 가자 지구에 파견된 병사들과 지휘관들은 여러 재판들로부터 안전하며 이스라엘 정부는 이 문제에 대해 그들을 지원하고 변호할 것이라는 점을 반드시 알아야 한다" 고 예루살렘에서 열린 주간 내각 회의에 앞서 올메르트는 말했다.

해설_ 제일 첫 문장에 제시된, 군을 변호할 것이라는 총리의 발언에서 보듯이 범세계적인 행동주의자들이나 일부 국가가 조사를 요구했었다는 것을 알 수 있다.

어휘_ offensive 공격, 공세
    Gaza Strip 가자 지구
    pledge 맹세하다, 약속하다
    tribunal 법정

정답_ (d)

STEP 3 Actual Test

1.

해석_ 캘리포니아 주 와인 품평 대회의 심사위원들은 블라인드 테이스팅에서 자신들이 여러 번 맛 본 똑같은 와인에 대해 일관된 평가를 내리지 못했다. 그것은 훔볼트 주립 대학의 은퇴한 교수인 로버트 호지슨이 4년간 캘리포니아 주 와인 품평 대회의 판결을 연구한 뒤 내린 결론이었다. "소비자는 와인들이 각종 대회에서 수상한 메달에 대해 건전한 회의주의를 견지해야만 한다" 고 그는 말했다.

해설_ 윗글은 와인 감정가들이 와인에 대해 일관된 평가를 내리지 못한다는 내용이다. (a)처럼 대회 운영의 변화를 검토해봐야 한다거나 (c)처럼 심사 위원의 자질을 테스트한다는 이야기는 이 글만으로는 추론하기 힘들다.

어휘_ judge 감정가, 심사위원
    identical 동일한, 똑같은
    skepticism 회의론

정답_ (d)

2.

해석_ 두 남자가 시카고 남서부 지구에서 체포되어 250만 달러어치 이상의 코카인과 헤로인이 포함된 마약 거래를 시도한 혐의를 받고 있다고 시카고 경찰이 오늘 밝혔다. 경찰 공보실에 따르면, 목요일 밤에 마약 단속반 경찰관들이 소형 닷지 트럭과 빨간색 혼다 승용차를 남쪽 풀라스키 도로 6800블록에 있는 주차장에서부터 남 킬러 가

(街) 6800블록에 있는 차고까지 추격했다고 한다.

해설_ 지문 후반부에 경찰이 용의자를 추격하는 과정이 나왔기 때문에 그 다음에는 용의자를 체포하는 과정이 순차적으로 나올 것으로 추측할 수 있다.

어휘_ charge 혐의

narcotics 마약(류)

pick-up truck 소형 트럭

정답_ (a)

3.

해석_ 2008년 250만 명 이상의 미국인들이 직장을 잃었습니다. 그리고 2009년에는 최소 200만 개의 일자리가 사라질 것으로 예측됩니다. 그러나 직원 감축으로 고통을 당하고 있는 이는 비단 구조 조정 당한 인력뿐만이 아닙니다. 아직 고용을 유지하고 있는 이들조차도 역할이 불투명해지고 노동 강도 또한 거세져 알코올 소비량이 더욱 증가되고 우울증에 걸리는 이도 많아질 수 있습니다. 게다가 정리 해고에서 살아 남은 사람들은 흔히 건강의 악화를 경험합니다. 이러한 결과는 장기적인 것으로 행동 과학 연구소에서 발간한 연구 자료를 보면 구조조정에서 살아남은 이들의 심리적 후유증은 6년간 지속된다고 합니다. 그리고 여러 차례의 정리해고에서 살아 남은 경우에도 그런 영향은 계속 누적된다고 합니다.

해설_ 구조조정에서 살아남은 이들조차도 여러 가지 부정적인 영향을 받게 된다고 한다. (b) 실직자가 우울증을 겪는다는 내용은 없다. (c) 구조조정당한 이들이 고용주를 불신한다는 이야기는 나오지 않는다. (d) 구조조정에서 살아남은 이들이 죄책감을 느낀다는 말은 없다.

어휘_ evaporate 증발하다, 사라지다

laid-off 구조조정당한, 해고된

prone to ~하기 쉬운

contribute to ~의 원인이 되다

fallout 후유증, 악영향

cumulative 누적적인, 가중의

정답_ (a)

4.

해석_ 지난달 일어난 200만 달러어치의 희귀 동전 강도 사건에 깜짝 놀랄 만한 수사 진전이 있었다. 경찰은 우연히 얻은 정보로 잃어버린 동전의 모든 현금을 다 찾을 수 있었다. 이상하게도 동전은 한 백화점 주 매장 마네킹에 걸려 있는 작은 여행 가방에서 발견되었다. 동전이 거기에 어떻게 들어갔는지, 얼마나 오래 그곳에 있었는지 아무도 모른다.

해설_ 희귀 동전은 작은 여행용 가방에서 발견되었다. (a) 동전 강도가 과거에 얼마나 발생했는지에 대한 언급은 없다. (b), (d)는 주어진 지문 내용과 정반대이다.

어휘_ startling 깜짝 놀랄 만한

정답_ (c)

Type B _ 테마별 Approach
Cloning 유전자 조작과 복제

STEP 3 Clinic

1.

해석_ 소비자의 대변자들은 곡물의 추가적인 검사와 유전자 가공식품에 대한 의무적인 등급제를 요구한다. 정부 관계자들은 그것은 불필요하다고 말하고, 식품 업계에서는 그것이 생물 공학적으로 만들어진 식품에 불공정하게 오명을 씌울 것이라고 주장한다. 우리는 생명 공학에 관해 UN 주최의 긴급 세계 정상 회담을 열 필요가 있고, 다음에는 국제적인 합의를 이끌어내야 한다. 오늘 우리가 유전자 공학을 통제하지 못하면 내일 유전자 공학이 우리를 재설계할 것이다.

해설_ 정부 관료, 식품업계 사람들과는 대비되게 소비자의 대변자들만이 유전자 가공식품에 대하여 additional testing과 같은 까다로운 요구를 했음을 알 수 있다.

어휘_ advocate 대변자

additional 부가적인, 추가의

mandatory 강제의, 의무의

genetically engineered product 유전자 가공식품

stigmatize 오명을 씌우다, 비난하다

biotech 생물 공학 (=biotechnology)

summit 정상 회담

redesign 재설계하다

정답_ (a)

2.

해석_ 생물 복제는 원래 아버지나 어머니 어느 한 쪽의 완벽한 복사본을 만들기 위해 체세포 조작을 통해 식물이나 동물을 재생하는 방법이다. 우리는 가까운 장래에 인간 복제를 허용해야 하는지에 대해 결국 결정을 내려야만 한다. 이것은 복제 논쟁에 있어 가장 뜨거운 쟁점이다. 사실 우리들 중 많은 이들이 복제의 잠재적인 긍정적 효과들을 무시하면서 복제 그 자체에 대해 비판하기도 한다. 그들은 일단 복제 기술이 그 같은 과제들을 달성할 수 있게 된다면 그 기술이 인

간에게도 적용될 것이라는 점을 걱정하는 것이다.

해설_ 빈칸이 있는 문장의 바로 앞에 생물 복제에 반대하는 사람들이 나오는데 이들이 가장 염려하는 것은 복제 기술을 인간에게 적용하는 것일 것이다.

어휘_ manipulation 조작
　　　 volatile 불안정한, 일촉즉발의

정답_ (d)

STEP 4 Actual Test

1.

해석_ 인간 복제는 항상 대중의 상상력을 사로잡아 왔다. 우리는 오늘날 현대의 아인슈타인이나 음악적 천재 또는 신동에게서 약간의 세포를 추출해 그들과 정확히 똑같은 유전자를 가진 수백 명의 복제 아기들을 만들어낼 수 있는 기술을 갖고 있다. 클린턴 대통령은 1997년 5월, 복제 인간은 만들어져서는 안 된다고 선언했다. 그는 열렬한 박수갈채를 받았다. 하지만 이어진 그의 다음 말은 그 금지가 단지 5년간에 한한다는 것이었다. 그 결과 인간 복제는 미국 내의 상업적인 실험실이나 미국의 기술을 사용하여 다른 곳에서 이루어질 것으로 예상된다.

해설_ 클린턴은 복제를 금지한다고 했지만 1997년과 그로부터 5년간인 2002년까지에 한해서 한 언급이었다. 따라서 그 이후는 알 수 없다.

어휘_ prodigy 천재

정답_ (b)

2.

해석_ 일부 비평가들은 생식을 돕기 위해 과학과 기술을 사용하는 정책에 대해 의구심을 가질 수도 있다. 아이를 바라는 부모에게 이러한 새 방법들은 신을 대신하는 것이다. 하지만 그 같은 진보된 생식 방법을 이용함으로써 우리는 진화의 가장 기본적인 법칙에 역행하고 있다. 만약 진화의 목적이 부적절한 유전자를 개체군에서 걸러내고 우월한 유전자의 영속화를 돕는 것이라면 인공 수정은 예측하지 못한 수많은 반향을 불러일으킬 것이다. 생식 요법이 얼마나 매력적인가 하는 것과는 무관하게 우리가 거기에 대해 할 수 있는 일이 많지 않을 때가 되어서야 우리는 이 기술의 부정적인 측면을 알게 될 것이다.

해설_ 마지막에서 '우리는 이 기술의 부정적인 측면을 알게 될 것이다'라고 했으므로 side effect를 조심하라는 내용이 맞다.

어휘_ reproduction 재생, 번식
　　　 evolution 진화

screen out 가려내다

perpetuation 영속화, 영구 보존

a multitude of 다수의, 수많은

repercussions 반향, 영향

정답_ (c)

Chapter 8

Type A _ 유형별 Approach
Part II 글의 분위기나 목적을 묻는 질문

STEP 1 Pattern Study
Sample
해석_ 마약과의 전쟁에 있어 진정한 영웅은 빈민가의 출세 가도에 저항하는 10대들이다. 그들은 집에 있으면서 학업을 계속하고 저임금을 받으며 일하면서도 꿋꿋이 공부하는 아이들이다. 놀라운 것은 그런 아이들이 많다는 사실이다. 미시간에 있는 한 청소년 법정의 수석 판사는 "대부분의 아이들은 약물에 관여하지 않습니다" 라고 말한다. "대부분의 아이들은 총을 갖고 돌아다니지 않아요. 사람을 죽이지도 않습니다. 대부분은 아주 잘하고 있는 거죠. 엄청난 유혹에 맞서서 말입니다." 이 아이들이야말로 제시 잭슨 목사의 말, 즉 "여러분은 빈민가에서 태어났지만 빈민가가 여러분에게서 태어난 것은 아닙니다" 에 부합하는 존재들인 것이다.

해설_ 마지막 문장의 but the slum wasn't born in you, 즉 빈민가가 그 청소년들 때문에 생긴 것은 아니라는 서술은 빈민가 청소년들에 대한 긍정적인 서술로 봐야 한다. 따라서 정답은 (b)가 된다.

어휘_ ghetto 빈민가
　　　　fast track 출세 가도
　　　　juggle 잘 병행하다
　　　　juvenile 청소년(의)
　　　　run around 돌아다니다
　　　　odds 가능성

정답_ (b)

STEP 2 Clinic
1.
해석_ 어떤 사람들은 "첫눈에 반하는 사랑" 을 고집하지만 나는 마음을 가라앉히고 다시 한 번 볼 것을 권한다. 첫눈에 반하는 사랑 같은 것은 없다. 첫눈에 매력 있는 특징들 가운데 일부는 진정하고 영속적인 것으로 드러나기도 하겠지만 동화책의 뻔한 공식을 기대하진 마라. 또 다른 격언인 "사랑은 맹목적인 것이다" 가 훨씬 더 현명한 말이다. 자신이 사랑에 빠졌다고 믿는 어린 소녀는 사랑하는 남자에게서 바람직하지 않은 특징들은 보지 못하는데 왜냐하면 그것들을 볼 수 없기 때문이다.

해설_ 첫 문장에 제시된 Some people insist에서 보듯이 일부 사람들은 그렇게 주장하지만 자신은 그렇지 않다는 식으로 글을 전개하고 있으므로 글쓴이는 첫눈에 반하는 사랑에 대하여 비판적인 태도임을 알 수 있다.

어휘_ genuine 진짜의
　　　　durable 영속성 있는, 오래 가는

　　　　count on 믿다, 의지하다
　　　　formula 방식, 공식

정답_ (b)

2.
해석_ 미국의 16대 대통령인 에이브러햄 링컨은 꿈에서 자신의 죽음에 대한 메시지를 받았을지도 모른다. 1865년 어느 날 밤 그는 이상한 꿈을 꾸었다. 그는 백악관에 있는 꿈을 꾸었다. 백악관의 동편 집무실에 한 무리의 사람들이 관을 둘러싸고 서 있었다. 그들 중 많은 이들이 울고 있었다. "누가 죽었나요?" 라고 그는 물었다. "대통령이요." 누군가가 대답했다. "그는 암살자에 의해 죽었습니다." 이 일이 있고 며칠 후인 4월 14일, 링컨은 워싱턴의 포드 극장에서 연극을 보던 중 총에 맞아 죽었다.

해설_ 꿈에서 암시된 것과 똑같은 일이 링컨에게 발생했다는 이야기이므로 글의 전반적인 분위기는 신비롭다(mysterious).

어휘_ coffin 관
　　　　assassin 암살자

정답_ (b)

STEP 3 Actual Test
1.
해석_ 미국 치과 협회에 의하면 치아는 평생 동안 존속되는 것으로 여겨지지만 칫솔은 그렇지 않고 매 4개월마다 교체되어야 한다. 그래서 캘리포니아 레드우드 시에 있는 오랄비 연구소는 교체 신호 기능이 있는 최초의 칫솔인 인디케이터를 내놓았다. 푸른 색깔이 칫솔모 아래로 절반 정도 사라질 때까지 일반적으로 약 3~4개월이 걸리는데 바로 그때가 새로운 칫솔을 살 때이다. 가격은 3달러.

해설_ 글의 분위기나 목적은 지문의 뒤쪽을 본다는 관점에서 이 문제는 가격을 제일 뒤에 제시했기에 글의 목적이 물건에 대한 정보를 제시하고 물건을 사라고 유인하는 광고 글이라고 봐야 한다.

어휘_ toss out (불필요한 것을) 버리다
　　　　introduce (신제품 등을) 발표하다, 출시하다
　　　　bristle (솔 등의) 털
　　　　indicator (신호) 표시기

정답_ (b)

2.
해석_ 마을의 모습은 말로 표현하기 어려울 지경이었다. 산더미 같은 진흙과 모래가 온 마을을 뒤덮고 있었다. 중앙로가 어디인지는 거의 알아볼 수 없었다. 두 개의 거대한 물줄기가 마을 중앙을 관통하

며 지나가고 있었다. 집들은 홍수에 떠내려가거나 주저앉았다. 거리
에는 몇 구의 불운한 희생자들의 사체가 쌓여 있었으며 폐허 속에서
수많은 사람들이 사라진 그들의 가족과 친척들을 찾고 있었다.

해설_ 앞에서도 마찬가지지만 특히 이 글의 뒷부분을 보면 폐허가
등장하고 수많은 시체가 쌓였다는 이야기가 제시되어 있으므로 글의
분위기는 비참하다고 봐야 한다.

어휘_ heap (쌓아 올린) 더미
　　　blow down 불어 넘어뜨리다
　　　bring down 주저앉히다

정답_ (d)

3.

해석_ 나중에 기억하는 누군가가 있다면, 20세기는 감옥의 그림자가
지구 전역에 드리워진 시기로 보여질 수 있다. 이 시기는 그들이 믿
거나 믿지 않는 것에 대해 사람들 안에 있는 사악한 독창성을 일깨웠
다. 이 중에서 조지 오웰은 이런 전개를 예견하고 경각심을 일깨우는
가장 무서운 이야기 중 하나인 '1984'에서 그것을 미리 선보이려 했
다.

해설_ 소설 '1984'의 내용으로 들어가기 위한 전 단계로서 소개를
하고 있다. 따라서 정답은 (d)가 된다.

어휘_ fiendish 사악한
　　　ingenuity 독창성
　　　forestall 선수를 치다, ~에 앞서다
　　　cautionary tale 경고하는[경각심을 일깨우는] 이야기

정답_ (d)

4.

해석_ 지난 몇백 년 동안 하늘에서 떨어지는 이상한 물체에 대한 많
은 보고들이 있었다. 1680년 노르웨이의 한 마을에서는 수백 마리의
살아 있는 쥐들이 떨어졌다. 물고기, 개구리, 도마뱀, 벌레들이 소나
기처럼 떨어졌다는 기록도 있다. 1977년 잉글랜드의 브리스톨에 있
는 교회에서 집으로 걸어가던 한 커플은 맑은 하늘에서 떨어지는 수
많은 헤이즐넛을 맞았다. 1984년 랭커셔의 한 단독 주택은 사과 세
례를 받았고, 1989년 호주의 작은 마을에는 정어리가 쏟아져 내렸
다. 1994년 프랑스의 한 연금 수령자는 일주일치 쇼핑을 하기에 충
분할 만큼의 동전 벼락을 맞았다.

해설_ 글 전반적으로 이해하기 힘든 미스테리한 이야기들이 펼쳐지
고 있다. 그래서 정답은 (d)의 Mysterious이다.

어휘_ shower 쏟아짐
　　　rat 들쥐
　　　rain 비처럼 내리다

bombard 퍼붓다
sardine 정어리
pensioner 연금 수령자

정답_ (d)

Type B _ 테마별 Approach
Albert Einstein 아인슈타인

STEP 3 Clinic

1.

해석_ 잘 알려진 과학 분야의 천재에 관해 생각할 때면 우리는 흔히
늙고 희끗희끗한 외모를 가진 누군가를 떠올린다. 예를 들면 우리는
알베르트 아인슈타인의 산발한 머리, 찰스 다윈의 위엄 있는 수염,
아이작 뉴턴의 주름진 얼굴을 생각하는 것이다. 그러나 진실은 우리
의 삶을 변화시킨 대부분의 위대한 과학적 발전들은 보통 아직 30대
에 불과한 사람들에 의해 이루어진다는 것이다. 아인슈타인이 그랬
으며 뉴턴과 다윈이 그렇다. 당연한 일이겠지만 실제로 젊은 과학자
들은 나이 많은 과학자들보다 당대의 지적인 정설에 영향을 덜 받는
다. 그들은 본능적으로 권위에 대해 의심한다. 그들은 어떤 새로운
아이디어를 사람들이 미친 것이라고 말해도 그 말을 믿지 않으며 따
라서 불가능한 일을 해내는 데 있어 자유로운 것이다.

해설_ 당시의 구습에 덜 얽매인다는 것이 전반적인 내용이므로 (d)
the intellectual dogma of the day가 타당하다.

어휘_ disheveled 부스스한, 헝클어진
　　　majestic 위엄 있는
　　　visage 얼굴
　　　breakthrough (과학 등의) 큰 발전, 약진

정답_ (d)

2.

해석_ 민주주의 이론은 아인슈타인이 세기말에 자신의 성찰을 시작
했을 때의 그 이론 물리학의 상태와 유사하다. 그 당시 받아들여졌던
학설은 대부분 뉴턴이 몇백 년 전에 발표한 것이었다. 그의 사고의
근간은 공간과 시간에 대한 개념이었다. 뉴턴은 그 둘을 서로 다른
별개의 것으로 생각했다. 한편 아인슈타인은 시간과 공간이 분리되
어 있지 않다고 했다. 더구나 그는 덧붙여 말하기를 에너지와 질량은
동등하고 서로 변환 가능하다고 했는데, 이는 질량 에너지 동등성이
라고 일컬어진다: $E = mc^2$.

해설_ 문맥상 (뉴턴이) '발표했다'는 말이 나와야 한다.

어휘_ akin to ~와 유사한

어휘_ akin to ~와 유사한

theoretical physics 이론 물리학

speculation 사색, 성찰

in the main 대체로, 대부분

fundamental 중요한, 기본의

conceive of A as B A를 B라고 생각하다

equivalent 동등한, 같은 값의

transmutable 변형 가능한

equivalence 등가(성)

정답_ (a)

STEP 4 Actual Test

1.

해석_ 아인슈타인은 자주 신에게 기원하고는 했는데 그의 신은 어느 쪽인가 하면 비인격적인 (범신론적) 신이었다. 아인슈타인은 존재하는 모든 것의 조화 속에서 스스로를 드러내는 신을 믿는다고 말했다. 이와 같은 신의 조화에 대한 그의 믿음은 그로 하여금 우주가 무작위성과 불확실성에 좌우된다는 관점을 거부하게 했다. 신은 이해하기 힘든 존재지만 악의를 갖고 있지는 않다. 신의 계획에 대한 탐구는 모든 진실한 예술과 과학의 원동력이라고 그는 말했다. 이 탐구는 겸손의 원인이 될 수도 있지만, 또한 우리의 삶에 의미와 존엄을 부여하는 것이기도 한다.

해설_ 마지막 문장의 Although this quest may be a cause for humility라는 표현에서 볼 때, 신의 계획에 대한 탐구는 사람으로 하여금 겸손함을 불러일으키게 할 수 있다.

어휘_ invoke 기원하다, 의지하다

depersonalize 비인간화하다

deity 신(성)

divine 신의

subject to ~의 지배를 받는, ~할 수밖에 없는

randomness 무작위(성)

subtle 이해하기 어려운, 불가사의한

malicious 악의 있는

humility 겸손

dignity 존엄, 품위

정답_ (a)

2.

해석_ 캘리포니아의 한 연구원에 의하면 알베르트 아인슈타인의 뇌는 보통 사람의 뇌와 분명한 차이점들이 있다고 한다. 하지만 이 차이점들과 아인슈타인의 비상한 지능 사이에 어떤 가능한 연관성이 있는지는 여전히 밝혀지지 않았다고 그녀는 덧붙였다. 천재의 뇌가 특별히 두드러진 특징이 있는지 조사하기 위해 UCLA의 달리아 W. 자이델 박사는 그 물리학자가 1955년 76세의 나이로 사망한 직후 뇌에서 채취한 것으로 만들어진 두 장의 슬라이드를 검사했다. 슬라이드에는 아이슈타인의 해마상 융기 샘플이 포함되어 있었는데 그것은 뇌에서 기억과 언어 연상에 관련된 부분이었다. 자이델은 아인슈타인의 뇌 조직을 사망 시 22세에서 84세에 이르는 보통 지능을 가진 10명의 뇌 조직과 비교해 보았다. 이 노벨상 수상자의 해마상 융기 좌측 신경 세포들은 우측 신경 세포들보다 일관되게 더 컸다. 자이델은 이러한 연구 결과는 보통 지능을 가진 사람들의 뇌에서 보이는 것과 "현저하게 다르다"고 말했다. 그녀는 연구 결과를 월요일 캘리포니아 샌디에이고에서 열린 신경 과학회 연례 모임에서 발표했다.

해설_ 뇌의 일정 부분의 크기와 관련되는 것이지 texture and hardness of his brain, 즉 재질과 강도에 따른 것은 아니다.

어휘_ gray matter 두뇌, 지능

hippocampus (뇌의) 해마상 융기

word association 언어 연상

neuroscience 신경 과학

정답_ (c)

Chapter 9

Type A _ 유형별 Approach
Part III 문맥상 어울리지 않는 것 찾기

STEP 1 Pattern Study

Sample

해석_ 척추 통증은 수백만 명의 환자들에게 짜증이나 고통 또는 심지어는 장애의 원인이다. (1) 수술을 받는 것은 비싼 치료법이며 환자들에게 큰 도움이 되지 않을 수도 있다. (2) 그럴듯한 광고에 등장하는 비싼 치료법들이 사실은 겉보기처럼 그렇게 좋지 않을 수도 있다고 시애틀의 워싱턴 대학 건강 서비스 연구원인 브룩 마틴은 말한다. (3) 약한 근육은 척추가 더 많은 하중을 지탱하게 함으로써 문제를 유발할 수도 있다. (4) 이제 많은 전문가들은 의사들이 칼(수술)에 의존하기 전에 좀 더 생각해볼 필요가 있다고 주장한다.

해설_ 윗글은 척추 통증에 수술이 만병통치약이 아니라는 것이 주된 내용이다.

어휘_ sufferer 환자

　　　 annoyance 짜증, 불쾌감

　　　 misery 고통

　　　 disability 장애

　　　 glossy 그럴듯한, 겉만 번지르르한

　　　 spine 척추

　　　 resort to ~에 의지하다

정답_ (c)

STEP 2 Clinic

1.

해석_ 그녀는 남편인 버락 오바마가 대통령에 출마하고 싶다고 했을 때 그것이 가능한 일인지 확신이 서지 않았다. (1) 그녀는 의문점이 있었고 그에 대한 대답을 원했다. 그녀는 어떻게 선거 운동 자금을 모을 것이며 또 선거 전략은 무엇인지 알고 싶어 했다. (2) 그러한 계획들이 더욱 현실적이고 분명해졌을 때 그녀는 가능성을 보기 시작했다. (3) 미셸은 남편이 여름 인턴십으로 일하는 동안 그와 함께 일하면서 버락을 지도하라는 임무를 맡았다. (4) 그런 뒤 그녀는 남편의 선거 운동을 돕기 위해서 자신의 재능을 이용하기 시작했다.

해설_ 윗글은 미셸이 남편 버락 오바마의 선거 운동을 돕게 되는 과정을 그리고 있다.

어휘_ run for ~에 출마하다

　　　 summer associate 여름 인턴십

정답_ (c)

2.

해석_ 정거장의 승무원을 3명에서 6명으로 두 배 늘리려는 계획으로 인해 러시아는 올해 이후에는 국제 우주 정거장에 관광객을 보내지 않을 것이다. (1) 2001년 이후 그 수지맞는 러시아 우주 관광 프로그램은 2,000만 불을 지불한 6명의 '민간 우주 비행 참가자' 를 (우주로) 보냈다. (2) 소유즈 우주선에 탑승한 가장 최근의 민간인은 컴퓨터 게임 개발자인 리차드 개리엇으로 그는 여행을 위해 3,500만 불을 지불했다고 한다. (3) 아마 그들은 선진국 내에서 아직도 평균 수명이 가장 낮은 국민들에게 더 많은 루블(러시아 화폐)을 써야만 할 것이다. (4) 우주 정거장 승무원은 우주 정거장에서 살기 위해 오랫동안 기다려온 캐나다인과 유럽인, 일본인 우주 비행사들을 수용함으로써 6명으로 확대될 것이다.

해설_ 이 글은 우주 정거장의 승무원 수를 늘리기 위해 더 이상 민간 여행자를 보내지 않는다는 것이 주된 내용이다.

어휘_ lucrative 돈이 벌리는

　　　 spaceflight 우주 비행

　　　 astronaut 우주 비행사

정답_ (c)

STEP 3 Actual Test

1.

해석_ 작고 동그란 진주와 세련된 드레스를 입은 미셸 오바마는 패션 리더로서 제2의 재클린 케네디가 될 수 있을 것인가? (1) 대중들은 미셸 오바마가 취임식에 어떤 옷을 입고 나타나 놀라게 하든 준비가 되어 있었다. (2) 그리고 그녀는 실제로 그랬는데 레몬색 코트와 특이하게도 녹색 구두에 녹색 장갑을 맞춘 패션을 선택했다. (3) 여성들의 패션은 항상 변화하기 때문에 어떤 유행이 뜰지 어떨지를 말하는 것은 더욱 어렵다. (4) 그날 밤 흰색 나비넥타이를 한 대통령과의 첫 번째 춤에서 그녀는 한쪽 어깨를 드러낸 흰색 드레스를 입었는데 그것은 덜 호평 받았다.

해설_ 윗글은 미셸 오바마의 패션에 관한 구체적인 이야기인데 (3)은 패션에 대한 일반적인 내용이다.

어휘_ chic 멋진, 세련된

　　　 inauguration 취임(식)

　　　 populace 대중

　　　 throw ~ a curve ball ~를 놀라게[당혹하게] 하다

　　　 idiosyncratically 특이하게

　　　 bow tie 나비넥타이

정답_ (c)

2.

해석_ 오늘 저녁 나와 이야기했던 마이크로소프트의 직원들은 회사

로부터 중대한 발표—아마도 해고에 관한 소식—를 기다리고 있었다. (1) 한 사람은 오전 7시에 통지를 받을 것으로 예상하고 있었다. (2) 나와 이야기했던 직원 중에는 해고의 규모나 이번 해고 사태에 영향을 받을 특정 그룹에 대해 자세히 아는 사람은 아무도 없었다. (3) 마이크로소프트는 6월 30일 현재 전 세계 고용 규모가 총 20,561명에서 91,259명으로 340% 이상 성장했다. (4) 모두들 심란한 해고 소문이 잠잠해지고, 안정된 환경이 조성될 가능성을 고대하고 있었다.

해설_ 이 글은 마이크로소프트의 직원 감축 소식에 관한 글이다. (3)과 같이 고용 규모가 늘었다는 내용은 지문의 전체적인 흐름에 부합하지 않는다.

어휘_ layoff 해고

　　　distracting 마음을 산란케 하는

정답_ (c)

3.

해석_ 과학자들은 남극 대륙이 지구 온난화의 추세에 저항하고 있다고 믿어왔지만 그렇지 않다. (1) 최근 남극 동쪽이 추워졌지만 그 대륙의 나머지 지역은 그 추위를 상쇄할 만큼 더워지고 있다. (2) 지구 온난화에 대해 회의적인 사람들은 남극의 냉각이 기후 변화에 대한 연구자들의 컴퓨터 예상치가 잘못되었다는 증거라고 지적했다. (3) 우리는 이제 온실가스에 대한 반응으로서 모델이 예측한 대로 지구의 모든 대륙에서 온난화가 일어나고 있는 것을 보고 있다. (4) 지난 50년간 모든 대륙의 기온은 십 년에 평균 화씨 0.2도씩 상승했다.

해설_ (2)를 제외하고 나머지는 모두 지구 온난화가 진행되고 있다는 내용이다.

어휘_ Antarctica 남극 대륙

　　　offset 상쇄하다, 벌충하다

　　　projection 예상, 예측

　　　skeptic 회의론자

　　　presumed 추정된

　　　in accord with ~에 맞게, ~와 일치하여

정답_ (b)

4.

해석_ 퀀타스가 로스앤젤레스 국제공항에 에어버스 A380기를 착륙시킬 때마다 공항의 일부가 기능을 멈춘다. (1) 세계에서 가장 큰 여객기가 도착할 때 활주로는 비행장 트럭, 차 그리고 다른 민간 비행기들이 들어갈 수 없다. (2) 그 비행기는 너무 커서 항공 관제사들은 그것에 우선권을 부여한다. 그래서 A380은 흐린 날씨에도 공항의 활주로 끝에서 이륙을 기다릴 필요가 없는데 왜냐하면 그것이 공항의 계기 착륙 장치에서 나오는 무선 신호를 교란시킬 수 있기 때문이다. (3) 이러한 비행기들은 항공 산업의 미래이다. (4) 다른 어떤 항공기보다 A380은 특별한 절차를 필요로 하는데 그것은 로스앤젤레스 국제공항이 그러한 크기의 항공기를 수용하도록 건설되지 않았기 때문이다.

해설_ 지문 전체가 A380기의 거대함을 설명하고 있는데 (c)만 문맥에 어긋난다.

어휘_ come to a halt 멈추다, 정지하다

　　　immense 거대한

　　　air traffic controller 항공 관제사

　　　instrument-landing system 계기 착륙 장치

　　　aviation 비행, 항공기 산업

　　　disrupt 혼란시키다, 불통으로 만들다

정답_ (c)

Type B _ 테마별 Approach
Global Warming & the Greenhouse Effect
지구 온난화와 온실 효과

STEP 3 Clinic

1.

해석_ 오존층에 구멍이 생기는 것은 온실효과와 어떤 관계가 있는 것일까? 그 모든 실질적인 이유들에도 불구하고 (둘 사이에는) 어떤 관계도 없다. 산소에서 자연적으로 발생되는 오존은 다른 이유 때문에 걱정거리가 되고 있다. 오존은 대기권 상층부에서 태양의 자외선으로부터 우리를 보호해 주는데 자외선은 피부암을 유발시킬 수 있다. 1985년 과학자들은 남극 상공의 오존층이 일시적으로 얇아졌다는 사실을 발견했는데 이것은 새로운 걱정을 불러일으킨다. 만약 오존층이 얇아지는 현상이 인구 거주 지역에까지 퍼지게 된다면 질병의 증가를 초래할 수 있기 때문이다.

해설_ 오존은 피부암을 유발하는 자외선을 차단해주는 역할을 하는데 인구 거주 지역의 오존이 얇아지게 되면 피부암 같은 질병이 당연히 증가할 것이다.

어휘_ ultraviolet 자외선

정답_ (b)

2.

해석_ 전 세계에 걸친 공해의 원인은 무엇일까? 장기간에 걸친 논쟁은 과소비에 집중되었다. 선진 산업국에 사는 대략 10억 명의 사람들이 전 세계 환경 문제의 거의 대부분에 책임이 있다. 그것(환경 문제)

이 오존 감소에 대한 온실 효과의 영향이든 심지어는 남벌이든 간에
선진국에 사는 우리가 바로 문제이며, 우리는 이 사실을 벗어나서는
우리의 삶의 방식대로 소비할 수 없다. 우리는 물질의 대량 소비에서
아마도 좀 더 적합한 생활 방식으로 주안점을 바꿔야만 한다.

해설_ 지문 마지막의 '우리는 물질의 대량 소비에서 아마도 좀 더 적
합한 생활 방식으로 주안점을 바꿔야만 한다' 는 내용으로 보아 과소
비가 문제를 발생시켰다는 것을 알 수 있다.

어휘_ culprit 범인, (문제의) 원인

ozone depletion 오존 감소

deforestation 삼림 벌채, 남벌

정답_ (b)

STEP 4 Actual Test

1.

해석_ 일부 전문가들에 따르면 우리는 자녀들과 후손들에게 무서운
유산을 남기고 있다. 대기 속에 축적된 이른바 온실가스의 증가와 이
것이 가져올지도 모를 잠재적으로 끔찍한 기후 변화가 바로 그것이
다. 하지만 과학계의 의견은 분분하다. 다른 과학자들은 지구 온난화
에 대한 증거가 결정적이지 않다고 주장하며 이에 기초한 예측도 의
문스럽다고 주장한다. 과학적인 논란은 뜨거웠다. 이것은 또한 있을
수 있는 기후 변화의 문제를 다루기 위해 만약 취할 수 있는 조치가
있다면 어떤 조치들이 취해져야 하는지에 대한 정치적인 논쟁을 부
채질했다.

해설_ 첫 문장의 some experts의 견해와 빈칸 다음에 나오는
Other scientists의 견해가 서로 다른 것을 볼 때 지구 온난화에 대
한 과학계의 의견이 일치돼 있지 않다는 것을 알 수 있다.

어휘_ inheritance 유산

accumulation 축적(물)

inconclusive 결정적이 아닌

intense 격렬한

fuel 자극하다, 부채질하다

정답_ (a)

2.

해석_ 다음 세기의 후반에는 환경의 상태가 주로 한 가지 요인에 의
해 결정될 것이다. 그것은 바로 인구이다. 만약 최악의 상황이 발생
한다면 수백만이나 되는 무수한 사람들이 환경 난민이 될 것이며 땅
과 물, 산림을 보존하기 위해 노력한 국가들을 궁지에 몰아넣을 것이
다. 현재의 젊은이들의 증손자들은 쥐와 바퀴벌레, 잡초와 세균들이
우위를 차지하는 적응력 강한 종들과 함께 지구를 공유해야 할 것이

다. 그들이 생존해가는 지구는 대부분 사막과 군데군데 남은 열대 우
림 그리고 침식된 산들로 이루어져 있을 것이다.

해설_ 분위기 문제는 주로 지문의 뒷부분에서 답이 결정된다. 마지
막 부분을 보면 '그들이 생존해 나가는 지구는 대부분 사막과 군데군
데 남은 열대 우림, 그리고 침식된 산들로 이루어져 있을 것이다' 라
는 다소 비관적인 내용을 담고 있다.

어휘_ swamp 궁지에 빠뜨리다

cockroach 바퀴벌레

microbe 미생물, 세균

patch 파편, 일부

정답_ (c)

Final Test 01

1.

해석_ 민주당 의원들은 다음 주 초에 흔들리는 디트로이트의 자동차 업계에 최소 150억 불의 구제 금융을 제공하고 연방 정부에게 그들의 경영에 대한 광범위한 구조조정 권한을 부여하는 법을 입안하고 있다. 이르면 내일 의회에서 표결에 붙여질 그 법안은 비틀거리는 업계를 수익성 있게 복구하기 위한 단기적인 자금 지원과 장기적인 노력 모두를 감독하기 위해 부시 대통령이 지명한 내각 관료들과 의장으로 구성된 7인 "자동차 위원회"를 구성할 것이다. 만약 해당 업체들이 자금을 받는다면 (그들이 내리는) 거의 모든 조치와 2,500만 불 이상의 모든 거래에 대해 정부에 보고해야 할 것이다.

해설_ <both A and B> 구문에서 A와 B는 서로 상반된 내용이 오는 경우가 자주 있다. B에서 long-term~이 나왔기 때문에 A에서는 mid-term~보다는 short-term~에 관한 내용이 나오는 것이 더 자연스러울 것이다. 게다가 지문 첫 단락에서 150억 불의 구제 금융 지원을 언급하고 있으므로 빈칸에는 short-term loans가 오는 것이 적절하다.

어휘_ Congressional 미 국회의, 연방 의회의
draft 기초[기안]하다
teeter 흔들리다, 동요하다
emergency loan 긴급 차관, 구제 금융
restructuring 개혁, 개편, 구조조정
falter 비틀거리다
be accountable to A for B B에 대해 A에게 설명할 의무가 있는
transaction 거래

정답_ (c)

2.

해석_ 대통령 당선자 버락 오바마는 일요일에 금융 시스템의 취약성과 15년 사이에 가장 높은 실업률을 기록중인 미국을 나타내는 최근의 수치들을 지적하며 국가의 경제 문제가 "더 나아지기 전에 더 나빠질 것"이라고 경고했다. 그는 이후 구조조정 및 높은 연료 효율성과 연계시킬 자국의 자동차 업계에 대한 정부의 새로운 긴급 구제책에 대해 지지를 표하면서 경제의 미래에 대한 냉정한 평가와 낙관주의의 균형을 맞추기 위해 노력했다.

해설_ 오바마가 빈칸 부분을 지적하며 경제가 더욱 나빠질 것이라고 했다면 빈칸에는 부정적인 내용이 들어가야 한다. 문맥상 (a)가 적합하다.

어휘_ fragility 부서지기 쉬움, 약함
seek to ~하려고 애쓰다
stark 적나라한, 단호한

assessment 평가
bailout (기업에 대한) 긴급 구제

정답_ (a)

3.

해석_ 석유 업계가 태도를 바꾸자 자동차 업계 역시 그렇게 하고 있다. 정유 업계가 97% 더 무해한 유황 성분의 디젤 연료를 생산함에 따라 디젤 차량들은 보다 깨끗하게 주행할 수 있게 되었다. 차량이 많은 캘리포니아와 뉴욕을 포함한 9개 주에서는 배출 기준을 매우 엄격하게 채택하여 보다 깨끗한 그 연료가 낡은 차들이 없어지도록 돕는 데 장애가 되었던 디젤 차량의 판매를 효과적으로 억제했다. 2009년형 메르세데스 벤츠는 50개 주에서 세 종류의 디젤 SUV 차량을 판매하고 있는데 ML, GL 그리고 R이 바로 그것이다. 각각의 차량들은 특수 용액을 촉매 변환 장치에 주입하여 질소 산화물을 휘발유와 같은 수준으로 줄여주는 기술 때문에 블루텍이라고 불린다.

해설_ 빈칸 다음의 내용을 보면 메르세데스 벤츠 같은 회사도 유해 배기가스 배출 억제를 위해 노력하고 있다는 것을 알 수 있다.

어휘_ petroleum 석유
clean up one's act 행실을 고치다
petrol 휘발유
noxious 유해한
sulfur 유황
emission 배출
bar 방해하다
hurdle 장애물
oil burner 낡은 차
catalytic converter 촉매 변환 장치
oxide 산화물
nitrogen 질소

정답_ (b)

4.

해석_ 작사 작곡가인 내 친구는 어떤 사람들은 동네 거리를 돌아다니면서 전 세계를 볼 수 있는 반면 다른 사람들은 세계 곳곳을 돌아다니면서도 아무것도 보지 못한다고 말한 적이 있다. 음식도 그와 같을 수 있다. 인터넷 덕분에 거의 모든 곳의 거의 모든 것을 당장 구할 수 있기 때문에 우리는 가끔 바로 이곳 남부 캘리포니아에서 생산되는 훌륭한 제품들을 간과하기 쉬운 것이다. 그래서 이번 크리스마스에는 집과 가까운 곳에서 선물을 사는 것이 어떨까? 근처에서 쇼핑에 몰두하다 보면 이전에는 결코 보지 못했던 지역을 발견할 수도 있으며 심지어는 생산자를 직접 만날 수도 있을 것이다.

해설_ 빈칸 다음에 오는 내용을 보면 제품, 생산자 등의 이야기가 나오므로 선택지 가운데에서는 (d) 음식이 가장 적합하다.

어휘_ observe ~라고 말하다, 깨닫다

정답_ (d)

5.

해석_ 영화감독 크리스토퍼 놀란은 슈퍼히어로 리얼리즘을 '다크 나이트' 에서 현기증 나는 수준까지 끌어올렸는데, 그 영화는 크리스찬 베일의 도덕적으로 갈등하는 배트맨과 히스 레저의 소름끼치는 조커를 멀리 떨어진 환상적인 영화 세트가 아닌 현대 미국과 심란하게 닮은 고담 시티에 가져다 놓았다. "영웅과 악당은 정말 그렇게 다른가?" 에 관한 놀란의 철학적인 설명의 상당 부분은 진부하지만 그의 인상주의적인 이미지들은 강한 힘을 가지고 있으며, 정체성과 잃어버린 이상이라는 그가 자주 사용하는 주제를 탐구하기 위해 인습적인 캐릭터를 쓴 그의 대담한 선택 역시 그렇다.

해설_ 빈칸 다음을 보면 '멀리 떨어진 환상적인 영화 세트' 가 아니라고 했기 때문에 그와 상반되는 곳, 즉 영화가 만들어졌던 장소와 시기가 일치하는 '현대 미국' 이 가장 적합하다.

어휘_ dizzying 현기증이 날 것 같은

creepy 소름끼치는

disturbingly 불안하게, 심란하게

villain 악당

philosophize 철학적으로 설명하다

overcook 지나치게 익히다

gutsy 대담한

iconic 인습적인

정답_ (a)

6.

해석_ 75세의 여성을 납치해서 음식이나 물을 주지 않고 그녀의 스테이션 왜건 뒤쪽에 26시간 동안 묶어놓은 혐의로 기소된 세 명의 청소년들이 고문과 다른 혐의들에 대해 무죄를 주장했다. 세 명은 금요일에 샌디에이고 카운티 상급 법원에 탄원서를 제출했다. 그녀는 심하게 맞고 묶인 상태로 발견되었다. 그녀는 월요일 밤 늦게 그녀의 집에서 납치되었다. 피고들은 고문, 강도와 납치를 포함한 혐의를 받고 있다.

해설_ 지문 중간을 보면 '세 명의 청소년들이 고문과 다른 혐의들에 대해 무죄를 주장했다' 는 내용이 나온다. 따라서 그들은 역으로 고문 혐의를 받고 있다는 사실을 알 수 있다.

어휘_ plead not guilty 죄상을 인정하지 않다

torture 고문

plea 탄원, 청원

bound 묶인

abduct 유괴하다, 납치하다

defendant 피고

정답_ (d)

7.

해석_ O. J. 심슨의 라스베이거스 재판의 핵심 증인이 전 NFL 스타에게 매수당했다는 것을 인정했다고 그를 심문한 네바다 주 조사관이 오늘 아침 산타모니카에서 판사에게 밝혔다. 조사관은 심슨이 증인에게 자신의 변호를 위해 증언을 번복하는 대가로 명예의 전당 반지를 주었다는 것을 증인이 인정했다고 말했다. "당신은 증언을 번복하기 위해 무엇을 받았느냐고 나는 물어봤습니다" 라고 심슨에 대한 무장 강도와 납치 사건을 맡은 검사들과 함께 일하는 빌 포크너는 말했다.

해설_ 빈칸 뒤에 증언을 번복하는 대가로 심슨이 반지를 주었다는 내용이 있기 때문에 정답은 (a)가 된다.

어휘_ Hall of Fame 명예의 전당

investigator 조사관, 수사관

in exchange for ~에 대한 대가로

alter 변경하다

testimony 증언

prosecutor 검사

정답_ (a)

8.

해석_ 바티칸의 생명 윤리학 문서는 많은 커플들이 이용하는 인공 수정 및 다른 기술들을 비난했으며 또한 인간 복제, 배아 줄기 세포 연구, 사후 피임약 역시 부도덕한 것이라고 말했다. 바티칸의 교리 체제에서 도출된 오랫동안 기다려왔던 그 문서는 바티칸이 생명 공학에 개입하게 되는 중요한 단계를 의미한다. 그 문서는 또한 자궁 내에 착상된 수정란을 유지하는 데 필요한 호르몬의 움직임을 차단하는 사후 피임약 같은 임신을 막는 약도 비난한다.

해설_ 빈칸 뒷부분을 보면 자궁 내에 착상된 수정란을 유지하기 위해 필요한 호르몬의 움직임을 차단한다는 내용이 나오는데 이는 곧 임신을 못하게 막는다는 의미이다.

어휘_ bioethics 생명 윤리(학)

condemn 비난하다

fertilization 수정

embryonic 배아기의

morning-after pill (성교 후 다음날에 복용해도 효과가 있는)

사후 피임약

doctrinal 교의상의

fertilized egg 수정란

uterus 자궁

정답_ (a)

9.

해석_ 존 트라볼타의 10대 아들인 제트가 바하마에 있는 그의 가족 별장에서 발작을 일으킨 뒤 머리를 부딪쳐 사망했다. 별장 관리인은 금요일 아침 늦게 화장실에서 의식을 잃은 제트를 발견했다. 그는 구급차에 실려 프리포트 병원으로 이송되었으며 그곳에서 사망했다. 발표에 따르면 소년은 목요일 날 화장실에 들어가는 것이 마지막으로 목격되었으며 발작 병력을 가지고 있었다. 부검이 있을 예정이다.

해설_ 지문의 첫 문장을 보면 소년이 발작을 일으켰다는 내용이 나오는데 그 사실이 힌트가 된다.

어휘_ seizure 발작

caretaker 관리인

unconscious 의식 불명의

autopsy 부검, 검시

정답_ (a)

10.

해석_ 2008년의 폭락 이후 세계 주식시장은 새해 들어 강세로 출발하고 있다. 다우존스 산업 평균 지수는 228포인트, 즉 2.6%가 올라 9,004포인트에 달했다. 오늘은 월 스트리트에 근무하는 사람이 얼마 없어 이 상황을 즐기지 못하는 것이 너무 안타까울 뿐이다. 거래는 매우 적은데 대부분의 투자자들이 주말을 포함한 4일간의 새해 연휴를 즐기고 있기 때문이다. 그리고 그것은 오늘 있었던 어떠한 의미 있는 시장의 움직임도 의심스럽다는 것을 의미한다. 대형 자금이 2009년의 주식시장에 대해 어떻게 생각하는지 알아보려면 월요일까지 기다리는 게 낫다.

해설_ 빈칸 앞의 내용을 보면 대부분의 투자자들이 연휴를 즐기고 있기 때문에 오늘 있었던 투자 움직임만으로는 상황 파악이 힘들다고 나온다. 따라서 빈칸에는 (b)와 같이 월요일까지 기다리는 것이 낫다는 내용이 적합하다.

어휘_ be off 출발하다

significant 의미 있는

정답_ (b)

11.

해석_ 하와이의 한 커피 농장에서는 새로운 커피로 수익을 올리기를 기대하고 있다. 대통령 당선자 버락 오바마의 다국적 뿌리에 경의를 표하기 위해 하와이와 케냐, 인도네시아의 커피 원두를 부드럽게 혼합한 버락 오 블렌드가 바로 그것. 지금까지는 그것이 효과가 있는 것 같다. 아버지가 케냐인이었던 오바마는 하와이에서 태어나 수년간 인도네시아에서 살았다. 버락 오 블렌드에 대해 설명해달라고 하자 생산자는 "(맛이) 매우 풍부하고 마시기에 편합니다"라고 말했다. 독점의 이유 때문에 그는 커피의 정확한 혼합에 대해서는 밝히지 않았다.

해설_ 지문 중간에 보면 버락 오바마의 다국적 출신 성분에 대한 설명이 나온다.

어휘_ plantation (대규모) 농원, 재배지

perk up 올리다, 향상시키다

brew 달인 차 (커피 등)

medley 혼합

proprietary 독점적인

정답_ (d)

12.

해석_ 시위자들이 최근 가자 지구에서 자행된 이스라엘의 군사 공격에 항의하기 위해 시카고 시내에 모였다. 그 시위는 이스라엘의 가자 지구 공습에 대해 전 세계에서 일어난 최근의 많은 시위 가운데 하나였다. 유엔은 하마스 무장 단체에 대한 이스라엘의 공습에서 사망한 400명 이상의 팔레스타인 인 중 20%에서 25%가 민간인이었던 것으로 추정한다. 시카고의 많은 시위자들은 민간인들의 죽음을 비난했다. "죽는 것은 죄 없는 사람들일 뿐이다. 우리가 반대하는 것은 죄 없는 사람들을 죽이는 것이다"라고 몇 명의 학우와 함께 시위에 참가한 하마드 하크는 말했다.

해설_ 하마드 하크는 빈칸에서 앞에서 했던 말을 다시 부연하고 있다.

어휘_ turn out 모여들다, 떼지어 나서다

air strike 공습

decry 비난하다

정답_ (b)

13.

해석_ 과학자들은 집 근처에 있는 주류 판매점의 접근성과 17세 미만 청소년들의 음주 관계를 조사했다. 캘리포니아에서는 보통 주택가에서 100피트 또는 학교에서 600피트 내에서는 판매 면허를 내주지 않지만 접근성 자체는 면허를 거부하기에는 충분치 않다. 접근성 규정에 대한 더 많은 관심이 필요하며 청소년들이 상가에서 술을 구입할 기회를 억제하기 위한 환경적인 조정이 필요하다.

해설_ but이라는 역접 접속사가 있기 때문에 빈칸에는 그 앞의 내용과 반대되는 내용이 와야 한다. 마지막 문장을 보면 기존의 접근성 규정이 다소 허술하다는 것을 알 수 있는데 이것이 힌트가 된다.

어휘_ proximity 근접, 접근
　　　residence 거주지
　　　attention 주의, 관심
　　　intervention 조정, 개입
　　　curb 억제하다

정답_ (a)

14.

해석_ 일요일 밤 시애틀 지역에 내렸던 눈은 밤사이 비로 변해 오늘 주요 도로의 통행이 약간 지저분하게 되었지만 그렇게 미끄럽지는 않았다. 국립 기상 서비스에 따르면 총 1인치에서 3인치가 예상되었지만 5인치가 내렸다. 일부 지역에서는 더 많은 눈이 보고되었는데 예를 들면 시애틀 북쪽의 브로드뷰 부근에는 6인치가 쌓였다.

해설_ 눈이 쌓이던 것에 비가 뒤섞였다면 통행하기에 길이 지저분하긴 하겠지만 눈만 쌓였을 때보다는 덜 미끄러울 것이다.

어휘_ commute 통근
　　　messy 지저분한, 성가신

정답_ (d)

15.

해석_ 암트랙은 보유 열차 중 한 대가 남부 일리노이의 선로를 막고 있던 트랙터 트레일러와 부딪쳐서 9명의 승객과 한 명의 승무원이 다쳤다고 밝혔다. 암트랙의 대변인인 마크 마그리아리는 그 10명의 부상자들은 진단을 받기 위해 병원으로 이송되었지만 생명이 위독한 사람은 없다고 말했다. 매커핀 카운티의 보안관인 돈 알브레히트는 트럭 운전사가 월요일 오전 11시 15분경 교차로에서 꼼짝 못하고 있다가 세인트루이스에서 시카고로 가던 열차 소리를 듣고 차를 떠났다고 말했다.

해설_ 빈칸의 앞과 뒤는 문맥상 10명이 병원에 있지만 크게 다친 사람은 없다는 내용으로 빈칸에는 역접의 접속사가 적합하다.

어휘_ slam into ~에 꽝 부딪치다
　　　sheriff 보안관

정답_ (b)

16.

해석_ 라이언 캘러 상사는 작년 이라크에서 돌아왔을 때 사실상 오늘날 퇴역 군인이 겪을 수 있는 거의 모든 증상을 지닌 걸어다니는 게시판이었다. 그는 외상(外傷) 후 스트레스 장애와 외상 두뇌 부상이

라는 진단을 받았다. 그는 어디든 장전된 권총을 갖고 다녔다. 그는 필름이 끊길 때까지 술을 마셨고 자해를 하곤 했다. 그는 또한 담배로 자기 피부를 지지기도 했고, 단지 자신이 피 흘리는 것을 보기 위해 혀를 깨물기도 했다. 그러나 부모에 의해 강하게 떠밀려 서서히 카운슬링과 치료를 인정하고 받아들인 그는 이제 회복하기 시작했으며 그의 부모는 계속 노력하고 있다.

해설_ 빈칸 앞의 내용과 뒤의 내용이 상반된다.

어휘_ Sgt. 상사 (=Sergeant)
　　　billboard 광고판, 게시판
　　　affliction 고통, 불행
　　　veteran 퇴역 군인
　　　post-traumatic 외상(外傷) 후의
　　　loaded 장전한
　　　handgun 권총
　　　pass out 의식을 잃다

정답_ (a)

17.

해석_ LA 타임스, 시카고 트리뷴, 그리고 야구팀 시카고 컵스를 소유한 회사가 은행 및 다른 채권자들과의 120억 불에 달하는 부채에 관해 재협상을 시도하면서 파산 신청에 대한 가능성을 준비하고 있다고 트리뷴사의 중역이 일요일에 밝혔다. 내부 소식에 정통한 사람들이 회사가 여러 옵션을 탐색 중이라고 말했음에도 불구하고 그 시카고 언론 대기업은 가능한 파산 신청에 대한 조언을 구하기 위해 1주일 조금 전에 래저드사를 고용했다.

해설_ 윗글은 빚에 쪼들린 트리뷴사가 파산 신청을 고려하고 있다는 것으로서 (d)가 정답이며 (c)(트리뷴사를 둘러싼 어려운 재정적·경제적 상황)는 그 범위가 너무 넓어서 주제로 적합하지 않다.

어휘_ creditor 채권자
　　　conglomerate 대기업

정답_ (d)

18.

해석_ 교통 당국은 운전자들이 문자 메시지를 읽고 쓰거나 보내는 것을 불법으로 규정한 새 법률을 칭찬하면서도 휴대폰을 들고 이야기하는 것을 금지했던 작년 법안이 실제로 사고를 방지했는지에 대해 별 증거가 없다는 것을 인정하고 있다. 작년 7월부터 휴대폰을 들고 귀에다 가져가는 것이 교통 위반이 되면서 캘리포니아 고속도로 순찰대는 48,000장의 딱지를 끊었다. 그러나 그 법이 얼마나 효과적인지에 대해서는 아무도 알 수 없다.

해설_ 운전 중 휴대폰 사용을 금지한 법안의 효과에 대해 논란의 여

지가 있다는 내용이다.

어휘_ ban 금지(령)

　　　patrol 순찰(대)

　　　violation 위반

정답_ (d)

19.

해석_ 5만 명 이상이 참가한 장기간의 실험에서 비타민 C와 E 보충제가 전립선암과 폐암의 위험을 줄여주지 않는다는 새로운 증거가 나왔다. 최근의 다른 연구들은 의사의 처방 없이 구할 수 있는 비타민과 미네랄이 다른 암들, 뇌졸중 또는 심장 질환과 싸우는 데 아무런 도움을 주지 않는다는 것을 밝혀냈다. 연구에서는 심지어 어떤 상황 하에서는 보충제가 안전하지 않을 수 있다는 것도 알려주었다. 일부 의사들은 이제 그들의 환자들에게 그 약들에 신경 쓰지 말고 대신에 필요한 비타민과 미네랄을 공급하기 위해 건강식을 활용하라고 조언한다.

해설_ 윗글은 비타민 보충제가 기존의 생각처럼 암이나 다른 질병들과 싸우는 데 도움을 주지 않는다는 내용이다.

어휘_ trial 실험

　　　prostate 전립선(前立腺)의

　　　over-the-counter (약이) 의사의 처방 없이 팔 수 있는

　　　stroke 발작, 뇌졸중

　　　cardiovascular 심장 혈관의

　　　supplement 보충제

정답_ (b)

20.

해석_ 여러분은 더 이상 신문에서 식료품 쿠폰을 자를 필요가 없습니다! 온라인에서 출력 가능한 식료품 쿠폰으로 쉽게 절약을 시작하세요. 슈퍼마켓에 가기 전에 여기 쿨세이빙즈의 식료품 인쇄용 쿠폰 페이지를 방문하여 좋아하는 브랜드의 쿠폰을 선택하여 출력하세요. 매주 쿠폰이 바뀌며 총 50-100달러까지 절약할 수 있습니다. 이 쿠폰들을 놓치지 않도록 모든 쿠폰 페이지를 꼼꼼히 살펴보세요.

해설_ 윗글은 온라인상에서 출력 가능한 할인 쿠폰에 관한 이야기이다.

어휘_ printable 출력 가능한

정답_ (a)

21.

해석_ 이번 선거는 부시 대통령에게 관심의 대상이다. 그는 주간 라디오 연설에서 세계의 신흥 민주주의 국가들에게 좋은 예를 보여줄 수 있도록 국민들에게 투표에 참여할 것을 당부했다. "그루지아와 우크라이나부터 아프가니스탄과 이라크에 이르는 신흥 민주주의 국가들은 민주 정치가 지속될 수 있다는 증거로 미국을 보면 될 것입니다. 그리고 아직도 폭정과 억압에 시달리는 국가들도 자유에 대한 우리의 헌신을 통해 희망과 영감을 얻을 수 있을 것입니다." 부시 대통령은 부재자 투표를 통해 이미 투표권을 행사했다. 다른 주들이 줄을 서서 기다리고 있는 가운데 30개 이상의 주들이 선거일 전 조기 투표를 허용한다. 선거 전문가들은 투표율이 1960년 선거 이래 가장 높을 것으로 전망하고 있다.

해설_ 윗글은 부시 대통령이 주간 라디오 연설을 통해 국민에게 대통령 선거 투표 참여를 독려하는 것에 관한 글이다.

어휘_ draw the attention to ~의 주목을 끌다

　　　self-government 민주 정치

　　　tyranny 폭정

　　　oppression 억압

　　　cast a ballot 투표하다

　　　absentee 부재자

　　　voter turnout 유권자의 투표수

정답_ (a)

22.

해석_ 중국의 가장 추운 도시 중 하나인 하얼빈은 극도의 혹한을 매년 열리는 얼음과 눈 축제로 맞이하고 있다. 수백 개의 거대한 조각들이―중국 궁전에서부터 프랑스의 성당까지―매년 1월 그 도시의 결빙된 강에서 잘라낸 얼음 조각으로 만들어진다. 거의 백만 명의 사람들이 이번 달 얼음 작품들을 구경하러 올 것으로 예상된다.

해설_ 윗글은 중국의 한 도시의 얼음 축제에 관한 이야기이다.

어휘_ freeze 혹한

　　　cathedral 성당

　　　creation 작품

정답_ (c)

23.

해석_ 친애하는 젠킨스 여사에게,

저는 시카고에서 파리로 해외 근무지 승진 발령을 제의 받았습니다. 저의 새 직위에 대한 봉급은 현재 받고 있는 것보다 훨씬 높을 것이며 저는 항상 저희 회사의 프랑스 지점에서 일하기를 원했습니다만 파리 생활이 지금보다 돈이 훨씬 더 많이 들 것 같아 걱정이 됩니다. 만약 그러하다면 아마도 봉급이 인상된다 하더라도 별다른 차이가 나지 않을 것입니다. 저에게 파리의 생활비에 대해 알려주시겠습니까?

당신의 데니스 앨리스가

해설_ 윗글은 파리의 생활비에 대해 조언을 구하는 편지이다.

어휘_ promotion 승진

make a difference 차이가 있다, 효과가 있다

정답_ (d)

24.

해석_ 디지털 사진의 유연한 형태는 소비자들에게 혜택을 주어왔다. 이미지를 집에서 인쇄할 수 있고 그것들을 인터넷에 업로드하거나 잘 나온 사진을 휴대폰으로 엄마에게 보낼 수 있다. 어떤 카메라들은 물속에서 사진을 찍을 수도 있다. 그러나 디지털 시대에 카메라에서 사진을 직접 인쇄할 수 없었다.—60년도 더 전에 폴라로이드가 개발했던 기술. 이제는 바뀔 때가 되었다.

해설_ 마지막 부분에서 카메라에서 사진을 직접 인쇄할 수는 없었지만 바뀔 것이라고 했기에 윗글의 다음에서는 프린터가 내장된 디지털 카메라에 대해서 이야기할 것으로 예상된다.

어휘_ boon 혜택, 이익

built-in 내장된

정답_ (d)

25.

해석_ 첫째 딸이 나에게 무엇이 잘못되었는지 묻자 나는 내 몸에 대해 내가 행복하지 않다는 것을 깨달았다. 나는 옷방에서 (내 모습을 본) 이 날까지 그것에 대해 정말로 생각해본 적이 결코 없었다. 나는 무언가를 바꾸어야 한다는 것을 알았지만 어떻게 해야 할지는 확신이 없었다. 25파운드를 빼는 것은 생각보다는 쉬웠다. 나는 TV에서 보았던 2가지 식이요법 보충제를 혼합 이용하였으며, 체중을 빼기 위해 요즘 유행하는 식이요법은 이용하지 않았다. 결국 내가 한 모든 것은 간단한 두 단계의 과정이었으며 그것은 나의 인생을 영원히 바꾸었다. 1주일 후 나는 5파운드를 뺐고 한 달 후인 지금은 내 목표를 이루었고 기분은 날아갈 듯하다.

해설_ 옷방에서 자신의 모습을 본 날부터 다이어트를 생각하게 됐다는 내용이 있다.

어휘_ take into consideration 고려하다

combination 결합, 배합

정답_ (b)

26.

해석_ 2004년 중반 이후 보잉사에서의 최초 일자리 감소를 보여주는 최근 발표된 수치에 따르면 2008년의 마지막 2개월간 워싱턴 주의 보잉사 고용이 줄어들었다. 워싱턴 주의 전체 보잉 직원은 10월 말 76,869명에서 연말에는 76,417명으로 감소했다. 보잉은 감축에 대해 발표하지 않았으며 대부분의 감소는 장기 계약자를 내보낸 것으로 발생한 것 같다. 기계공 조합의 국제 협회 대변인인 코니 켈리허는 그 감축은 육체노동 부문에서 발생한 것이 아니라고 말했다.

해설_ 글의 후반부에서 대부분의 감원은 장기 계약자의 퇴사로 발생한 것으로 보인다는 내용이 힌트가 된다.

어휘_ slip 하락하다

machinist 기계 기술자, 기계공

blue-collar 육체 노동(자)의

정답_ (b)

27.

해석_ 9백만 불 이상의 예산 삭감을 앞두고 있는 주 정신 건강부는 심각한 정신 질환자들을 관리하고 그들이 필요한 서비스를 받을 수 있게 하는 병상 관리자의 1/4 정도를 해고했다. 약 100명의 병상 관리자가 해고 통지서를 받았거나 오늘 받을 것이다. 주 관리는 약 3,000명의 고객이 그들의 병상 관리자를 잃을 것이라고 말했다. 그 고객들은 남아 있는 350명의 다른 병상 관리자가 맡게 될 것이다.

해설_ 윗글의 첫 부분에 나오는 9백만 불 이상의 예산 삭감이 힌트가 된다.

어휘_ pink slip 해고 통지서

정답_ (c)

28.

해석_ 1800년대 중반 콜레라가 런던에 창궐했을 때 사람들은 그 병이 수증기에 의해 전염된다고 믿었다. 한 초기 유행병 학자는 그 병이 공기에 의해 전염될 것이라 예상한 경우 부합하지 않는 사례들을 밝혀냈다. 콜레라 희생자 사이의 공통적인 요소는 전염된 이웃과 사는 것이 아니라 특정한 공동 우물에서 물을 길어오는 것이었다. 콜레라는 이제 박테리아에 의해 발생하는 것으로 알려져 있으며 현대 수도관 형태의 위생은 선진국에서의 발병을 예방한다.

해설_ 글의 마지막 부분에서 "콜레라는 이제 박테리아에 의해 발생하는 것으로 알려져 있다"는 내용이 힌트가 된다.

어휘_ scourge 천벌, 재앙

vapor 증기, 수증기

epidemiologist 역학(疫學)자, 유행병 학자

plumbing 수도(관)

정답_ (a)

29.

해석_ 캘리포니아 의회는 온실가스를 줄이기 위한 국가의 첫 번째 광범위한 계획을 채택했다. 그 야심찬 청사진은 다음 12년 동안 주의 배기가스 배출을 15% 줄여 1990년도 수준으로 다시 떨어뜨린다는 것이다. 주 대기 자원 위원회에서 만장일치로 채택되어 자동차에서 빌딩, 산림 그리고 쓰레기 매립지까지 사실상 경제의 모든 영역을 대상으로 한다. 그 법안은 캘리포니아 전력의 3분의 1을 태양열, 풍력 그리고 다른 재생 가능한 자원으로부터 충당하도록 되어 있다.

해설_ 캘리포니아는 자원을 화석 연료보다는 재생 가능한 자원으로부터 얻을 계획이다.

어휘_ regulator 규정자, 단속자

　　　 slash 대폭적으로 인하[삭감]하다

　　　 unanimous 만장일치의

　　　 landfill 쓰레기 매립지

정답_ (b)

30.

해석_ 모리스 F. 콜린은 건강관리를 개선하기 위해 컴퓨터의 엄청난 힘을 이용하는 데 선구자이다. 그는 조제 약품이 장년층에게 영향을 주고 해를 입힐 수 있는 방법에 대해 연구하고 있다. 그는 6번째 책을 열심히 쓰고 있다. 그러나 그는 새로 딴 운전면허증이 훨씬 더 자랑스러울 것이다. "당신이 다시 보지 못할 것을 보여줄까요?" 라고 콜린이 물어보며 자신의 지갑을 잡았다. 그는 사각형 플라스틱을 꺼내며 생일을 가리켰다. 1913년 11월 20일. 그는 (면허) 만료 기간을 가리켰다. 2013년 11월 20일. 그는 웃었다. "앞의 것은 20세기이고, 뒤의 것은 21세기의 것이죠. 100년을 나타내죠."

해설_ 그의 생일과 면허증의 만기일이 100년 차이가 났던 것이지 그가 100년을 살았던 것은 아니다.

어휘_ harness 이용하다

　　　 interact 상호 작용하다, 서로 영향을 끼치다

　　　 billfold (둘로 접는) 지갑

　　　 rectangle 직사각형

　　　 grin 이를 드러내고 싱긋 웃다

정답_ (b)

31.

해석_ 오늘날 아이들은 개인 오디오 장치 때문에 소음으로 인한 청각 저하에 노출되어 있다. 휴대용 음악과 관련하여 큰 걱정거리는 사람들이 자주 헤드폰으로 너무 크게 듣는 것인데, 그것은 더욱 더 많이 청각 저하 문제를 일으킨다. 소아과 학회에 따르면 85데시벨에서 위험한 소음 수준이 시작된다고 여겨진다. 또한 음악을 듣는 시간의 길이도 문제가 되는데 아이들은 음량 수준에 관계없이 오랫동안 계속적으로 들어서는 안 된다.

해설_ consider나 deem은 둘 다 '간주하다' 의 의미로 85dB은 위험 수준의 시작이다.

오답 피하기_ (a) MP3 플레이어와 같은 기구로 인해 청각 저하 문제가 초래된다. (b) 새로운 헤드폰이 청각 저하를 막는다는 이야기는 없다.

어휘_ pediatric 소아과(학)의

　　　 threshold 문턱, 발단

　　　 stretch 연속된 시간

정답_ (c)

32.

해석_ 육군이 이라크와 아프가니스탄에서 사망한 병사들의 가족에게 "친애하는 아무개 씨" 라는 인사말로 편지를 보낸 후에 그들에게 공식적으로 사과를 했다. 12월에 육군은 2001년 이후 이라크와 아프가니스탄에서 전사한 3,544명의 병사의 가족에게 7,000장의 편지를 보냈다. 편지 봉투는 이름 표기가 잘 되었으나 소프트웨어 문제로 에러가 발생하여 인사말에 "친애하는 아무개" 라는 문구가 편지의 문두에 인쇄되었는데, 그것은 민간 기업이 인쇄한 것이다. 사과와 더불어, 육군 참모총장 조지 W. 케이시 주니어 장군은 가족들에게 실수를 설명하는 새로운 편지를 보낼 예정이다.

해설_ printed by a private contractor에서 인쇄를 민간 기업에서 했다는 것을 추론할 수 있다.

오답 피하기_ (a) 죽은 병사에게 사과한 것이 아닌 그 병사의 가족에게 사과한 것이다. (b) 3,500여 장이 아닌 7,000장을 보냈다.

어휘_ salutation (편지 서두의) 인사말

　　　 John Doe 아무개

　　　 address 주소를[성명을] 쓰다

　　　 Gen. 대장, 장성, 장군 (=General)

정답_ (d)

33.

해석_ 콘돌리자 라이스 미 국무부 장관은 중동 평화 협상을 진전시키기 위한 새로운 외교적 움직임 중에 이스라엘 외무장관과 회담을 가졌다. 라이스와 치피 리브니의 만남은 이스라엘이 서안 지구의 정착촌 확대 계획을 승인한 이후 이뤄졌는데, 미국은 이것이 "도움이 되지 않는다" 고 단언했다. 리브니의 워싱턴 방문은 하마스가 다스리는 가자 지구에서 이스라엘과 팔레스타인 사이의 전투가 소강된 다음에 이어진 것이다. 딕 체니 미국 부통령 역시 곧 이 지역을 방문할 예정이다. 회담 전에 조지 W. 부시 미 대통령은 내년 1월 임기를 마

치기 전에 중동 평화 협정이 맺어질 것을 여전히 낙관적한다고 말했다.

해설_ 제시된 여러 인물들 중 조지 W. 부시 대통령은 제일 뒤에 나온다. 그가 여전히 낙관적이라고 견해를 표하는 것은 평화 정착을 희망한다고 보아야 한다.

오답 피하기_ (c) 부통령은 예루살렘이 아닌 가자 지구의 정착촌을 방문할 예정이다. 따라서 틀렸다.

어휘_ settlement 촌락, 부락

　　　 follow ~의 뒤에 일어나다

　　　 lull 진정, 소강

정답_ (d)

34.

해석_ GM은 미국 밖에서 더 큰 존재감을 가지고 있으며 이곳보다 다른 나라에서 더 많은 직원을 고용하고 실제로 상파울루에서 상하이까지 해외에서 차를 팔며 돈을 벌고 있다. GM의 미국 수입은 지난 3년간 24% 줄어들었지만 세계의 다른 나라에서 GM은 28%의 수익 증가를 자랑한다. 현재 미국의 입법자들이 디트로이트에 기반을 둔 회사 GM의 붕괴를 막기 위해 수십억 불을 대출해줄지에 대해 숙고하고 있는 이때, GM의 해외 개척은 여러 면에서 가장 간과된 자산이며 궁극적인 생존의 열쇠가 되었다.

해설_ 윗글은 GM의 생존 또는 파산을 피하기 위한 방법은 해외 시장에 있다는 내용이다.

어휘_ revenue 수입, 소득

　　　 mull 숙고하다

　　　 boast 자랑하다

정답_ (b)

35.

해석_ 종합격투기가 점점 더 많은 관객들을 끌어 모으고 네바다, 캘리포니아, 일리노이, 그리고 뉴저지를 포함한 여러 주에서 규제하는 안전 규칙을 채택하면서 상당한 진전을 이루었지만 수년 동안 그 스포츠의 폭력성에 대한 비판은 여전히 남아 있다. 존 매케인의 고향인 애리조나는 9월까지 프로 종합격투기를 허가하지 않았으며, 뉴욕은 여전히 그 스포츠를 금지하고 있다. "그런 것들을 보고 있노라면 터프한 남자 콘테스트로밖에 안 보인다"라고 복싱 프로모션 회사 톱 랭크의 회장 토드 드뵈프는 말했다.

해설_ (b) 지문에 미국 내에서 종합격투기에 대한 비판이 있다는 내용이 있다. (c) 애리조나는 9월까지 프로 종합격투기를 허용하지 않았다는 내용이 있기에 그 이후에는 허용했을 것이라는 추측이 가능하다.

어휘_ Mixed Martial Arts 종합격투기

　　　 strides 진보, 발전

　　　 lingering 여전히 남아 있는

정답_ (b)

36.

해석_ 북아메리카에서 최근 발견된 극소형 다이아몬드들은 13,000여 년 전 혜성이 불, 홍수, 황폐화의 대변동을 발생시켜 매머드를 멸종시켰음을 나타낸다고 과학자들이 말했다. 그 나노 다이아몬드들은 혜성의 잔해물로 사료되는데, 그 혜성은 공룡을 멸종시켰던 훨씬 더 큰 충돌이 있은 지 약 6,500만 년 후에 부딪쳤던 것이었다. 그 이론에 의하면 혜성이 떨어져나가면서 대륙 전체에 불꽃이 내려 평원과 숲들을 불태우고 숨막히는 연기층을 만들어냈다.

해설_ 지문 중간에서 나노 다이아몬드가 혜성의 remnant, 즉 '잔해물'이라고 했기에 혜성 충돌의 결과나 영향이라고 봐야 한다.

오답 피하기_ 혜성 충돌은 공룡의 멸망 이후의 일이다.

어휘_ microscopic 극히 작은, 초소형의

　　　 comet 혜성

　　　 cataclysm 지각 변동, 대변동

　　　 devastation 유린, 황폐

　　　 remnant 나머지, 찌꺼기

　　　 ignite ~에 불을 붙이다, 태우다

　　　 choking 숨막히는

정답_ (d)

37.

해석_ 아메리칸 리그 챔피언 탬파베이 레이스는 관심을 표명한 한 팀이라고 그리피의 에이전트인 브라이언 골드버그가 SI.com에게 말했다. 지난해 그리피의 친구 한 명은 앞으로 명예의 전당에 오를 그(그리피)가 올란도 집에서 두 시간 이내의 거리인 탬파 베이에서 뛰고 싶어 할 것이라고 말했다. 그리피가 레이스의 (스카우트) 명단에 있긴 하지만 바비 어브레유와 팻 버렐 같은 좀더 젊은 두 명의 타자가 (그리피보다) 우위에 있을 것이다. 그리피의 다른 가능한 종착지는 메이저리그 경력을 시작했던 시애틀이 될 수 있다. 팀을 재건중인 매리너스는 그리피를 그들의 젊은 선수들을 도와주고 팬을 끌어 모으는 수단으로 볼 수도 있는 것이다.

해설_ 그리피와 같은 베테랑 선수들은 선수 경력의 말년을 고향 근처의 팀에서 뛰길 원하는 경우가 많다. 지문에도 그가 올란도에 있는 자신의 집과 가까운 탬파에서 뛰길 원한다는 내용이 있다.

어휘_ Hall of Famer 명예의 전당에 든 사람

　　　 aid 조력자, 보조자

draw (인기나 사람을) 끄는 것

정답_ (b)

38.

해석_ 비행기가 항공모함의 갑판에서 이륙했을 때, 조종사는 아마도 비행기의 엔진 중 하나에 고장이 나서 자신이 곤경에 처했다는 것을 재빨리 알았다. (a) 그는 미라마의 해병대 기지국의 항공 관제사와 교신을 했는데, 항공 관제사는 비상 착륙을 하라고 명령했다. (b) 비행기가 미라마로 가는 도중에 토리 파인스 상공을 가로지를 때 두 번째 엔진의 "연소 정지"를 포함하여 더 많은 문제가 터졌다. (c) 100명 이상의 소방관들이 몇 분 내에 해병대의 추락 전문가들과 함께 현장에 도착했다. (d) 몇 초 내에 그 비행기는 급강하해 엄마, 할머니 그리고 두 아이가 살고 있던 캐더 가의 한 집에 내리꽂혔다.

해설_ 소방관들이 비행기 추락 전에 추락 현장에 도착하는 일은 불가능하다.

어휘_ lift off 이륙하다

carrier 항공모함

en rout to ~로 가는 도중에

flame out (제트 엔진의 갑작스런) 연소 정지

smash into 세게 충돌하다

정답_ (c)

39.

해석_ 매섭도록 차가운 폭풍이 북동부 지역을 휩쓸어 도로를 두꺼운 얼음으로 덮고 전선을 내려앉힌 후에 그 지역의 100만 가구 이상이 하루 종일 전기 없이 보냈다. (a) 일부 지역에서는 눈이 녹기 시작했다. (b) 지난밤 그 지역에 강하게 불기 시작한 폭풍은 학교와 공공 기관의 문을 닫게 했고 매사추세츠와 메인 주로 가는 교통을 두절시켰다. (c) 모든 지역이 전기가 나갔다. (d) 주민들은 양초와 장작을 태우면서 춥고 어두운 주말을 준비하며 집 안에서 하루를 보냈고, 한편 다른 이들은 가정용 발전기 연료를 실어오기 위해 주유소로 달려갔다.

해설_ 아직 날씨가 추운데 눈이 녹기 시작했다는 이야기는 어울리지 않는다.

어휘_ gust (바람이) 갑자기 강하게 불다

travel 왕래, 교통

frigid 몹시 추운

scramble 허둥지둥 가다

generator 발전기

정답_ (a)

40.

해석_ 평면 TV는 큰 단점을 가지고 있다. 에너지를 많이 먹는다는 것이다. (a) 주 의회는 판매자들에게 에너지 효율이 가장 좋은 모델만 팔도록 요구함으로써 TV의 증가하는 에너지 소모를 제한하기 위한 준비를 하고 있다. (b) 가전 산업은 그 규정에 반대하며 가게 진열대에서 일부 TV를 치우고 소비자 가격을 조금 올릴 수도 있다고 주장하고 있다. (c) 그러나 캘리포니아 에너지 위원회는 전기망의 과도한 부담을 덜 방법을 모색하고 있다. (d) 그것은 판매업을 망칠 것인데, 사람들이 아마존에서 물건을 사고 배송을 요청하며 판매세를 내지 않을 것이기 때문이다.

해설_ 판매망이나 인터넷 구매, 판매세와 지문의 내용과는 관계가 없다.

어휘_ hog 돼지, 욕심꾸러기

gluttony 폭식

strain 큰 부담, 과중

power grid 전기망

정답_ (d)

Final Test 02

1.

해석_ 세상에 공짜 점심은 없지만 앤호이저 부시 테마 공원에서는 공짜 맥주를 항상 기대할 수 있었다. 지금까지는 말이다. 그 양조업자는 올란도와 샌안토니오, 샌디에이고의 씨월드 고객 센터에서 공짜 맥주 제공을 그만두었다. 앤호이저 부시 어드벤쳐 공원의 대변인 프레드 제이콥스는 공짜 맥주가 일부 공원 고객에게만 효과가 있었다고 말한다. 제조자는 아이들이 있는 가족들을 겨냥한 식당을 더 많이 지을 계획이다. 고객들은 여전히 일부 공원에서 맥주를 구입할 수 있다.

해설_ 빈칸 뒤에 공짜 맥주가 일부 고객에게만 효과가 있었다는 내용과 식당을 더 건설한다는 내용이 있다.

어휘_ count on 기대하다
brewer 맥주 양조(업)자
hospitality 환대, 접대
geared toward ~에 맞춘, ~를 대상으로 한

정답_ (a)

2.

해석_ 만약 당신이 크리스마스 선물로 새로운 휴대폰을 선물 받는다면 헌 휴대폰을 어디에다 버릴지 찾아보라. 미국 환경 보호청은 휴대폰 재활용을 위해 버스에 일련의 광고를 게재했는데, 매년 20% 이하의 휴대폰만이 재활용되기 때문이다. 휴대폰은 값진 금속들, 동, 플라스틱으로 만들어진다. EPA에 따르면 백만 대의 휴대폰을 재활용하는 것만으로 1,368대의 차가 일 년 동안 도로에 내뿜는 만큼의 온실가스 배출을 줄여준다.

해설_ 재활용을 위한 광고를 게재하는 이유는 휴대폰 재활용 실적이 낮기 때문일 것이다.

어휘_ drop off 떨어뜨려 놓다
copper 구리, 동(銅)

정답_ (d)

3.

해석_ 샌프란시스코의 게이바 11곳이 리신으로 공격하겠다고 위협하는 편지를 받았다. 익명의 편지들에는 "나는 약 67그램의 리신을 가지고 있으며 당신의 고객 중 최소 5명을 무작위로 공격할 것이다. 나는 그들이 병원에서 고통스럽게 죽어갈 것이라고 예상한다"고 씌어 있었다. 샌프란시스코 경찰서는 그 위협을 심각하게 생각한다고 말했다. 경찰은 편지를 압수해서 조사하고 있으며 FBI 및 다른 연방 기관들과 공동으로 노력하고 있다. 미국 질병 통제 및 예방 센터는 리신은 섭취하거나 흡입 시 치명적일 수 있는 독이라고 밝혔다.

해설_ 빈칸 뒤에서 "경찰이 편지를 압수해서 조사하고 있으며 FBI

및 다른 연방 기관들과 공동으로 노력하고 있다"는 내용이 있기에 빈칸에는 "그 위협을 심각하게 생각한다"는 내용의 (a)가 적합하다.

어휘_ ricin 리신 (피마자에서 채취한 백색의 유독한 단백질 가루)
anonymous 익명의
indiscriminately 무차별적으로
seize 압수하다
ingest 섭취하다
inhale 흡입하다

정답_ (a)

4.

해석_ 눈이 무릎까지 차올라 몇 발자국 걷기조차 힘들었다. 바람은 그의 (몸의) 균형을 흔들었고 내리치는 눈은 그의 숨을 차게 했다. 그는 눈 속을 뚫고 앞으로 나아가며 언덕을 내려갔다. 그의 몸 전체는 꽁꽁 얼었다. 그의 발은 다른 사람의 발처럼 느껴졌다. 그 아래에는 하얀 땅밖에 보이지 않았다. 눈이 모든 것을 뒤덮었다. 그는 아웃사이드 몰이 언덕 밑에 있다는 것을 기억했지만 그의 눈에 보이는 것은 눈뿐이었다.

해설_ 빈칸 뒤에 "눈이 모든 것을 뒤덮었다"는 문장이 있기에 "하얀 땅" 밖에 보이지 않았다는 내용이 적합하다.

어휘_ suffocate 숨이 막히게 하다
wade 힘들여 나아가다

정답_ (d)

5.

해석_ 미국은 북한이 시리아가 "평화 목적이 아닌" 원자로를 건설하는 것을 돕고 있다고 비난했다. 북한에 있는 장소와 유사하다고 전해지는 이곳은 2007년 이스라엘의 폭격을 당했다. CIA 관리들이 의회에 브리핑한 이후 백악관은 성명을 통해 시리아는 비밀 핵 프로그램에 대해 "실토해야" 한다고 말했다.

해설_ 문맥상 시리아는 핵 개발을 공개하고 포기해야 한다는 내용이 들어가야 적합하다.

어휘_ accuse A of B B에 대해 A를 비난하다
nuclear reactor 원자로
come clean 실토하다, 사실을 말하다

정답_ (b)

6.

해석_ 적십자 국제 위원회는 가자 지구의 산산이 부서진 집들에서 최소 15명의 시체를 발견했다고 말하며 이스라엘이 그 지역으로 가려는 앰뷸런스들을 막았다고 비난했다. 적십자 관계자는 구조원들

이 그 집들에 사상자가 있다는 구체적인 정보를 받고 그 지역으로 앰뷸런스들을 보내려 했었으나 이스라엘 군이 허락하지 않았다고 말했다. 제네바 본부에서 발표한 이례적인 공식 성명에서 적십자는 그 사건을 "용납할 수 없다"면서 이스라엘 군이 "국제 인도법에 따라 부상자를 치료하고 후송해야 할 의무를 저버렸다"고 말했다.

해설_ 빈칸 뒤의 내용은 이스라엘이 가자 지구의 사상자를 구출하려는 앰뷸런스를 허락하지 않았다는 내용이다.

어휘_ shattered 산산이 부서진

casualties 사상자

obligation 의무

humanitarian 인도주의의, 박애(주의)의

evacuate (부상병 등을) 후송시키다

정답_ (b)

7.

해석_ 주가는 폭락하고 있고 신용 시장은 경색되어 있다. 이는 공장 주문의 하락으로 인해 뜻밖의 신규 실업 수당 신청 건수가 증가하고 있다는 소식에 따른 것이다. 하원이 상원에 이어 개정된 구제 금융 법안을 통과시킨다 하더라도 이 모든 것이 경제가 직면한 문제들을 강조하고 있다. 경제학자 마크 랜지는 경제적인 압박이 고용 시장을 긴장시키고 있다고 말한다. "금융 위기에 대한 공포가 사업가들의 확신을 무너뜨려 이제 직원들을 해고하고 있습니다. 그리고 수천 수백만 개의 일자리가 없어지는 것을 지금부터 내년 초까지 보게 될 것입니다."

해설_ 빈칸 앞쪽에 they're now laying off workers가 힌트가 된다.

어휘_ tumble (가격이) 폭락하다

unemployment claim 실업 수당 청구

the House 하원

the Senate 상원

reworked 개정된

bailout bill 구제금융 법안

정답_ (d)

8.

해석_ 버락 오바마가 11월 4일 선거에서 승리한 이후에 미국 경제는 더 높은 실업률, 추락하는 소비자 지출, 그리고 마이너스 성장에 대한 추후 판단으로 심각하게 후퇴했다. 경기 후퇴(악화)는 다음과 같은 의문을 떠오르게 한다. 나빠지고 있는 환경이 차기 대통령으로 하여금 선거 운동 기간 중에 내놓았던 경제 전략을 버리고 새로운 전략을 짜게 할 것인가?

해설_ 빈칸 뒤에서 높은 실업률, 추락하는 소비자 지출의 내용이 나오기에 빈칸에는 경제가 심각하게 후퇴했다는 내용이 와야 한다.

어휘_ plunge 떨어지다, 추락하다

retrogression (경기) 후퇴

jettison 내던지다, 버리다

formulate 조직적으로 세우다

정답_ (c)

9.

해석_ 부시 대통령은 주간 라디오 연설에서 구제 금융에 투입되는 7천억 달러의 대부분을 손실로 보고 있지 않다고 말했다. "정부가 구입할 자산의 상당 부분이 매우 잠재적 가치를 지니고 있습니다. 시간이 흐름에 따라 그 가치는 상승할 것이고 이는 정부가 본래 지출의 전부는 아니더라도 상당량을 되찾을 수 있다는 것을 의미합니다." 부시 대통령은 구제 금융 법안이 하원을 통과한 뒤 바로 법안에 서명했다.

해설_ 빈칸 뒤에서 부시 대통령이 구제 금융이 투자된 자산의 가치가 상승할 것이라고 말한 내용이 힌트가 된다.

어휘_ underlying 잠재적인

the House 하원

recoup (손실 등을) 되찾다

정답_ (c)

10.

해석_ 베스트셀러인 지프렉사, 리스페달, 그리고 세로퀼을 포함한 일반적으로 널리 사용되는 항정신성 약들은 치명적인 심장마비를 초래할 수 있다고 연구자들이 말했다. 오래된 믿음과는 달리 그 연구 결과는 이러한 종류의 약에 대한 비판을 들끓게 한다. 지프렉사, 리스페달, 그리고 세로퀼은 세계에서 가장 일반적으로 처방되는 10개의 약에 속하며 일 년 판매액은 145억 불에 달한다.

해설_ 기존에 많이 이용되었던 약품에 대해 비판이 들끓는다고 했기에, 빈칸에는 기존의 믿음과 상반된다는 내용이 들어가야 한다.

어휘_ antipsychotic 항(抗)정신병성(性)의

drumbeat 요란한 주의[주장]

add to 가중시키다

정답_ (b)

11.

해석_ 하루에 8시간 이하로 잔 사람들이 8시간 이상 잔 사람들보다 감기에 걸릴 확률이 거의 3배가 높다는 새로운 연구 결과가 나왔다. 수면의 질은 양보다 훨씬 더 중요하다고 그 연구는 밝혔다. 25분 정

도 잠을 뒤척이는 사람들은 코를 훌쩍이고 재채기할 확률이 5배 이상이 된다. 잠을 잘 자야 한다는 옛말은 의학 연구로 잘 뒷받침된다.

해설_ 빈칸 뒤에서 잠을 잘 못 자는 사람들은 코를 훌쩍거리고 재채기를 할 확률이 높다는 내용이 힌트가 된다.

어휘_ toss and turn (잠을 이루지 못해 몸을) 뒤척거리다

sniffle 코를 훌쩍이다

sneeze 재채기하다

age-old 옛날부터의

정답_ (a)

12.

해석_ 건즈 앤 로지스의 리드 보컬은 닥터 페퍼가 그의 밴드와 그들의 신보로 이익을 취하고 있다고 말한다. 닥터 페퍼의 제조 회사는 몇 달 전 건즈 앤 로지즈가 오랫동안 연기해온 앨범을 올해 발매하면 전 미국인에게 무료 음료를 제공한다고 말했다. 건즈 앤 로지즈의 변호사는 밴드는 약속을 지켰지만 닥터 페퍼 측은 약속을 어겼다고 말한다. 소비자들에게 무료 음료를 제공하던 일요일 24시간 동안 닥터 페퍼의 홈페이지는 다운되어 버렸다. 이 날은 'Chinese Democracy'의 발매일과 같은 날이다. 지금까지 닥터 페퍼는 이 록 밴드의 불만에 대응하지 않고 있다.

해설_ 문맥상 건즈 앤 로지스는 약속을 지켰지만 닥터 페퍼는 그러지 않았다는 내용이 적합하다.

어휘_ profit from ~로 이익을 얻다

overdue 늦어진

crash 갑자기 기능을 멈추다, 다운되다

정답_ (a)

13.

해석_ 제너럴 모터스의 프리츠 헨더슨 사장은 사업을 유지시키기 위한 절차를 밟고 있으며 여기에는 회사 규모 축소도 포함된다고 말했다. "우리는 우리가 처한 환경에 대응해야 하며, 그에 대한 일환으로 지금과 같은 어려운 경제 환경에 대처하기 위해 회사의 규모를 크게 변화시켜야만 합니다." 헨더슨 사장은 CBS 얼리쇼(Early Show)에서 이와 같은 모든 변화에도 불구하고 GM이 생존하기 위해서는 수십억 달러가 필요하다고 말했다. 월 스트리트의 오전 거래장에서는 다우 지수가 172포인트 하락했다.

해설_ 빈칸 뒤에 회사의 규모를 크게 변화시켜야 한다는 내용이 있기에 빈칸에는 구조 조정 등의 내용이 나와야 한다.

어휘_ take steps 조치를 취하다

address 다루다, 처리하다

정답_ (a)

14.

해석_ 버락 오바마 대통령 당선인은 민주당 경선 경쟁자였던 힐러리 클린턴을 국무 장관에 임명할 것이라고 한다. 큰 장애물이었던 빌 클린턴 전 대통령의 국제 재단 문제가 해결되었다. 클린턴 전 대통령은 많은 기부자들이 자신의 신원이 밝혀지지 않는다는 조건 하에 기부를 했다고 말하며 자신의 재단 기부자들의 신원을 밝히기를 오랫동안 거부해왔다. 클린턴 전 대통령은 이제 기부자들이 누구인지 밝히기로 했으며, 자신의 아내가 오바마 정권에서 일하는 동안 일상적인 재단 운영에서 물러나 있겠다고 말했다.

해설_ 빈칸 앞에 큰 장애물인 빌 클린턴 국제 재단이 나오고 결국 그 장애물이 제거 또는 해결되었다는 내용이 나온다.

어휘_ name 지명하다, 임명하다

Secretary of State 국무부 장관

disclose 공개하다

identity 신원, 정체

step away from 물러나다

정답_ (a)

15.

해석_ 러시아의 천연가스 독점은 우여곡절 끝에 우크라이나를 경유하여 유럽으로 가는 (가스 공급) 흐름을 차단해서 혹독한 겨울 동안의 연료 부족 우려를 심화시켰다. 유럽 연합의 경고에도 불구하고 가즈프롬(러시아의 국영 에너지 회사)과 우크라이나 사이의 심각한 가격 논쟁은 가스 공급이 축소된 이후에도 잦아들 징조가 보이지 않았다. 두 당사자가 서로 비난하면서 6일 동안 협상은 결렬된 상태다.

해설_ 빈칸 앞뒤의 문맥을 살펴보면 "~에도 불구하고, ~을 무릅쓰고"의 뜻을 가진 despite가 적절하다.

어휘_ monopoly 독점

dramatically 극적으로

sharpen 더욱 심하게 하다

tense 팽팽한

dwindle 줄어들다, 감소하다

let up 그만두다, 가라앉다

accusation 비난

정답_ (a)

16.

해석_ 차량 내부의 위성 TV는 지금까지는 정말 형편없어서 가로등이 신호를 막을 때마다 그림과 소리가 멈추었다. 이 효과를 집에서 재현하려면 1분에 20번 정도 TV의 일시 정지 버튼을 누르면 된다. 그러나 AT&T CruiseCast의 새로운 시스템은 큰 발전을 이루었다.

차량 테스트 시연에서 라스베이거스 인근을 운전하는 중 생방송 케이블 채널이 거의 끊김 없이 방영되었다. 그 시스템은 인터넷 상에서 패킷 변환과 유사한 버퍼 통제를 사용하여 (신호기) 잠시 막혔을 때에도 채널의 방송을 가능하게 유지한다.

해설_ 빈칸의 앞과 뒤가 상반된 내용이기에 빈칸에는 역접의 접속사가 와야 한다.

어휘_ a disaster 엉망진창인 것

light pole 가로등

duplicate 되풀이하다, 다시 하다

seamlessly 고르게, 끊김 없이

momentarily 일시적으로

regimen 관리, 통제

정답_ (b)

17.

해석_ 미국 자동차업계가 빅 3 구조에서 빅 2 구조로 재편될 것이라는 소문이 돌고 있다. 제너럴 모터스와 크라이슬러는 합병 또는 GM이 크라이슬러를 인수하는 거래에 관한 예비 회의를 가졌다. 자동차 분석가 링컨 메리휴는 어떤 계약이 체결되든 간에 막대한 비용이 따를 것이라고 말한다. "공장을 폐쇄시킨다든가 하는 일에는 비용이 들지요. 종업원의 수를 줄이는 것도 돈이 들어갑니다. 직원들에게 돈을 주고 해고해야 할 수도 있어요. 브랜드를 없애거나 대리점을 철수시키는 이런 모든 것에는 비용이 발생합니다."

해설_ 윗글은 미국 자동차업계의 빅 3에 속하는 GM과 크라이슬러의 합병에 관한 이야기이다.

어휘_ preliminary 예비의, 준비의

merger 합병

buy out 돈을 주고 포기하게[손떼게] 하다

정답_ (b)

18.

해석_ 실제 보험 납부액은 구입한 보험 금액과 여타 요인에 따라 다를 것입니다. 30,000달러는 2개의 방을 가진 일반적인 아파트의 개인 자산 가치에 관한 대강의 국가적 견적입니다. 실제 가치는 다를 것입니다. 보험은 보상이 제한되거나 제외되는 손해 유형과 개인 재산을 포함해 유효성, 자격 그리고 보험 증권 약관에 따라 결정됩니다. 보다 상세한 사항에 관해서는 여러분의 보험 증권을 읽어보시기 바랍니다.

해설_ 윗글은 보험료와 보험의 보장 범위에 관한 간략한 글이다.

어휘_ premium 보험료

rounded 대강의

availability 유효성

exclusion 제외, 배제

policy 보험 증권

정답_ (b)

19.

해석_ 친애하는 여러분,

제가 여기까지 오는 것은 험난한 여정이었으며 저는 사람들을 위한 봉사에 대해 충심으로 믿음을 가지고 있었지만, 최선에는 못 미친 게 사실입니다. 심지어 저의 큰 실수를 되돌릴 수는 없지만 진심으로 일을 바로잡고 싶으며, 이러한 생각을 공개하고 공유함으로써 여러분의 마음에 믿음을 복구하고 싶습니다. 제가 이 장소까지 오는 데는 시간이 걸렸지만 결국 저의 목표는 아무리 늦더라도 해야 할 일을 하는 것이며 저의 말이 그들의 정부와 다른 이들에 대한 사람들의 믿음을 회복하는 치료 과정에 도움이 되기를 소망합니다.

당신의 존 피츠제럴드가

해설_ 윗글은 어떤 실수에 대해 충심으로 사과하는 내용이 담긴 글이다.

어휘_ undo (일단 해버린 것을) 원 상태로 돌리다

blunder 큰 실수, 터무니없는 실책

tardy 늦은

정답_ (c)

20.

해석_ 여러분이 이곳에 커피를 주문하기 위해 오셨든 저희 지점 중 한 곳을 마지막으로 방문했던 것에 대해 이야기하기 위해 오셨든 DunkinDonuts.com을 방문할 때마다 즐거우시길 바랍니다. 그러니 안심하세요. 여러분의 이메일 주소에서부터 여러분이 가장 좋아하는 도넛까지 여러분이 저희와 공유하는 모든 정보는 여러분의 신용카드 번호와 다른 주문 및 배송 정보를 암호화하는 산업-표준 보안 소프트웨어를 이용하여 안전하게 보호될 것입니다. 던킨 도너츠는 이 개인 정보 정책을 어느 때라도 변경할 수 있는 권리를 보유하고 있습니다. 업데이트를 위해 이 페이지를 정기적으로 체크하시기 바랍니다.

해설_ 윗글은 DunkinDonuts.com의 개인 정보 정책에 관하여 고객에게 알리는 글이다.

어휘_ rest assured 안심하고 있다

encrypt 암호화하다

reserve 보유하다

periodically 주기적으로, 정기적으로

정답_ (c)

21.

해석_ 이 특별한 "아웃백 에어패스" 상품을 구매하기 위해서는 콴타스 베이케이션스와 함께하는 노던 테리토리에서 3일 밤의 숙박을 예약해야 합니다. 아웃백 에어패스는 다음의 오지 지역 중 최소 1구역을 방문하는 것을 포함합니다. 다윈, 에어즈 록, 앨리스 스프링즈가 그곳입니다. 좌석은 엄격하게 제한됩니다. 앨리스 스프링즈 사막 공원이나 다윈의 야생 공원에 무료 어른 입장 티켓은 아웃백 에어패스 상품의 일부이며 먼저 예약한 100분에게만 제공됩니다. 입장 티켓은 2009년 8월 31일까지 유효합니다. 야생 공원 티켓의 선택은 제한되며 선착순으로 지급될 것입니다. 현재의 가격을 아시려면 전화 주십시오.

해설_ 이 글은 여행 상품의 각종 조건에 대하여 고객에게 설명하는 글이다.

어휘_ outback (호주의 미개척의) 오지(奧地)

　　　　strictly 엄격하게

　　　　complimentary 무료의

　　　　promotion 판매 촉진용 상품

　　　　booking 예약

　　　　first-come basis 선착순

정답_ (c)

22.

해석_ 신체의 어떤 조직도 될 수 있는 잠재력을 지닌 배아 줄기 세포를 복제하기 위해 인간의 피부 세포가 두 과학자 단체에 의해 재구성되었다. 이번의 중대한 발전은 많은 질병의 새로운 치료법을 찾아내는 데 사용될 세포들을 풍부하게 공급해줄 새로운 원천이 될 것으로 보인다. 결정적으로, 이번 발견은 이러한 연구가 상당한 논란의 여지가 있는 것으로 밝혀진 인간 배아의 세포에 더 이상 의존하지 않아도 된다는 것을 의미할 수도 있다.

해설_ Crucially 뒤에서 더 이상 인간 배아의 세포에 의존하지 않아도 된다고 했으니 지금까지는 인간 배아의 세포에 의존했다는 것이 사실이다.

어휘_ mimic 복제하다

　　　　embryonic stem cells 배아 줄기 세포

　　　　breakthrough 비약적 발전, 눈부신 발견

　　　　controversial 논의의 여지가 있는

정답_ (a)

23.

해석_ "정통한 소식통"이라는 사람의 말을 인용하여 남한의 연합 뉴스는 북한의 지도자 김정일이 3남 중 막내인 김종운에게 결국 북한의 정권을 맡겼다고 최근 보도했다. 바로 이틀 전에는 김정일의 장남인 김정남을 단지 명목상의 국가 원수로 하여 집단 지도 체제가 구성될 것이라고 일본의 한 일간지가 보도했다. 북한은 세계에서 가장 비밀스러운 국가 중 하나이기에 그 보도들을 확인할 방법은 없다. 그리고 평양의 공식 선전을 모니터해온 분석가들은 후계가 정해졌다는 어떠한 변화도 발견하지 못했다.

해설_ 김정일의 막내 아들 또는 장남이 후계자로 결정되었다는 등 여러 소식이 있지만 그것을 확인할 길이 없기 때문에 지금 현재로서 답은 (d)가 적합하다.

어휘_ verify 입증하다

　　　　propaganda 선전 (활동)

　　　　successor 후계자

정답_ (d)

24.

해석_ 운동 프로그램의 첫 번째 주에 사람들은 결심이 실천보다 훨씬 쉽다는 것을 알게 될 것이다. 많은 이들은 이미 그들의 운동 목표에 대해 머뭇거리며 아침이나 저녁의 추위에 맞서는 것이 어렵다는 것을 알게 된다. 운동 프로그램을 시작하는 4부분 중 둘째 주에 우리는 전 올림픽 출전자이며 현 미국 사이클 국가 대표팀 코치인 데이빗 브리튼으로부터 도움을 얻었다. 그는 프로처럼 운동하고 초보자가 체력 소모를 피하는 방법을 알려주며 그 과정을 쉽게 할 수 있는 몇 가지 도구들을 제안한다.

해설_ 윗글의 후반부에 한 전문가가 운동하는 방법을 알려준다는 내용이 있다.

어휘_ falter 주춤하다, (용기가) 꺾이다

　　　　elite 선발된, 정예의

　　　　burnout 극도의 피로, (심신의) 소모

정답_ (d)

25.

해석_ 월동 준비를 위해 내 차를 손보던 주유소 직원은 타이어를 갈아야 하며 그 비용은 500달러 정도 될 것인데 자기가 그 일을 하면 기쁠 것이라고 말했다. 나는 여분의 500달러가 없었다. 그리고 만약 그 돈이 있다 하더라도 가장 불만족스러운 구매는 자동차 부품일 것이다. 내가 타이어에 돈을 쓰기 싫다면 당신도 그러하리라 확신한다. 그래서 나는 당신을 위해 이런 고약한 상황을 되도록 스트레스 안 받고 비용 효과적으로 대처할 수 있게 도와줄까 한다.

해설_ 보통 지문 뒤에 어떤 내용이 나올 것인지 추정하는 문제는 그 지문의 하단에 힌트가 있다. 윗글에서는 새 타이어를 갈 때의 스트레스 받는 상황과 그러한 상황에 현명하게 대처하는 방법을 도와주려

고 한다는 내용이 있기에 이 지문 뒤에는 타이어 교체를 현명하게 하는 방법에 대한 이야기가 나올 것이다.

어휘_ miserable 괴로운, 고생스러운

정답_ (b)

26.

해석_ 의사나 병원이 많지 않았던 과거에는 사람들은 병을 낫게 하기 위해서 민간요법을 사용했다. 이번 주에는 가장 대중적인 민간요법 몇 가지를 배워보자. 민간요법은 집에서 병을 치료하는 전통적인 방법이다. 오래 전에는 누군가 조금 아프거나 심하지 않은 감기가 걸리면 엄마들은 병을 낫게 하기 위해서 오래된 치료법을 사용했다. 민간요법은 세대에서 세대로 전해져 내려왔다. 여러분은 그것들이 효과적이지 못하다고 생각할 수도 있다. 하지만 많은 민간요법이 정말 효과가 있다! 다음번에는 여러분이 직접 시도해보는 것이 어떨까?

해설_ 지문의 앞부분에 "가장 대중적인 민간요법 몇 가지를 배워보자" 라는 내용이 힌트가 된다.

어휘_ folk remedy 민간요법

　　　 be handed down 전해 내려오다

정답_ (d)

27.

해석_ 어린 시절 가족들과 헤어져야만 했던 수천 명의 호주 원주민들이 아무런 보상도 받지 못하게 될 것이라고 호주 정부가 밝혔다. 시위대는 정부가 약속했던 사과의 일환으로 거의 8억 7천만 달러에 이르는 배상 기금을 요구했었다. 하지만 원주민 담당 제니 매클린 장관은 이 돈이 보건 및 교육 계획에 투입될 것이라고 밝혔다. 많은 원주민 자녀들이 1915년부터 1969년까지 백인 가정에 위탁되었다. 이들은 정부가 백인과 원주민을 동화시키려 했던 시도의 일환으로 백인 가정에 의해 양육되었다.

해설_ 윗글의 마지막 부분에 힌트가 있다.

어휘_ Aborigine 오스트레일리아 원주민

　　　 campaigner (정치 · 사회의) 운동가

　　　 reparation 배상(금)

　　　 indigenous 토착의, 원산의

　　　 scheme 계획

　　　 assimilate (문화적으로) 동화시키다

정답_ (d)

28.

해석_ 오스카상을 두 번 수상한 엠마 톰슨을 포함하여 환경주의자, 과학자, 배우들이 모여 영국 정부가 히드로 공항에 활주로를 건설하려는 계획을 완전히 망쳐놓기로 결심했다. 그 혼합 팀은 추가 활주로가 생길 그 개발 지역의 중심부에 땅을 조금 샀다. 정부가 그 땅을 모두 사들이거나 압류하려고 하면 정부가 꼼짝 못하도록 그 그룹은 그 땅을 수천 개의 단위로 나누어 전 세계의 환경 운동가들에게 팔기로 했다. 그들은 세 번째 활주로의 경제적 이득이 과장되었으며 환경적, 인간적 손실이 너무 크다고 주장한다.

해설_ 엠마 톰슨은 다른 환경주의자들과 모여 영국 정부의 히드로 공항 추가 활주로 건설을 막으려 하고 있다.

어휘_ coalition 연합, 제휴

　　　 scupper (계획 등을) 망쳐 놓다

　　　 motley 잡다한, 뒤섞인, 혼성의

　　　 plot 작은 구획의 땅

　　　 vow 단언하다, 맹세하다

　　　 subdivide 다시 나누다

　　　 bog down 꼼짝 못하게 하다

　　　 buy up 모두 사들이다

　　　 seize 빼앗다, 압류하다

정답_ (c)

29.

해석_ 샐리시 롯지의 온천이 조조할인으로 당신을 유혹하려 합니다. 오전에 일찍 오시는 분은 매주 월요일에서 금요일 오전 8시에서 9시 사이에 40달러의 가격으로 온천 서비스가 제공됩니다. 스노퀼미까지 운전해서 가기에 시간이 조금 일러 보입니까? 집을 떠나 롯지에서 전날 밤을 보내는 것은 어떻습니까? 멋지죠! 자세한 사항을 알고 싶으면 1-800-272-5474로 전화 주십시오. 이 광고는 다음 금요일까지 유효합니다.

해설_ 윗글은 온천의 아침 조기 입장 할인을 선전하고 있다.

어휘_ seduce 유혹하다

　　　 make a getaway 도망치다

정답_ (b)

30.

해석_ 미 의회에서 민주당이 제시한 보고서에 따르면 이라크와 아프가니스탄에서 미국이 치르고 있는 전쟁은 기존에 예상되었던 비용의 두 배 가까이 들고 있다. 민주당에 따르면 "숨은 비용" 이 요청되었던 8천 4십억 달러의 거의 두 배에 가까운 1조 5천억 달러에 가깝게 총 비용을 증가시켰다고 한다. 높은 유가, 부상 당한 퇴역 군인에 대한 치료 비용, 그리고 예비군을 직장에서 소환하여 경제에 미치는 비용 등이 고려되었다. 백악관에서는 이 보고서가 정치적인 목적을 띠고 있다고 비난했다.

해설_ 총비용에서 요청되었던 비용을 빼면 숨은 비용이 산출된다. (1,500 - 804 = 696)

어휘_ trillion 1조(兆)(의)

veteran 퇴역 군인

reservist 예비병

정답_ (d)

31.

해석_ 중국에서는 1월, 폭설에 의해 가격 상승에 대한 압력이 악화되어 인플레이션이 지난 11년 중 최고에 이르렀다. 치솟는 식료품 가격이 소비자 물가 상승을 12월의 6.5%에서 지난달에는 7.1%까지 밀어붙인 주요 원인으로 파악되고 있다. 중국 정부에서 경기 과열을 방지하기 위해 이자율을 높이고 다른 조치들을 취하고 있음에도 불구하고 중국의 인플레이션은 지속적으로 상승하고 있다. 지난 수십 년 중 최악의 겨울을 보낸 탓에 식량 공급에 차질이 생겨 식료품 가격이 18%나 상승했다. 폭설이 농작물을 망쳐놓고 수백만 마리의 가축을 폐사하게 만들었다. 하지만 분석가들은 식료품 가격 상승의 원인이 가혹한 날씨뿐만은 아니라고 충고하며, 가격이 아직도 더 상승할 수 있다고 경고했다.

해설_ 눈이 많이 온 것은 곡물 가격 상승의 한 원인일 뿐이며 그것이 전부가 되지는 못할 것이다. 따라서 그것보다 포괄적인 의미인 "곡물가의 급상승" 이 식료품 가격 상승의 원인이 된다는 내용이 더 자연스럽다.

어휘_ wreck 망치다

livestock 가축

정답_ (b)

32.

해석_ 산타 카탈리나 섬의 동물 병원이 바지선으로 바다를 건너 트럭으로 아발론의 새 둥지에 도착해 그곳에서 1년에 약 2,400명의 고객을 맞을 것이다. 시설 공개는 발렌타인 데이에 예정되어 있으며, 그때 방문자들은 시설을 살펴볼 수 있을 것이다. 그곳은 장애인 편의 시설을 갖추고 있으며 수술실과 32×14피트 면적의 대기실을 보유하고 있다. 그 섬의 유일한 수의사인 데니는 자신의 310평방 피트의 사무실에서 계속 일할 것이다.

해설_ 데니는 veterinarian, 즉 '수의사' 이다.

어휘_ veterinary clinic 동물 병원

surgery suite 수술실

veterinarian 수의사

정답_ (d)

33.

해석_ 1963년 11월 비틀즈는 영국 여왕 앞에서 공연을 하였다. 그것은 그 그룹에게는 대단한 영광이었다. 1963년 말경 비틀즈는 영국에서 가장 인기 있는 밴드였다. 비틀즈는 1964년 처음으로 뉴욕에 가서 순식간에 성공을 이루었다. 뉴욕에 간 지 2주 만에 상위 5개의 베스트셀러 음반을 석권한 것이다. 1964년 말경 그들은 전 세계적으로 유명해졌다. 1964년에는 또한 "당신의 손을 잡고 싶어요" 라는 곡으로 비틀즈 열풍을 일으켰다.

해설_ 1964년 말이라고 해야 올바른 내용이다.

어휘_ incredible 믿을 수 없을 정도의, 엄청난

정답_ (d)

34.

해석_ 부시 대통령이 의회에서 통과된 법률에 대해 거부권을 행사하면서 워싱턴의 논쟁이 연방 정부 차원의 줄기 세포 연구 자금 지원으로 바뀌었다. 대통령의 거부권을 지지하는 사람들 쪽은 연구 사용 목적으로 버려지는 배아의 개인적 권리를 지적하면서 배아 줄기 세포 연구에 반대한다. 다른 한쪽은 배아는 어차피 버려질 것이며 이 연구는 심각한 질병으로 고통 받고 있는 사람들에게 귀중한 치료책을 제공할 수 있을 것이라고 주장한다. 하지만 이 논쟁에서 어느 쪽도 납세자의 권리를 둘러싼 도덕성을 고려하고 있지 않는 것 같다.

해설_ 지문의 하단에서 "이 논쟁에서 어느 쪽도 납세자의 권리를 둘러싼 도덕성을 고려하고 있지 않는 것 같다" 는 내용이 힌트가 된다.

어휘_ stem cell 줄기 세포

embryo 태아, 배아

veto 거부(권 행사); 거부하다

discard 폐기하다, 버리다

정답_ (d)

35.

해석_ 달 과학자들은 그때 이후로 달에 관하여 많은 것을 알게 됐다. 달 정착의 가장 큰 어려움 중 하나는 7피트부터 아마도 100피트 이상의 깊이까지 실질적으로 달 전체를 덮고 있는 표토와 함께 어떻게 살 것인가이다. 그 표토는 거대한 지표석부터 지름이 몇 나노미터에 불과한 소립자까지 모두를 포함하지만 대부분은 30억 년 이상 동안 대기의 방해를 받지 않고 달에 부딪친 셀 수 없이 많은 고속의 미소 운석(隕石)에 의해 만들어진 수프와 같은 것이다.

해설_ 지문에 "먼지가 7피트부터 아마도 최대 100피트 이상의 깊이까지 실질적으로 달 전체를 덮고 있다" 는 내용이 있다.

어휘_ boulder 큰 알돌, 표석

puree 퓨레 (채소와 고기를 데쳐서 거른 것으로 수프 등을 만

듧), 퓨레로 만들다

micrometeorite 미소 운석, 우주 먼지

unimpeded 방해 받고 있지 않은

정답_ (b)

36.

해석_ 1750-1850년은 직장과 화이트칼라 범죄의 역사에서 분수령을 이룬 시기였다. 예전에는 "의례적인 권리"라는 개념으로 정당화되었던 도용이 이제는 점점 "도둑질"로 간주되었다. 같은 시기에 직장을 새로운 취약점에 노출시킨 상업 세계의 변화에 의해 직원의 절도 기회는 확대되었다. 이 시대에는 신분 좋은 중산층 범죄자들에 의해 사기와 횡령 같은 예전에 없던 재정적 범죄들이 생겨나 만연했다.

해설_ 전반적인 주제 의식 자체가 1750-1850년대 사이의 시기에 절도의 기회가 증가하였다는 내용이므로 (c)가 정답이다.

오답 피하기_ (b) 도용은 과거에는 "의례적인 권리"라는 개념으로 정당화되었다.

어휘_ watershed 분수령, 중요한 시기

appropriation 도용

legitimate 정당화하다

notion 개념, 생각

customary 습관적인, 통례의

pilfer 좀도둑질하다, 훔치다

arena 투기장(鬪技場), 경기장, 활동 무대

epoch 시대

embezzlement 횡령, 착복

정답_ (c)

37.

해석_ 수에즈 운하는 수에즈 만의 수에즈 항에서 지중해의 포트사이드까지 대략 200킬로미터를 흘러간다. 이 운하의 일부 지역은 너무 좁아서 배 두 척이 동시에 지나갈 수 없다. 배 한 척은 특별한 장소나 호수 가운데 하나에서 배가 지나갈 수 있게 될 때까지 기다려야만 한다. 프랑스의 기술자인 페르디낭 드 르쎄가 수에즈 운하 건설의 책임자였다. 1859년에 착공해서 1869년에 완공되었다. 수에즈 운하의 완공을 기념하여 유명한 이탈리아 작곡가인 조셉 베르디가 특별한 오페라를 작곡했다. 이 오페라 '아이다'는 지금까지 작곡된 가장 유명한 오페라 중 하나이다.

해설_ 프랑스 인 페르디낭 드 르쎄가 건설을 책임졌다고 언급하고 있으므로 정답은 (c)이다

어휘_ canal 운하

approximately 대략

Mediterranean Sea 지중해

정답_ (c)

38.

해석_ 현대 자동차 미국 법인은 다음 12개월 동안 새로 현대차를 구입하는 고객이 구입 후 1년 이내에 "본의 아니게 수입을 잃게 된다"면 차를 반환할 수 있다고 말했다. (a) 현대는 할부금을 지불하지 않기로 결정한 고객에 대해 7,500달러만큼의 채무 가격을 흡수할 것이라고 하였다. (b) 많은 자동차 제조자와 딜러들은 이미 무이자 판매와 같은 많은 인센티브를 제공하고 있다. (c) 구매한 지 1년 동안 새 차 가치 25% 정도의 감가상각이 이루어질 수 있다. (d) 그러나 현대의 라인업이 저가와 중간 수준의 가격에 치중되어 있기 때문에 7,500달러는 대부분의 현대차의 가치 상실을 메울 것이다.

해설_ 윗글은 현대 자동차의 이야기를 하고 있으며, 다른 자동차 회사의 상황과는 거리가 있다.

어휘_ involuntary 본의 아닌, 내 의지가 아닌

opt to 선택하다, 택하다

negative equity 담보물의 시장 가치 하락으로 인한 채무

a raft of 많은

depreciation 가치 하락

skew 빗나가다, 비뚤어지다

정답_ (b)

39.

해석_ 당신의 약상자를 1년에 적어도 한 번은 정리하라고 미국 응급 의사 협회가 권고했다. (a) 그리고 당신이 정리를 할 때, 약을 욕실에서 모두 꺼내어 벽장의 높은 곳에 있는 선반으로 옮기는 것을 고려하라. (b) 1년치의 샤워와 목욕은 열기와 습기를 만드는데 그로 인해 약이 효력을 잃을 수도 있다. (c) 약이 효력을 잃으면 약의 필요 복용량을 얻지 못할 수 있기에 그것을 모두 버리는 것이 좋다. (d) 알링턴 하이츠와 같은 일부 지역에서는 매달 첫 번째 목요일의 오전 11시에서 오후 1시까지만 약을 허용한다.

해설_ 윗글은 약상자 정리에 관한 것이기에 일부 지역에서 약을 허용한다는 (d)의 내용은 어울리지 않는다.

어휘_ medication 약제, 약물

potency (약 따위의) 효능, 효력

dosage 복용량

정답_ (d)

40.

해석_ 삼성은 백라이팅에 LED를 이용한 새로운 LCD TV 제품군으

로 CES 무대에 오르게 되었다. (a) 그 LED 백라이팅은 LCD TV를 보다 밝고 보다 환경친화적이고 그리고 매우 얇게 만드는 것을 가능케 한다. (b) 삼성은 튜너를 포함하여 대략 1인치 두께밖에 안 되는 세트를 선보일 것이다. 이번 봄에 3개의 모델이 출시될 것이다. (c) 삼성은 야후와 연합하여 뉴스, 주식, 엔터테인먼트와 다른 컨텐츠를 전송할 계획이다. (d) 가격은 아직 공개되지 않았으나 삼성은 현재의 LED 백라이트 세트보다 최소 "몇백" 불 비쌀 것이라고 말했다.

해설_ 삼성의 새로운 LCD TV에 관한 글로 컨텐츠 전송에 관한 글이 아니다.

어휘_ CES 매년 초 미국 라스베가스에서 개최되는 전자제품 박람회
LED 발광 소자(=light-emitting diode)
disclose 공개하다
environmentally friendly 환경친화적인

정답_ (c)